THE IMPEACHMENT POWER

The Impeachment Power

THE LAW, POLITICS, AND PURPOSE OF AN EXTRAORDINARY CONSTITUTIONAL TOOL

KEITH E. WHITTINGTON

PRINCETON UNIVERSITY PRESS

PRINCETON & OXFORD

Published by Princeton University Press
41 William Street, Princeton, New Jersey 08540
99 Banbury Road, Oxford OX2 6JX

press.princeton.edu

Library of Congress Cataloging-in-Publication Data

Names: Whittington, Keith E. author.
Title: The impeachment power : the law, politics, and purpose of an
    extraordinary constitutional tool / Keith E. Whittington.
Description: Princeton : Princeton University Press, [2024] |
    Includes bibliographical references and index.
Identifiers: LCCN 2024018180 (print) | LCCN 2024018181 (ebook) |
    ISBN 9780691265391 (hardback) | ISBN 9780691265407 (e-book)
Subjects: LCSH: Impeachments—United States. | BISAC: POLITICAL
    SCIENCE / American Government / Legislative Branch |
    POLITICAL SCIENCE / Political Process / General
Classification: LCC KF4958 .W45 2024 (print) | LCC KF4958 (ebook) |
    DDC 342.73/068—dc23/eng/20240604
LC record available at https://lccn.loc.gov/2024018180
LC ebook record available at https://lccn.loc.gov/2024018181

British Library Cataloging-in-Publication Data is available

Editorial: Bridget Flannery-McCoy and Alena Chekanov
Production Editorial: Jaden Young
Jacket/Cover Design: Karl Spurzem
Production: Erin Suydam
Publicity: James Schneider and Kathryn Stevens
Copyeditor: Jennifer McClain

Jacket image: ASSOCIATED PRESS

This book has been composed in Arno

Printed in the United States of America

10 9 8 7 6 5 4 3 2 1

CONTENTS

Introduction   1

1 What Is the Impeachment Process?   7

2 What Is a Fair Impeachment Process?   40

3 What Is the Impeachment Power For?   78

4 What Are High Crimes and Misdemeanors?   116

5 When Does Abuse of Power Justify Impeachment?   150

6 Can the Supreme Court Intervene in
an Impeachment?   186

Conclusion   204

Further Reading 217
Acknowledgments 221
Notes 223
Index 239

THE IMPEACHMENT POWER

Introduction

I FIRST became interested in federal impeachments when I was working on my doctoral dissertation in the early 1990s. At the time, impeachments seemed like a particularly useful way to study how Congress exercised its constitutional responsibilities when it was working without a net. In an impeachment, the members of Congress have to take responsibility for their own actions because the Supreme Court is not going to bail them out if they make constitutional mistakes. Impeachments can reveal something about how Congress thinks about the Constitution when left to its own devices. Moreover, high-profile impeachments shed particular light on how the American constitutional system has developed over time. They mark moments when Congress—and America broadly—has contemplated the foundational principles that ought to guide government officials as they work in the public trust. They are moments of constitutional restoration, and sometimes of constitutional change.[1]

But no matter how interesting or illuminating such historical impeachments might be, they have been rare and seemed firmly anchored in the past. As with much scholarly work, my time spent studying impeachments seemed rewarding for its own sake but arcane and distant from ordinary political life. Of course, it has turned out that impeachments, even presidential impeachments, are not simply a thing of the past. We have lived through more presidential impeachments than has any previous generation of Americans. We will probably live through some more.

We live in an age in which every succeeding presidential administration has bred its own cottage industry of critics and opponents calling for impeachment. Before Donald Trump was sworn into office as president, books were being written calling for his impeachment. Before Joe Biden was sworn into office as Trump's successor, a newly elected member of the House of Representatives promised to introduce articles of impeachment against him. Such has been the way of our political life for more than two decades.

My goal for this book is different. I come neither to bury Caesar nor to praise him. I do not mean to mount a prosecution of the current president and explain why he should be impeached and removed from office, nor do I mean to mount a defense of a former president and explain why his impeachment was unjust. Such works have their place, and there are examples of them aplenty. This is not one of those books.

Instead, I hope to illuminate the constitutional nature, purpose, and history of the federal impeachment power not from the perspective of how it might help or hurt a particular government official but from the perspective of how we have thought and should think about it over the long run. It can be a useful exercise when thinking about constitutional powers to consider how we should understand that power not only when it is being used by our friends but also when it is in the hands of our opponents. My views on the impeachment power were shaped from the study of our history, before impeachment politics entered contemporary American life. They have been deepened and informed by the events and controversies of the past quarter century as I have sought to apply those early lessons to emerging problems, but my view of the impeachment power was not developed in the heated partisan environment of a particular impeachment. I have been both critical of and sympathetic to aspects of every impeachment that has been pursued over the course of my adult life. I have tried during those controversies to share the lessons of my studies of the Constitution and the impeachment power to improve the public understanding of the process and the political use of this important constitutional tool. I hope the reflections in this book can be helpful in thinking about the controversies yet to come, and that it can help shed light on the impeachment power without turning up the heat.

The conventional form of referring to the Senate when it tries an impeachment case is as the "high court of impeachment." This style is borrowed from the British practice, where the House of Lords sat as the "high court" in impeachments there. But the British Parliament was a high court in a broader sense as well since it traditionally exercised some judicial powers that were somewhat comparable to the role that the Supreme Court plays in the American system. Parliament was, quite simply, the highest court in the land. The U.S. Senate is not a high court in that sense. It only plays the role of a court in a single, special circumstance—when members of the House of Representatives come to the Senate chamber to impeach a federal officer.

The Senate has more rarely been referred to as the "constitutional court of impeachment," but that appellation has special significance. In the American context, the Senate sits as the *constitutionally specified* court of impeachment. When the Senate is gaveled to order as a court of impeachment, it does so under constitutional directive, in accordance with constitutional forms, and for designated constitutional purposes. It is a court specially constituted by the Constitution. Thus, advocates have sometimes referred to the constitutional court of impeachment in order to emphasize this constitutional form, and on occasion to question whether the Senate is living up to it in practice. The friends of President Andrew Johnson questioned whether it was even possible for the Senate in 1868 to "form a constitutional court of impeachment for its trial" because "almost one-third of its members [was] excluded" by the refusal of the Republicans to seat senators from the states of the former Confederacy that were still under Reconstruction.[2] His sympathizers wondered whether the Reconstruction Republicans appreciated that it was not the Senate *as a political body* that should have been trying the case. Only a properly formed "constitutional court of impeachment" was authorized to play that role.[3] President Johnson's attorney general had earlier tried to emphasize to the justices of the Supreme Court that a sitting president "cannot be made subject to the jurisdiction of any court, while in office, except only the Senate of the United States, as the constitutional court of impeachment."[4]

When the Senate sits as the constitutional court of impeachment, it does so as the highest and final court under the Constitution and thereby exercises an especially solemn constitutional responsibility. The constitutional court of impeachment is empowered to resolve the gravest of constitutional questions and to hold accountable the highest governmental officers in the land. When the senators assume that mantle, only the people themselves stand above them. Not long after the drafting of the U.S. Constitution, a member of the British House of Commons rose from his seat to defend, for nearly the last time, "the existence of that great constitutional instrument of public safety," the impeachment power.[5] That instrument might not always be used wisely or well, but it should call legislators to recognize and assume their most solemn place in the constitutional order.

In the following pages, I develop an explanation of the scope and purpose of the impeachment provisions of the U.S. Constitution. We have to understand the nature of the impeachment power in order to answer pressing questions about how it should be used and what we can reasonably hope to accomplish by its use. Answering such questions might not have been considered pressing during the long periods in American history when federal impeachments were rare, but calls for the use of the impeachment power are no longer rare and no longer confined to the political fringes.

The argument presented here draws on many sources. The constitutional text is an essential starting point, but the text by itself leaves us with many interpretive puzzles. The purpose and history behind that text is clarifying, as are our established practices in making use of the impeachment power. The impeachment power is an important piece in the intricate structure and design of the Constitution, and it reflects not only the worries that the founding generation had when imagining how republican politics might work in a new nation but also our persistent fears about how government power can be abused and how those abuses might be remedied. The impeachment power sits at the intersection of our dual commitments to democratic self-government and constitutional restraints on political power. Making sense of that power and how it should be responsibly used requires thinking through both our democratic and our constitutional commitments and how they operate in our modern political world.

My perspective throughout is one informed by history and politics. The impeachment power is not just a legal instrument. It is also a political tool. There is a meaningful law of the impeachment power, rooted in our text and tradition, that bounds its use. Within those bounds, however, political judgment is required to know whether and when and how it should be used. The impeachment power is designed to remedy a distinctly political problem of the misconduct of an officeholder. It is exercised by political officials who must not only make contextualized assessments of whether another political official has engaged in grievous misconduct, but also consider the range of options that might be available to address that misconduct. When legislators reach for the impeachment power, they should know what they hope to accomplish and have some idea of how the impeachment power might be used to reach that goal. Exercising the impeachment power involves choices—choices about how politics is to be conducted, how misbehavior is best remedied, and how we can best secure our highest constitutional ideals.

Choosing well depends on the wisdom and experience of the elected members of the legislature who serve in the constitutional court of impeachment. Those choices can be informed by lawyers, scholars, and experts, but they cannot be dodged. Ultimately, legislators are held to account for how they make those choices by their constituents, and they alone bear the burden of persuading their colleagues as to what actions are needed and of justifying to the voters what has been done. Legislators need to understand for themselves and be able to explain to others the reasons for their choices. Why did they act, or fail to act? Why did they pursue action in this way? What other options were available to them, and how did they assess the risks and rewards of the path that they chose? Were they satisfied with how events played out? Did the proper people learn the proper lessons, or were mistakes made along the way? Voters should demand answers to such questions, and members of the legislature should be confident in their ability to provide an adequate response.

In the following chapters, I both clarify the law of federal impeachments and illuminate the choices that political officials must make when contemplating whether to use the impeachment power. For the general reader, there are points explained here that are widely accepted by scholars on these topics. But there are many claims developed here that remain points of contention. If this book can help enlighten and inform our scholarly and political debates about how the impeachment power should be used, then it will have done its job.

1

What Is the Impeachment Process?

MORE THAN a century before the American Revolution, the impeachment power enjoyed its heyday in the House of Commons of the British Parliament. The memory of those days was fading but not yet forgotten when Americans were drafting their state and federal constitutions after shaking loose from the British empire. The Americans remained impressed with the parliamentary battles with the British monarch in the seventeenth century, and they were happy to borrow the weapons that Parliament had used in those battles in order to help defend their own republican aspirations.

In 1624, King James I gave a prophetic warning to a favorite courtier, George Villiers, the Duke of Buckingham; and to the prince, the future King Charles I. Both had encouraged the impeachment by the British Parliament of a rival at court, Lionel Cranfield, the Lord Treasurer. James was not pleased. Using his pet name for the duke, James declared, "By God, Stenny, you are a fool, and will shortly repent this folly, and will find, that, in this fit of popularity, you are making a rod, with which you will be scourged yourself." The prince was eight years the duke's junior, but old enough to anticipate wearing the crown himself. James had words for him as well. "That he would live to have his belly full of parliament impeachments: and when I shall be dead, you will have too much cause to remember, how much you had contributed to the weakening of the crown, by the two precedents he was now so fond of."[1] Within just a few years, James would be dead and the freshly coronated King Charles I would have to dissolve Parliament in order to head off the impeachment of the Duke of Buckingham.

Two decades before issuing that warning to his son, James had unified the kingdoms of Scotland and England under his own rule. His reign saw the flowering of English literature and the arts, from the writing of the plays of William Shakespeare to the translation of the Bible into English. But not everything was running smoothly in England at the beginning of the seventeenth century. The Catholic terrorist Guy Fawkes had tried to blow up Parliament just after James had assumed the English Crown. While still ruling over Scotland alone, James had published a controversial tract laying out his theory of the divine right of kings and his expansive views of monarchical power. He had advised his eldest son, Henry, who was felled by typhoid fever as a young man, "hold no Parliaments, but for necessitie of new Lawes, which would be but seldome: for few Lawes and well put in execution, are best in a well ruled common-weale."[2] King James had never been a fan of quarrelsome legislatures.

James had offered that written advice when Prince Henry was still a small child and when James ruled only over Scotland. When Queen Elizabeth died in 1603, James united the two kingdoms under his own rule. It did not take long for the English Parliament to give James new reasons to wish them out of session. The first Parliament to meet under King James I wound up petitioning the king for permission to arrest and sue some of his minor functionaries, who the House of Commons thought were abusing their offices. James informed Parliament that only the king had the authority to punish his servants and would do so "as he saw fit."[3] Not long after, James dissolved the Parliament. When his other schemes to pay off the royal debt failed, James was obliged to call Parliament back into session but quickly dissolved it again when he thought he had found an alternative source of funds. Some members of Parliament were left to wonder whether they would ever be called into session again or whether this was the end "not only of this, but of all parliaments."[4]

But eventually the king wanted money to raise an army, so he once again summoned Parliament to assemble. Rather than simply raising taxes and going home, that Parliament too began investigating abuses by friends of the king and questioning the king's foreign intrigues (including the negotiations with Spain's King Phillip III for a marriage between his daughter and Prince Charles). Such impertinence led James to issue a proclamation explaining to his Parliament that while he was an indulgent king who would "allow of convenient freedom of speech," his patience had limits and the parliamentarians should henceforth avoid an "excess of lavish speech" and stop talking "of matters above their reach or calling."[5] Sir Edward Coke, a famed jurist and now a member of Parliament, took the lead in developing a response, and eventually the House of Commons put before the king a bold assertion of a liberty to speak freely "as in their judgements shall seem fittest."[6] The king allowed the members to return home for Christmas, but when the festivities were over, he had the elderly Coke sent to the Tower of London (where he was held for nine months) and ordered the journal of the House of Commons brought to him so that he could personally rip out the page recording the Protestation. He then promptly dissolved the Parliament.

In addition to adopting its Protestation in defense of a freedom of speech in Parliament, the House of Commons made another bold move in 1621—it revived the impeachment power. Parliament had not impeached anyone since the reign of King Henry VI more than a century and a half earlier, and the possibility of such a power was barely remembered. The notorious outrages of Sir Giles Mompesson spurred Parliament to search its dusty records for a power to act. Mompesson had proven entrepreneurial in securing monopolies from the king that allowed him to harass and extort businessmen and enrich himself and members of the king's inner circle. Sir Edward Coke reported to the House of Commons that the "searchers have discharged their duties" and had discovered that "according to former precedents" the House should "address ourselves to the Lords." And so "it was agreed to go to the Lords, and that the committee examine all his offenses."[7] The king chose not to waste political capital trying to protect Mompesson, and the disgraced knight fled to France before the House of Lords could pass sentence on him.

Having rediscovered this medieval power, the Commons became enthusiastic about its use. It is not clear that Coke or anyone else in 1621 had settled on a name for this practice of the Commons "acquainting the Lords that we had fallen upon some Grievances" that the two chambers together "might all join in the punishing," but at some point it began to be referred to as an impeachment.[8] John Pym, another leader in the House of Commons, boasted that "the high court of parliament is the great eye of the kingdom to find out offenses and punish them."[9] He was zealous in ferreting out those offenses, but his targets were rarely close to the king.

Indeed, the king held the trump cards in the game of impeachment, and Parliament's enthusiasm for it proved to be short-lived. In one of his last addresses to members of Parliament, King James I warned that they were treading on thin ice in impeaching the Lord of Middlesex. Parliament should remember that "they should make the punishment no greater than his crime." Ultimately, the king would have the last word. "And now how far I find they have proceeded according to my rules, so far I will punish; how far I find they have exceeded, I will add mercy. As for bribes, if he have taken any to the detriment of the party, I will punish it." The king cautioned the Commons as follows:

> But as it is lawful for grieved men to complain, so I would not have an inquisition of Spain raised in England that men should seek to inquire after faults; but if complaints come to you, judge of them accordingly but search not for them. . . . But I must warn you for the time to come of one thing. Men shall not give information against my officers without my leave. If there be cause, let them first complain to me, for I will not have any of my ser-

vants and officers, from the greatest lord to the meanest scullion, complained on by any without my leave first asked but I will make them smart sorer that complain than he is complained of. Neither will I have any man to presume to go to complain as if there were no king in Parliament. I will not suffer it.[10]

Even Pym recognized that Parliament might be able to declare through the impeachment power that a punishment should take place, but "for execution, left to the king wholly, who hath the sword."[11] It was left to the king to strip an officer convicted in the court of impeachment of his titles and offices, imprison or exile him, or worse—and the king might instead choose not to follow up on Parliament's judgment at all. The king might pardon an individual who fell under the "great eye of the kingdom." The king might even suspend or dissolve the Parliament and put an end to its investigations.

When Parliament turned its sights on the Duke of Buckingham, the intimate friend of the king, in 1625, King Charles I played his card, informing Parliament that, "the king, perceiving the commons resolved . . . to reflect upon some great persons near himself . . . this parliament was declared to be dissolved."[12] When Charles called the Parliament back the next year, he gave them a stern reminder of where they sat in the British constitutional order as he understood it. "Parliaments are altogether in my power for the calling, sitting and dissolution. Therefore as I find the fruits of them to be good or evil, they are to continue or not to be."[13]

The conflict at the beginning of his reign between King Charles I and the Parliament did not bring an end to the British practice of impeachments, but its limitations were already visible. In the 1640s, the Commons attempted to take on "great persons" near the king, and the results were not encouraging. What the Parliament really wanted and needed was an instrument for taking control of the government, and the impeachment power was too crude a tool to serve that purpose. As the Commons pleaded with the king in the Great Remonstrance of 1641, it hoped that he would "employ such Counselors, Ambassadors, and other Ministers in managing his business at home and abroad, as the Parliament have cause to confide in," even if "we may be unwilling to proceed against them in any legal way of charges or impeachment."[14] That conflict between king and Parliament degenerated into civil war and Charles lost his head in 1649.

In the century and a half before American independence, impeachments were part of the process by which Parliament tried to gain control over how public policy was formulated and administered, to realize in practice what one pamphleteer in the early eighteenth century said was a "noble Maxim of our Constitution, (which expressly makes the Ministers accountable for all Transactions contrary to the Interest and Honour of their Nation) by punishing those who have so many times brought Us to the brink of Ruin."[15] Convincing the king to adopt the practice of dismissing ministers who had lost the confidence of the Parliament realized that goal more effectively than did impeachment. The impeachment power was just a way station on the road to votes of no confidence.

When the first edition of what would become a classic treatise on the law and practices of Parliament appeared in 1844, its author could safely treat impeachments as a thing of the past. The power of parliamentary impeachment was, to be sure, "a safeguard to public liberty well worthy of a free country, and of so noble an institution as a free Parliament. But, happily, in modern times, this extraordinary judicature is rarely called into activity."[16] The British constitutional system had discovered better tools than impeachment for remedying most political ills.

Perhaps if the U.S. Constitution had been written a few decades later, the American founders would have emulated the system of ministerial accountability that eventually developed in England. In the mid-nineteenth century, the third Earl Grey could say the ministers of government exercised "the powers belonging to the Crown" but were "considered entitled to hold their offices only while they possess the confidence of Parliament, and more especially of the House of Commons."[17] No impeachment power was necessary if executive officers were understood to serve at the pleasure of the legislative majority.

But that was not the system that the American founders imagined or designed. Executive officers in the American system were to be independent agents of the people and were not mere instruments of the legislature. The founders imagined that the executive branch and the legislative branch of the American republic could clash as they had in seventeenth-century England (though hopefully without the necessity of the chief executive losing his head). The executive would not be subordinate to the legislature, but rather the executive and legislature would be yoked together in a system of checks and balances. The impeachment power was part of that system, helping to keep the executive under control.

Few principles were so central to the founding era thinking about constitutional design as that power ought to be made to check power. The records of the Philadelphia Convention, where the delegates met in the summer of 1787 to haggle over a new set of constitutional rules, are replete with discussions of how adequate checks on power were to be established. Although only thirty-four years of age, Edmund Randolph was one of the elder statesmen of the convention. He had served for a decade as the first attorney general of the state of Virginia, and he was taking a break from his duties as governor when he traveled north to lead his state's constitutional delegation. Once the delegates had assembled in Independence Hall, Randolph was chosen to launch the substantive business of the convention by introducing the Virginia Plan—the first outline for a new federal constitution. As the debate got under way, Randolph urged the convention to accept the proposal for a bicameral national legislature. The evils that plagued the United States since the end of the American Revolution could be attributed to "the turbulence and follies of democracy." "Some check therefore was to be sought for against this tendency of our Governments," and he hoped the Senate would do the trick. North Carolina's Hugh Williamson similarly hoped that a legislature divided into two chambers could "serve as a mutual check," while James Madison hoped to provide Congress with a "check" against the "mischiefs" of the states. (The delegates would accept only a watered-down version of that particular check.)[18]

When the convention began to consider Virginia's proposal for a council of revision that could veto bills from the legislature, Elbridge Gerry of Massachusetts thought that judges should be left off any such council since they would already "have a sufficient check against [legislative] encroachments on their own department." The judges, Gerry thought, would hold a power of deciding on the constitutionality of legislation and would therefore be able to "set aside laws as being against the Constitution." Gerry thought there should be a check on both the constitutionality and the wisdom of legislative proposals, but that judges should concern themselves only with the former. Benjamin Franklin dissented from the council idea at least, which he thought "was a mischievous sort of check" that would encourage corrupt bargains between the legislature and the executive. His fellow Pennsylvanian, the future Supreme Court justice James Wilson, worried instead that if the legislature could override a presidential veto too easily, the "Executive check" might prove inadequate, in "tempestuous moments," to the task of allowing the executive "to defend itself" against an overweening legislature.[19] Checks had to be put in place everywhere, the Federalists believed, so that no actor or interest could become too powerful or abusive.

The ultimate and most powerful of these checks—the impeachment power—was entrusted to the Congress. With this power, the legislative branch alone was vested with the authority to remove, when necessary, members of the other branches of the federal government. Members of the legislature could themselves be removed by the chamber as a whole (through expulsion) or by their constituents at regular intervals (through elections). The other branches of government were designed to be powerful and independent, but the legislature held the trump card. Though

Madison was among those who worried about "a powerful tendency in the Legislature to absorb all power into its vortex," there was no other body that could be entrusted to exercise a power to impeach and remove misbehaving members of the judicial and executive branches.[20]

An extraordinary power, but how should it be used? Other checks within the American constitutional system get regular use. The impeachment power, as the constitutional framers probably expected or hoped, has been used far more sparingly. As a result, the impeachment power is less familiar than other aspects of our constitutional system. The threat of its use can be disconcerting. American politicians are perhaps not as bewildered by the ancient precedents as the English parliamentarians in the reign of King James I, but they too often struggle to understand the nature of the impeachment power and its uses. The stakes of its use might not be as high as they were when Britain teetered on the brink of civil war, but the impeachment power is too important to be neglected.

The impeachment power is also too important to be left to the lawyers. Central to this work is thinking about the impeachment power as a political tool. It is ultimately a constitutional power created by politicians for the use of politicians. It is a tool intended to solve political problems, and it both represents and helps secure the centrality of Congress in the constitutional enterprise.

The founders sought to create three branches of government, each independent of the others and enmeshed in a system of checks and balances. They thought that if government power rested with a single set of officials, civil liberty and political effectiveness would be compromised. Each branch of government was armed with its own set of powers and responsibilities and given sufficient tenure and resources to be able to act on its own judgment.

But the desire for independence had to be balanced against a concern for accountability. Government officials needed to be independent enough to be able to act in the public interest, but not so independent as to be able to exercise unchecked power.

When the founders wanted to ensure accountability, they mostly relied on elections and the voters to hold government officials responsible for their actions. But for cases in which abusive behavior could not be tolerated until the next election, they provided for the possibility of impeachment and removal. That power they were only willing to entrust to the most democratic branch of the government: the legislature.

There are risks associated with either a narrow or broad reading of impeachable offenses. A narrow reading of the power risks making the impeachment power inflexible and unable to respond to unanticipated bad behavior on the part of government officials. A broad reading of the power risks creating a partisan weapon that can be used by legislators to undermine the independence of other government officials.

The broader the category of impeachable offenses is understood to be, the easier it is for mere political disagreements to become grounds for impeachment investigations. It is all too common for partisans to believe that their political foes are not just wrong but dangerously wrong, not just mistaken but willfully mistaken, not just erroneous but abusive. If the impeachment power is used to settle political scores, then the independence of the separate branches of government is undermined. If routine impeachments were to become a tool for overcoming policy disputes and political obstructions, then political power would gradually be centralized in Congress, with the judiciary and the executive reduced to little more than extensions of the legislative will. The Constitution was not designed to have presidents and judges sit only at the pleasure of the Congress.

The founders left a powerful weapon in the hands of Congress in the form of the impeachment power. Like all powers, the impeachment power is subject to misuse and abuse. The ultimate check on how that power is used is public sentiment. The burden is on those who think that an impeachment is appropriate to persuade others that the circumstances warrant taking such drastic measures. Successfully exercising the impeachment power requires the ability to reach across the political aisle and forge a consensus that the danger of leaving an individual in power is too great to be risked. In the absence of that consensus, legislators are forced to rely on the more mundane tools they have at their disposal to check abuses of power and advance the public welfare.

To understand the impeachment power, it helps to begin with the constitutional text. The text alone does not tell us what the impeachment power is for or how it is best used, but it does establish the basic framework within which we must operate. With that framework in place, we can begin to explore more controversial questions about the impeachment power in subsequent chapters.

Unfortunately, the constitutional text establishing the impeachment power in the federal constitution is remarkably scant. Worse yet, the drafters did not lay out the impeachment power in one compact constitutional provision. The constitutional language relating to impeachments is spread across the document. State constitutions are often much clearer than the federal constitution in how they describe the impeachment power. While the constitutional text tells us something about the impeachment power, a great deal of detail is left to historical background, structural logic, and congressional practice.

The Power to Impeach in the House

As the Constitution describes the House of Representatives in Section 2 of Article I, it simply concludes, "The House of Representatives shall chuse their Speaker and other Officers; and shall have the sole Power of Impeachment." This is not terribly helpful, and it clearly leaves much to the congressional imagination.

Notably, this clause tells us nothing at all about what process the House must follow when it chooses to exercise its sole power of impeachment. We have to fill in the gaps by looking to a separate provision of Article I, which lays down the default rule that "Each house may determine the Rules of its Proceedings." Unless the Constitution tells us otherwise, it is up to the House to determine for itself how to conduct its business. It is up to the House itself to determine whatever process the chamber will use to impeach a government official. The House makes up its own rules for impeachment. Those rules might be guided by earlier House precedents, but the House can always change its mind and adopt a new process if it so prefers. Just because the House has proceeded in one way in the past does not mean that it must proceed in the same way in the future.

The Constitution does not impose any procedural constraints on how the House exercises this power. A government official being impeached has no constitutional warrant for expecting that the House will proceed in any particular way. The House might grant an officer a hearing, or it might not. The House might hold a public impeachment inquiry, or it might not. The House might vote to launch an impeachment inquiry before it votes to impeach a government official, or it might not. The constraints on how the House manages an impeachment are not imposed by constitutional rules. They are imposed by politics. The House need not ask how the Constitution dictates that it pursue an impeachment, but the House will inevitably have to ask how it can win public support of and legitimacy for an impeachment, how it can best prepare for a Senate trial, and how it can accomplish the political objectives that an impeachment is attempting to advance.

Likewise, the Constitution does not specify what the House must do to secure an impeachment. By default, the House, like other legislative bodies, operates by simple majority rule. When the Constitution deviates from that default assumption, it does so explicitly. The Constitution informs us that two-thirds of the House is required to override a presidential veto or propose a constitutional amendment or expel a member. It is silent on how articles of impeachment are adopted, and thus they can be adopted by a bare majority of the House.

Similarly, the Constitution does not specify a burden of proof that the House must satisfy in order to impeach an officer or what evidence it might consider. When exercising the impeachment power, the House is often likened to a grand jury. The comparison is helpful, even if not completely accurate. The House stands in the role of a prosecutor. It brings forth allegations of wrongdoing on the part of a government official. It need only satisfy itself that wrongdoing has occurred. The standard for doing so might be quite low. Like a grand jury in a criminal case, the House might think it sufficient that there is probable cause that impeachable offenses have been committed, or some House members might think that a somewhat greater showing of the preponderance of evidence is necessary to secure their vote to impeach. The House has generally not taken the view that any charges must be shown beyond a reasonable doubt. It is enough that allegations seem credible. Moreover, the House need not restrict itself to the kinds of evidence that might be admitted in a court of law, nor need it hear from the accused. The House could, in effect, impeach an officer in a summary proceeding with no real investigation or deliberation at all.

The House might be able to move precipitously to impeach an officer, but if it hopes to win its case in a Senate trial, it must anticipate what the Senate will need in order to be persuaded. Strictly speaking, an officer is impeached by the sole action of the House. President Bill Clinton was impeached by the House in 1998, and the fact that he was acquitted after a Senate trial does not change that fact. An officer can be impeached by the House even if the case never moves to a Senate trial at all, which might happen if the officer resigns after the impeachment and the House drops the case or even if the House just declines to move forward to a trial. But if the House wants to win a conviction in the Senate, it needs to assemble a case that will persuade the senators. At the very least, this means it needs to be prepared to present evidence to support its allegations; and it might be better situated to do that if it engages in a substantial impeachment inquiry that can gather evidence, and perhaps even if it allows the target of the impeachment inquiry to respond so that the House itself can assess the strength of its case.

Because an impeachment is inevitably political and the House must eventually persuade a body of elected senators (not to mention the House members' own constituents at the next election), the House would be wise to be cognizant of public opinion. One way to convince the senators is to go over their heads and appeal to their bosses, the voters. In most impeachments, the electorate is unlikely to pay much attention. The fate of a corrupt district court judge does not command the attention of the average voter. In some high-profile impeachments, such as the impeachment of a president, the public will certainly be paying attention, and a successful impeachment process will require that the House build a public case that will win over that political audience. A grand jury might be able to indict a ham sandwich, and the House might be able to railroad a federal officer in an impeachment vote, but such a process is unlikely to end well or achieve the goals that the House is attempting to achieve. Successfully impeaching an officer and successfully accomplishing something are not necessarily the same thing.

One thing that the Senate will demand if it is to proceed to trial are articles of impeachment. Articles of impeachment are comparable to a grand jury bill of indictment, in that they detail the charges that are being levied against a government official. The articles identify specific acts of misconduct that the House believes constitute impeachable offenses. They have sufficient specificity that the Senate can evaluate them and the impeached officer can mount a defense against them. That list of impeachable offenses might be quite lengthy, or the House might levy only a single charge stated in a single article of impeachment. In order to proceed to trial, it is not enough for the House to impeach an officer; it must draft articles of impeachment that can form the basis for a trial. The House can vote to impeach before articles of impeachment have been drafted and even before an investigation has taken place. But if it wants to move to trial, it will need to draft and adopt articles of impeachment.

The drafters of the Constitution relied on an English legal context when composing constitutional language, and that is true in the impeachment context as well. The Sixth Amendment does not detail what an "impartial jury" is; it relies on American lawyers knowing what that term entails. Similarly, the Constitution does not tell us what an impeachment is; it only tells us that the House has the sole power to do it. The fact that the House alone possesses the power to impeach is itself significant. Only the U.S. House of Representatives can file the charges necessary to initiate a Senate trial. There is no path to circumventing the House and going directly to the Senate. If the House stubbornly refuses to impeach an officer that the Senate clearly thinks should be removed, the Senate cannot act alone, nor can it act on the basis of charges filed by the Department of Justice, or a petition submitted by a group of voters, or a resolution adopted by a state legislature. Action in the House is a necessary condition for launching a Senate trial. Impeachment politics could play out very differently if the House did not possess the *sole* power to impeach.

But what is the "power of impeachment" that the House possesses? As Sir Edward Coke informed the House of Commons in 1621, it is the power to "address ourselves to the Lords," or, in the American case, to the senators. The power of impeachment is the power to go to the Senate and demand that it conduct a trial to determine whether a specified federal officer should be removed for having committed a high crime and misdemeanor. Since the House has the sole power to impeach, no one else may go to the Senate and demand such a trial. Importantly, the power of impeachment also does not mean anything more than that under the federal constitution. The House can level accusations and demand a trial, and that is all.

The situation is a bit different in some of the American states, and that difference is both informative and consequential. Some state constitutions specify that when an individual is impeached by the lower legislative chamber that individual is also suspended from exercising the powers of public office. Those powers are restored to the individual if the Senate acquits, but they are permanently removed if the Senate convicts. Note that this gives an important power to a single legislative chamber. By a bare majority vote, the House in some states can temporarily take away an officer's powers. If the Senate delays holding a trial, that temporary suspension can be quite lengthy. By statute, North Carolina has determined that "every officer impeached shall be suspended from the exercise of his office until his acquittal." When some Republicans were angered by rumors that the slim majority of Democrats on the state supreme court might vote to force two Republican justices to recuse themselves from participating in a case on a controversial voter ID law, they floated the possibility that state House Republicans might "effectively suspend those Democrat justices immediately and indefinitely by a simple majority vote." An impeachment vote could take justices out of play until they were acquitted in a Senate impeachment trial, and the House could take its time before bringing articles of impeachment to the Senate for trial or the Senate could delay beginning an impeachment trial in which the justices might win their acquittal. Indeed, a simple majority of the lower legislative chamber could deny the Democrats of their majority on the state supreme court until after the next election, when the voters themselves might hand control of the court to the Republicans.[21] Cooler heads prevailed in North Carolina in 2021. No justices were recused, and no justices were impeached. The voter ID law was struck down by the state supreme court, but Republicans won back the state supreme court in 2022 and the new majority reversed that decision. Pandora's box had been put in full view even if it had not been opened.

A legislative chamber with the power to suspend a judge or a governor can do quite a bit of mischief. On the other hand, a governor who deserves to be removed from office can do quite a bit of mischief while awaiting a trial. Some states have decided that the wiser course of action is to err on the side of suspension. The drafters of the federal constitution, probably without giving the matter much thought and relying on the English practice, decided to err on the side of preserving the status quo. There is a genuine risk that a tyrannical president could do a great deal of damage between the time that the House has impeached him and the Senate has convicted him, and that includes the possibility of a president conspiring to use the powers of his office to avoid a Senate conviction. Under the federal constitution, there is nothing to be done to prevent such misbehavior besides moving expeditiously to get a conviction. If a Congress truly feared what such a president might do, the solution available is to impeach and convict as quickly as possible—and that could be quite quick indeed. To date, Congress has never moved that quickly, but that reflects a political judgment on the part of the House and the Senate and not anything about the constitutional power itself. It seems probable that the House thought that President Donald Trump had been practically stripped of power when it voted to impeach him for a second time in January 2021. The House did not move quickly to impeach the president after the events of January 6, and it waited until after Joe Biden was sworn in as president before getting around to demanding a trial in the Senate. One can only assume that the congressional leadership had received some assurances behind the scenes that President Trump would not misbehave in the nearly two weeks that he was allowed to continue to occupy the White House after the electoral votes had been counted. The second impeachment was not about incapacitating a dangerous president. It was about symbolically punishing an enfeebled president.

That state practice is also informative of what the "power of impeachment" even means. In December 2019, the House voted to adopt articles of impeachment against President Trump but was in no hurry to initiate a Senate trial. Apparently hoping that the House could influence the Senate's decision about what trial procedures to adopt, Speaker Nancy Pelosi decided to wait until after the holidays to present those articles to the Senate. This raised the interesting, but legally meaningless, question of whether President

Trump could celebrate the holidays without yet having the stain on his record of having been impeached, and the president took some joy in telling his supporters during those weeks that, "In fact, there's no impeachment." Pelosi, for her part, insisted that the House had ruined the president's holidays by having already impeached him. The answer as to when the impeachment of an officer by the House technically occurs is not entirely obvious, but there seems to be good reason for thinking that Pelosi was wrong and that Trump's record was unblemished when he enjoyed his Christmas feast in 2019.[22]

Nonetheless, it should be noted that Speaker Pelosi's view does reflect modern congressional practice, which began in 1912. In that year, for the first time, the House did not send one of its members to the Senate to demand that a trial be conducted to impeach an officer. Instead, the House simply gave directions to the clerk of the House "that a message be sent to the Senate to inform them that this House has impeached, for high crimes and misdemeanors, Robert W. Archbald, circuit judge of the United States." After 1912, the House voted on resolutions specifying that an officer "is impeached," and then simply sent a written notice to the Senate informing them of what the House had done. The modern *House Practice Manual* specifies that "the respondent in an impeachment proceeding is impeached by the adoption of the House of articles of impeachment." Since 1912, the Senate has learned about an impeachment in the past tense. If we think the constitutional meaning of the "power of impeachment" is something that evolves with congressional practice or is simply subject to congressional definition, then our current practice under the federal constitution dictates that an officer is impeached the moment the House adopts a resolution declaring that the officer is impeached. Once that is done, the House just sends the paperwork to the Senate letting them know what has happened. By that logic, Donald Trump was impeached for the first time on December 18, 2019.[23]

The modern view is not, however, consistent with the early historical practice and likely the original public meaning of the impeachment power. William Blackstone, the English jurist whom many early Americans relied upon for understanding English law, defined an impeachment as "a prosecution" and "being a presentment to the most high and supreme court of criminal jurisdiction by the solemn grand inquest of the whole kingdom." An early American constitutional commentator, William Rawle, thought it clear that the power "to impeach" simply is the power "to exhibit articles of accusation against a public officer before a competent tribunal."[24] When the U.S. House of Representatives decided to exercise its power of impeachment for the first time against Senator William Blount in 1797, it searched the English precedents for guidance as to how to do it. It concluded that it needed to pass a resolution designating someone to walk over to the Senate and impeach Senator Blount. The Senate journal records that the following message was delivered by Representative Samuel Sitgreaves from the House:

> Mr. President: I am commanded, in the name of the House of Representatives, and of all the people of the United States, to impeach William Blount, a Senator of the United States, of high crimes and misdemeanors; and to acquaint the Senate, that the House of Representatives will, in due time, exhibit particular articles against him, and make good the same.[25]

The House had commanded Sitgreaves to go to the Senate and impeach Blount. Once that was done, then the Senate could send notice to Blount that he had been impeached and could prepare for trial. The House would later draft and exhibit in the Senate articles of impeachment. This was the form that the House used to impeach officers all through the nineteenth century. An impeachment occurred when the Senate sergeant-at-arms announced the presence of a member of the House, who then addressed the Senate chamber and declared that "in obedience to the order of the House of Representatives we do appear before you, and in the name of the House of Representatives and all the people of the United States of America we do impeach" some miscreant federal officer. Up through 1904, an impeachment was an act performed by the House on the floor of the Senate. By that logic, Donald Trump was impeached on January 16, 2020.

The Power to Try All Impeachments in the Senate

In describing the Senate in Section 3 of Article I, the Constitution again concludes with the impeachment power, but here the text is somewhat more fulsome:

> The Senate shall have the sole Power to try all Impeachments. When sitting for that Purpose, they shall be on Oath or Affirmation. When the President of the United States is tried, the Chief Justice shall preside: And no Person shall be convicted without the Concurrence of two thirds of the Members present.

The constitutional text is more robust in regard to the Senate, and for good reason. Note that here the Constitution specifically departs from the default of simple majority rule. In order to do so, the text is explicit that conviction in a Senate trial requires more than a bare majority. Conviction requires a supermajority, in this case a supermajority of two-thirds. The constitutional drafters built in a bias toward acquittal and of leaving impeached officers in place, and a distinct minority of the senators can force that result. At the same time, the only votes that count are those of senators who are present to vote. Senators cannot impede a conviction by removing themselves from the Senate floor and refusing to be counted.

As it did with the House, the Constitution entrusts a "sole power" to try impeachments in the Senate. Just as the Senate cannot circumvent the House in order to launch an impeachment process, so the House cannot circumvent the Senate to secure a removal of a disfavored officer. There is only one constitutional court of impeachment, and that is the Senate. As we discuss further in chapter 6, this textual delegation arguably excludes the

Supreme Court from reviewing the actions of the Senate when it tries an impeachment. In this unusual class of cases, the Senate is the court of last resort.

The Constitution once again leaves to the Senate a great deal of discretion over what procedures it might choose to adopt when exercising its share of the impeachment power, but unlike with the House, the Constitution describes the Senate's role in a way that is pregnant with meaning. What happens in the Senate is described as a trial and the potential results as a conviction. The senators, unlike the House members, are instructed to take an oath when sitting for an impeachment trial. In at least one situation, the chief justice is instructed to preside over the trial. Such markers have long been understood to suggest that the Senate plays a more judicious role than the House. If the House acts like a prosecutor in leveling accusations, the Senate acts as a court in evaluating those allegations. In that impeachment trial, the House plays the role of prosecutor by sending a delegation of representatives to serve as "managers" of the case in the Senate. The impeached official is entitled to bring lawyers of his own to mount a defense. The Constitution itself does not specify what oath the senators will take, but the Senate has adopted a rule specifying that the senators will pledge themselves to "do impartial justice according to the Constitution and laws." Unlike the House, the Senate gavels itself in and out of its session as a court of impeachment. As a formal and procedural matter, the Senate exists as two separate bodies, one legislative and one judicial.

The Senate is a court of a very peculiar sort. The senators do not believe themselves to be bound by the federal rules of evidence that would apply in an ordinary court. They determine their own burden of proof for justifying a verdict, and some senators have preferred a very high standard comparable to criminal trials while others have preferred a lower bar. The senators need not accept defenses and immunities that are appropriately recognized in a criminal court. If senators wish to draw inferences from a witness's refusal to answer questions or wish to dismiss an officer's defense that his speech is protected from criminal punishment by the First Amendment, they have the freedom to do so. The senators are not passive jurors watching a trial and rendering a judgment at the end. They are also the judges, and judges of an extraordinary sort. The Senate as a body sets the rules for the trial and acts on motions from the parties to the case. The presiding officer, whether the chief justice, the vice president, or the president pro tempore, makes an initial ruling on motions, but ultimately the presiding officer has no power to substitute his or her will for the will of the Senate majority. The role of Chief Justice John Roberts in the impeachment trial of President Donald Trump was to do no more than interpret and implement the rules of the Senate, and his judgment could be overridden at any moment. The presiding officer in a Senate trial is more ceremonial than consequential. But the presiding officer does set a tone, and the fact that the Constitution designates the chief justice to preside over at least some Senate trials has emphasized that what the Senate is doing on those occasions is conducting a trial and acting in a solemn judicial capacity, not in a purely political one. The senators might not have to do what the chief justice says, but the chief justice's presence is a reminder of their oath.

The text of the Constitution empowers the Senate to hold an impeachment trial, but it does not mandate that the Senate have a trial. To impeach an officer, the House sends a representative to the Senate to demand a trial, but the constitutional text does not require any particular response to that demand from the Senate. The current Senate rules anticipate that the Senate will move to a trial when the House exhibits articles of impeachment, but such rules can be changed. If the Senate wants to take action against an officer, it must go through the constitutionally specified process of holding a trial; but if the Senate is content to allow an officer to remain in place, it is not clear that the Senate needs to follow any particular procedure. The status quo can be preserved by the Senate acquitting an impeached officer, but it can also be preserved by the Senate just never holding an impeachment trial. Moreover, the fact that the Senate has the "sole Power" to try impeachments emphasizes that the impeachment process is a cooperative one. There is no way to end-run a Senate that does not want to remove an individual from office. If the argument above is correct that the power to impeach is the power to address the Senate, then the Senate may decline to hold a trial—but it may not bar the doors to a delegation from the House seeking to impeach an officer. The House's power to impeach requires that the Senate hear the grievances, even if the Senate does not want to take any action to remedy those grievances. Of course, if Nancy Pelosi is correct that the impeachment is complete when the House has voted on a resolution, then the Senate could theoretically refuse to allow the House even to exhibit the articles of impeachment on the chamber floor. The constitutional power of the House to impeach is exhausted within its own chamber.

The fact that the Senate must conduct a trial in order to convict and remove an impeached official raises some important questions about what procedures might satisfy that constitutional requirement. We consider that in more detail in the next chapter.

Who Can Be Impeached and For What?

Oddly, the constitutional drafters tucked the scope of the impeachment power at the end of Article II, which describes the executive branch. Separating the provisions of the impeachment power in this way introduces some unfortunate ambiguities that a more compact impeachment clause might have avoided. Section 4 of Article II states, "The President, Vice President and all civil Officers of the United States, shall be removed from Office on Impeachment for, and Conviction of, Treason, Bribery, or other high Crimes and Misdemeanors."

This clause is generally understood to define the jurisdiction of federal impeachment power. It is possible that the text simply tells us what happens when a civil officer is impeached and convicted but does not tell us that *only* civil officers can be impeached and convicted. Congress has refused to go down that path. Military officers, members of Congress, state officials, and private individuals who have never held federal office are understood to be beyond the reach of the federal impeachment power. Even if that result is not textually required, it is a less dangerous interpretation. If Congress could proactively impeach and convict private individuals who might someday become rivals for political power, it tilts the balance of power too far in favor of incumbent politicians. Private individuals are ill situated to defend themselves against an overreaching Congress. State government officials might have more political resources to mount a vigorous defense against an impeachment, but intruding into the operation of the state governments in such a way would mark a sharp departure from traditional principles of American federalism. If the Senate were asked to take jurisdiction of such an impeachment case, it would be expected to dismiss the charges as beyond the reach of the constitutional impeachment power. It has been long held by the Senate itself that only presidents, vice presidents, and federal civil officers are subject to impeachment.

It is also here that the Constitution seems to specify the scope of impeachable offenses. It is evident from the debates in the Philadelphia Convention and the earliest commentary that this language was meant to establish the possible grounds for impeachment. To the extent that the "power of impeachment" as it was inherited from England encompassed a broader range of possible offenses, the text of the Constitution imposes a restraint. The American House of Representatives cannot impeach individuals for everything that the English House of Commons could. This limitation is part of the taming of the impeachment power as it was carried over into republican government.

The offenses of treason and bribery are familiar enough, but the phrase *high crimes and misdemeanors* is unique to the impeachment context. In practice, it has been those high crimes that have generated impeachment inquiries, and it has been high crimes that have generated controversy over the range of impeachable offenses. The meaning of that phrase is the focus of our attention in chapter 4.

Can Former Officers Be Impeached?

The second impeachment of President Donald Trump shone a spotlight on what was once a highly esoteric question: whether former officers can be impeached by the House and convicted by the Senate. This is not an easy question, and there is no scholarly consensus on the answer. Even so, I think the best answer is both that the House can impeach and the Senate can try a former officer. We can assume that the conventional understanding of the scope of the impeachment power is correct—that the House can only impeach presidents, vice presidents, and federal civil officers. The question is whether the House, the Senate, or both lose jurisdiction over those individuals once they leave office. Everyone agrees that private individuals are outside the scope of the impeachment power. Are former federal officers simply private individuals for purposes of the impeachment power? The powers of the House and the Senate in such circumstances create distinct puzzles, however, and the case for the Senate is admittedly stronger than the case for the House. Let us start with the easier case first.

As we have seen, the Constitution grants the Senate the power to "to try all impeachments." From a purely textual perspective, this would seem to suggest that the Senate has jurisdiction to try any case involving an individual who was the subject of a valid House impeachment.[26] The House has frequently chosen to drop its impeachment efforts when the officer in question has resigned; in those cases, it has generally either not voted on an impeachment resolution, not drafted articles of impeachment, or not presented articles of impeachment to the Senate. But the fact that the House frequently concludes that its goals have been accomplished by the officer's resignation does not mean that the House could not have seen the impeachment process all the way through to a Senate verdict.

It is true that Article II, Section 4, does specify what happens to designated officers upon conviction in a Senate impeachment trial. This language generally has been read, quite reasonably, to limit the potential scope of the impeachment power. The Constitution could have been written differently, but this extension of the jurisdictional scope of the impeachment power to other individuals would have departed from inherited practice and could be expected to require an explicit textual delegation. According to Section 4, incumbent officers "shall be removed" upon conviction, which is why the Senate does not take a separate vote on whether to remove—instead, removal is automatic and instantaneous upon conviction. Section 4 says nothing about what happens to former officers, and Article I states that the punishment that the Senate can levy after conviction "shall not extend further" than removal and disqualification. So while the Senate has limited punishments it can impose, Article I says nothing about whether Senate trials or punishments are limited to incumbent officers.

What about the purpose of the constitutional impeachment power? If the sole purpose of an impeachment is to remove from office an individual who might pose a danger to the nation, does that mean that former officers cannot be put on trial? If Congress is limited to considering the misdeeds of a current officeholder in their current office, could a current officer be impeached and tried for his misdeeds in a previous office? Precedent suggests the answer is yes. Circuit Judge Robert W. Archbald was impeached, tried, and convicted for corruption in office, and the articles of impeachment included his behavior in his previous position of district court judge. It is true that the House was unable to secure the necessary two-thirds majority for conviction on those articles stemming from his prior office, and at least some senators expressed doubts "as to his impeachability for offenses committed in an office other than that he held at time of impeachment." By contrast, the House argued that "it is indeed anomalous if this Congress is powerless to remove a corrupt or unfit Federal judge from office because his corruption or misdemeanor, however vicious or reprehensible, may have occurred during his tenure, in some other judicial office under the Government of the United States prior to his appointment to the particular office from which he is sought to be ousted by impeachment." Archbald is one of the few federal officers to suffer the penalty of disqualification from future federal office, suggesting that the Senate appreciated the gravity of Archbald's extended history of misconduct.[27]

If the House had been able to uncover corruption only from Archbald's days as a district court judge but not from his then brief tenure as a circuit court judge, it is easy to imagine that two-thirds of the senators would have voted to convict and remove rather than leave a demonstrably corrupt judge on the bench. Even if the Senate had been convinced that such a judge had reformed himself and thus was no longer going to further harm the nation from the office he then occupied, impeachment and removal for the past misdeeds might well have been sensible and sufficient.

But set that scenario aside. Is it the case that removal is the sole purpose of the impeachment power? Such a framing at the very least ignores the additional punishment available to the Senate after conviction—disqualification from future federal office. Removal is wholly sufficient to prevent the further harm an incumbent officeholder might do. Disqualification is necessary to ensure that the individual—such as a serially corrupt judge—has no opportunity to do similar harm in the future.

Even this reads the purpose of the impeachment power too narrowly. The impeachment power gives the first, most democratic branch of the government the ability to scrutinize the actions of individuals in the other branches of government and call them to account for their actions. What is more, the impeachment process serves as a warning to future officeholders. By clearly and decisively condemning certain actions as intolerable within the American system of government, Congress not only purges the particular malefactor but also attempts to purge the misdeeds from the system and set up a prophylactic to prevent their recurrence. If impeached officials can short-circuit that process of condemnation by resigning—as Secretary of War William Belknap attempted to do in 1876—then the bad actor has within his power the ability to deprive Congress of fully making an example of him and thereby sending the necessary signals to future officeholders. The Senate did not allow Belknap to avoid its jurisdiction by resigning. It proceeded to trial and delivered a verdict.

The Belknap and Archbald examples point to the more serious challenge with impeachment trials of former officers. In both cases, there was enough support in the Senate to proceed with a trial on the charges stemming from a previously held office, but not enough support to convict on those charges. The jurisdictional question of taking the case only required a simple majority in the Senate, but conviction required a two-thirds majority. Introducing an additional complication of a late impeachment trial makes it that much harder, as a practical matter, to convince a supermajority of senators to convict. At least some wavering senators are likely to be bothered by the timeliness of the proceedings, and when the Senate needs two-thirds to convict, there is no room for error.

The case of the House impeaching a former officer is more difficult than the Senate conducting a trial of a former officer. The starting point is once again the question of what the "power of impeachment" is understood to mean. The Constitution does not explicitly limit the impeachment power to current officeholders. If we think that former officers are beyond the reach of the House, then it must be because there is such a limitation implicit in the impeachment power itself.

It is not obvious that the impeachment power has such a built-in limitation. The founders borrowed this power from British parliamentary practice and state constitutional practice, which does not suggest that the power of impeachment was intrinsically limited to incumbent officers. Quite the contrary, in fact: British practice indicates that the "power of impeachment" is the power to lodge formal allegations that an individual engaged in misconduct while holding a governmental office. That an officer resigned or his misdeeds were not discovered right away did not prevent the House of Commons from impeaching him. Impeachments of former officers were both known and explicitly textually allowed. When the impeachment power was transplanted to American shores, it was explicitly shorn of some British features, but there was no American consensus that the impeachment power did not extend to former officers. In fact, some state constitutions explicitly authorized their legislatures to impeach former officers, sometimes while imposing a time limit on how long the former officer was at risk of impeachment. No state explicitly prohibited such impeachments. Especially when both terms of office and legislative sessions were short, the possibility that official misconduct could be investigated and condemned even after the wrongdoer left office was not only sensible but perhaps even imperative. The federal constitutional framers did not clearly rule out such "late" impeachments, though they were aware that such applications were understood to be within the scope of a legislative power of impeachment. When the constitutional drafters wanted to narrow the scope of the impeachment power as it was inherited from England, they said so. They did not say so in this case.[28]

Moreover, one can imagine circumstances in which such a use of the impeachment power would be justifiable. In 1862, the Senate for the first time disqualified someone from future federal office when it convicted Judge West Humphreys on articles of impeachment that included the charge that he "did unlawfully act as judge of an illegally constituted tribunal within said State, called the district court of the Confederate States of America." If Humphreys had bothered to send in his resignation rather than simply neglecting his duties as a federal judge under the U.S. Constitution, the House might not have taken the time to impeach him. But it would have been understandable if Congress had determined that, even if he had resigned, the secessionist Humphreys still needed to be barred from any future federal office of honor, trust, or profit. If Congress in 1974 had imagined the possibility of President Richard Nixon rehabilitating his reputation sufficiently to have a chance at holding a future office, it is not hard to imagine a bipartisan House and Senate steaming ahead with an impeachment and trial in order to bar that possibility through a judgment of disqualification. Worried that an infamous former officeholder might eventually live down his infamy, Congress might seek to make that recovery more difficult through the impeachment process.

The framers did not discuss the matter one way or another, but they could easily have understood that the "power of impeachment" implicitly includes a jurisdiction over former officials. The text is at best vague. And if the House can impeach them, then the Senate can try them, because the Senate has the power "to try all impeachments."

The House may have the constitutional authority to impeach a former president, but such acts are highly disfavored within our constitutional practice, and the House would have an extraordinary argumentative burden to bear to justify such an action. It might be the case that the House should impeach a former officer so as to fortify constitutional norms and send a clear message to other officers that the behavior in question is unacceptable. But we should not want to go down the road of using the impeachment power simply to settle scores with the leaders of the other political party. Such actions would quickly squander the solemnity and weight of the impeachment power while heightening partisan tensions and fostering greater animosity and distrust. Late impeachments might be possible under the Constitution, but the circumstances that might justify taking such a step should be exceptional.

What Are the Consequences of an Impeachment?

After entrusting the Senate with the sole power to try all impeachments, the Constitution in Section 3 of Article I goes on to impose a limit on the Senate:

> Judgment in Cases of Impeachment shall not extend further than to removal from Office, and disqualification to hold and

enjoy any Office of honor, Trust or Profit under the United States: but the Party convicted shall nevertheless be liable and subject to Indictment, Trial, Judgment and Punishment, according to Law.

In addition, when enumerating the powers of the president, the Constitution also makes clear that the president's pardon power does not extend to "Cases of Impeachment."

An American impeachment is a much more limited affair than the English impeachments of yore. The House of Lords was an alternative forum to the ordinary criminal courts for bringing criminal charges against some especially high-and-mighty individuals. As a consequence, the House of Lords could impose a wide range of quite drastic punishments when it convicted someone in an impeachment trial.

The Senate has no such power to punish. The potential consequences of an impeachment are purely political, and that has served to emphasize that the American impeachment power is a political process to remedy political problems. Impeachments are strictly separated from the ordinary criminal process. The conduct of a federal officer might merit indictment and trial in an ordinary criminal court, and it might also merit impeachment and trial in the Senate, but the two possibilities exist on completely different tracks. A criminal proceeding is unaffected by anything that the House and Senate might do, and the House and Senate can reach through the impeachment power conduct that is not criminally liable. It is not double jeopardy for an individual to face trial in a criminal court and then subsequently face trial in the Senate for the same actions.

The Senate can do no more than remove an individual from office and disqualify an individual from future office. The first, removal, is understood to be immediate and automatic upon conviction. Officers "shall be removed from office" upon conviction. Disqualification, on the other hand, has traditionally been understood as a discretionary step that the Senate might take after conviction. The Senate has required that the House request that such a punishment be imposed, and in those cases the Senate has taken a second and separate vote on whether to disqualify after it has rendered a guilty verdict. Somewhat controversially, the Senate has assumed that it can disqualify by a simple majority vote, even though the prior conviction requires a two-thirds majority.[29]

The limitation on the president's pardon power likewise emphasizes that the impeachment process and the criminal process are two completely distinct things. The president has no role whatsoever in the impeachment process. Since misconduct involving the president was precisely the kind of thing that motivated the framers to include an impeachment power in the Constitution, it was essential that the president not be able to rescue individuals from impeachment and removal. At the same time, just as individuals who have been impeached and convicted might still be liable in the ordinary criminal courts, so might they be pardoned by the president from that liability. If a judge was both impeached and convicted for bribery and also indicted and convicted for the same acts, the president could relieve the judge from punishments imposed by the ordinary criminal court but could do nothing about the judge's removal by the Senate.

These constitutional provisions regarding the consequences of an impeachment strengthen the hand of the American Congress at the same time that they impose limits. The English monarchs took care to inform Parliament that it was the sovereign ruler, not the Parliament, that held the trump card in the game of impeachments. Monarchs could dissolve Parliament. Monarchs could refuse to apply the punishments that the Parliament had imposed. Monarchs could pardon those who had been impeached. And, of course, the monarchs themselves were immune from impeachment. All those monarchal powers helped undermine what Parliament could hope to accomplish through the impeachment power. On the other hand, the constitutional drafters shifted power back to Congress. Presidents have no comparable power to dissolve Congress if they do not like what it does. Presidents cannot nullify the punishments imposed by the Senate after a conviction in an impeachment trial. Presidents cannot immunize officers from impeachment, and they themselves are not immune from the impeachment power. By limiting the impeachment power to political offenses, the constitutional drafters made Congress supreme in that more limited domain.

Such landmarks of the federal impeachment power are not entirely uncontroversial, but they set out the broad contours of the impeachment power. They leave some very important questions unanswered, however. They do not tell us when, how, and why Congress ought to exercise its impeachment power. Grappling with those questions is the task of the remainder of this book.

2

What Is a Fair
Impeachment Process?

THE CONSTITUTION famously did not anticipate political parties, and the founding generation severely distrusted them. The constitutional framers certainly understood the realities of political disagreement, ambitious politicians, and divergent interests. They strove to design a constitution that would organize and channel popular politics and political intrigues. They hoped that setting the new government on the firm republican foundations of public approval and regular elections would sap the energy away from party organizations, or what they frequently called political "factions."[1]

The first generation of American political leaders was not always consistent in its views on the sources and dangers of political parties, but saw great risk in their emergence. Political parties, in its view, were frequently little more than conspiracies for acquiring power. Alexander Hamilton was typical in expressing a fear of the "intolerant spirit which has, at all times, characterized political parties." Parties created political orthodoxies and heresies, measured political loyalty and disloyalty, and all too often sought by "fire and sword" to banish their enemies from the public arena. What is worse, Hamilton thought, they could become a source of foreign intrigue as enemy governments took advantage of American elections "for exciting cabals & parties."[2] Benjamin Franklin worried that men overtaken by the passions of "ambition and avarice" would "strive for this profitable pre-eminence through all the bustle of cabal, the heat of contention, the infinite mutual abuse of parties, [and the] tearing to pieces the best of characters."[3] Aggrieved by the growing chorus of critics during his second term of office, President George Washington was wont to characterize political parties as the seedbed of treason and insurrection. They were "incendiaries of the public peace and order" which sought to "poison and discontent the minds of the people against the government." The father of the nation recognized, of course, "the right of the people to meet occasionally to petition" the government, but that was quite different than the formation of "a self-created *permanent* body" (italics in original) that set about "endeavoring to destroy all confidence in the administration" and "disquiet the public mind." In his farewell address to the people of the country as he retired from public life, Washington sought to "warn you in the most solemn manner against the baneful effects of the Spirit of Party," which would "distract the Public Councils, and enfeeble the Public administration"—when it was not setting the stage for "a frightful despotism."[4]

Thomas Jefferson was more open than most of his generation to the possibilities of political parties in a free society. It was, after all, Jefferson and his allies like James Madison who were helping to orchestrate much of the public criticism of George Washington and his administration. Washington channeled their thoughts when observing that "there is an opinion that parties in free countries are useful checks upon the Administration of the Government, and serve to keep alive the Spirit of Liberty." Washington admitted that this might be true "in Governments of a Monarchical cast," but did not think it true in republican America.[5] Jefferson later tried to reassure his onetime rival and renewed friend, John Adams, that "in all governments where they have been permitted freely to think and to speak," people have divided into parties. Partisan disagreements might sometimes venture into "bitterness" and "indecency," but "differences of opinion and party differences" were inevitable as individuals worked to identify and advance the public good as best they could. "Like religious differences, a difference in politics should never be permitted to enter into social intercourse, or to disturb its friendships, its charities or justice," but parties could be "useful watchmen for the public."[6]

Even so, Jefferson was concerned about where the "spirit of party" might lead when he was awkwardly serving as vice president of the United States in 1798. One way in which the Constitution failed to anticipate the rise of political parties was in its design for the election of the president and vice president. Thinking that the important office of the "first magistrate" should be filled only by those individuals who were universally regarded as fit and worthy for the role, the Constitution simply designated that the vice president would be the runner-up in the presidential election. Who could be more ready to step into the president's shoes if circumstances called for it than the person who received the second-most ballots cast for the job? In the election of 1796, that meant that John Adams was chosen president, and his rival Thomas Jefferson became the vice president. Of course, as both Adams and Jefferson recognized, the two men were distinguished not merely by the relative esteem with which their fellow countrymen regarded their wisdom and judgment but also by their opinions about how the government should be run. Jefferson feared Adams harbored monarchical aspirations of his own; Adams feared that Jefferson was a revolutionary of the French sort, where mobs gathered to watch the guillotine claim thousands of heads. All things considered, Jefferson was relieved to have come in second place, for "a more tranquil and unoffending station could not have been found for me" since he could as vice president spend most of his time at home in Virginia.[7]

In the meantime, Jefferson partly occupied himself with the one constitutional duty that was entrusted to the vice president—sitting as the presiding officer of the United States Senate. Having decided that his office was "constitutionally confined to legislative functions," Jefferson thought he was both barred from taking "any part whatever in executive consultations" and free to complain (privately) that the friends of Adams were "all timid men who prefer the calm of despotism to the boisterous sea of liberty." As the Senate's presiding officer, Jefferson thought it imperative that he govern himself by "some known system of rules, that may neither leave himself free to indulge caprice or passion, nor open to the imputation of them." Legislative rules had the added benefit of providing "a shelter and protection to the minority, against the attempts of power" of the legislative majority. Jefferson's bookish efforts to write a manual of parliamentary practice that could guide Senate deliberations going forward were no doubt spurred in part by his recognition that his own political allies were only a small minority in the Fifth Congress (and picked up only two additional seats in the midterm elections of 1798). Some rules were needed to check the "wantonness of power" of "large and successful majorities."[8]

That concern was soon brought to the fore when Jefferson was called upon to preside over the very first federal impeachment trial of Senator William Blount of Tennessee. Blount was one of the few Jeffersonians in the Senate, and a man of some significant stature, having split his time in the summer of 1787 between serving as a delegate to the Constitutional Convention in Philadelphia and as a member of the Continental Congress in New York. The Senate was therefore shocked in July 1797 when President John Adams delivered to the clerk of the chamber an intercepted letter from Blount detailing a conspiracy to help Britain seize Florida and Louisiana, which were then held by Spain. The Senate quickly voted to expel Blount, the House voted to impeach him, and Blount fled back to Tennessee. The House was much slower, however, to draft articles of impeachment and present them to the Senate, and the Senate likewise took its time before beginning the trial. The unprecedented event forced both the House and the Senate to come up with some procedures for impeaching and trying an officer on impeachment charges.

Jefferson thought the Blount impeachment raised a host of thorny questions, not least of which was whether a senator could be impeached at all. In the end, it was that question that brought the case to a close. A majority of the Senate voted to dismiss the case for lack of jurisdiction on January 14, 1799. Jefferson was apt to view the jurisdictional issue as among the "many metaphysical niceties" that were being bandied about in the months leading up to the Blount trial.[9]

More interesting to him was how any such trial would be conducted, and how it related to the growing reality of political partisanship. With more than two-thirds of the Senate controlled by the president's party, and "under the probable prospect" that such would be the case "forever," the vice president feared that the impeachment power would become "the most formidable weapon for the purposes of a dominant faction that ever was contrived" and "the most effectual one for getting rid of any man whom they consider as dangerous to their views." Under such circumstances, whether the House should impeach and the Senate should convict might become "a question of pure party," and the impeachment power itself "an engine more of passion than justice."[10] Although the already exiled Blount seemed bound to escape a conviction on the theory "a Senator unimpeachable, absolutely," Jefferson suspected the Federalists were prepared to declare "that not only officers of the State governments, but every private citizen of the U.S. is impeachable." "No republic," Jefferson mused, "can ever be of any duration, without a Senate . . . strong enough to bear up against all popular storms and passions."[11] He was not convinced that so partisan a Senate could be counted on to be such a bulwark. Jefferson had hoped that the Senate might be convinced to send all impeachment trials to a jury, which might be "so composed as to be clear of the spirit of faction," wagering that this would "lessen the dangers of the court of impeachment under its present form."[12] Blount's attorney argued to the Senate that the disgraced senator, now a private citizen accused of criminal acts, should be held liable only "by the unanimous consent of a jury of his neighbourhood."

"Trial by jury, like every human institution, is liable to abuse," but the defense contended, it was "infinitely less so, than trial by Impeachment," where "the demon of Faction most frequently extends his sceptre over numerous bodies of men." The Senate declined to address the jury question directly, preferring to simply resolve "that this Court ought not to hold Jurisdiction of the said Impeachment."[13] The Federalists did not, as Jefferson feared that they would, turn their attention to impeaching state government officials, private citizens—or the sitting vice president of the United States.[14]

The Blount case raised the question of what procedures the House and the Senate should use when exercising the impeachment power, but it did not resolve it. It also highlighted how partisanship would complicate the impeachment process. The Constitution said practically nothing about how an impeachment would be conducted. It entrusted the House with the power to impeach and the Senate with the power to try impeachments. It specified that conviction required a two-thirds majority in the Senate. Beyond those most rudimentary landmarks, the Constitution left the members of Congress to their own devices.

What is a fair impeachment process, and is fairness even a relevant consideration? It is a fool's errand to try to take politics out of the impeachment process. Politics might even be desirable when deciding whether a political official should be removed from office, and, in any case, politics is inevitable when Congress assembles and deliberates. The founders might have hoped to create a constitutional republic that would be free of partisan politics, but those hopes immediately proved to be unrealistic. Partisanship was a natural feature of a free government. There was no possibility of purging the impeachment process of politics, but there was the possibility of considering whether and how partisanship might be moderated and restrained.

The constitutional framers all agreed that the power to remove misbehaving federal officers would have to be lodged somewhere. They had more difficulty agreeing on who should control the removal power and on what basis it should be exercised. There were essentially two options on the table in answer to both questions. The president might be removable by either the state governments or Congress. There was little interest among the nationalists who were working to rewrite the federal constitution in giving the states that kind of power over a branch of the national government, so they quickly settled on giving the power to Congress. If Congress had the authority to remove the president, it could be done either by impeachment or by what is sometimes known as *removal by address*. Impeachment was understood to require that a specific cause for removal be stated and a trial be held to determine whether the officer was guilty of those charges. Removal by address was a simpler process that merely required a vote, with no necessity that specific charges be made or proven or that a fair hearing be provided. Because the framers valued the independence of the three branches of government and did not want the president to be at the mercy of a hostile legislature, they preferred the route of impeachment. What kind of process would balance the need to address troublesome officers and to preserve the independence of the executive and judiciary from the legislature?

What Process Is Due for Political Misdeeds?

An important starting point for determining what process is due in an impeachment is to recognize that impeachments are a political process to rectify political problems and not a criminal process to punish crimes. This was not always true in England, where Parliament could hand down verdicts in criminal cases and impose criminal punishments, up to and including the death penalty, on wrongdoers. American legislatures were not to possess the unbridled power that Parliament sometimes wielded. The impeachment power had to be adapted to the American context and not just transferred wholesale from the British system.

The framers of the federal constitution took care to strip Congress of the power to impose criminal punishments. Thus, Congress was explicitly prohibited from exercising the parliamentary power of adopting *bills of attainder*, which singled out individuals, declared them guilty of a crime, and imposed a punishment. The Revolutionary-era Virginia judge St. George Tucker denounced bills of attainder as "state-engines of oppression" since they circumvented "legal forms, legal evidence, and of every other barrier which the laws provide against tyranny and injustice in ordinary cases." The possibility of such a despotic practice, Tucker thought, was itself "a decisive proof of the importance of the separation of powers of government, and of the independence of a judiciary."[15] Justice Joseph Story later explained that, "in such cases, the legislature assumes judicial magistracy, pronouncing guilt of the party without any of the common forms and guards of trial," and as such "may be properly deemed an irresponsible despotic discretion, being governed solely by what it deems political necessity or expediency, and too often under the influence of unreasonable fears, or unfounded suspicions."[16] A clear prohibition on bills of attainder was an important "constitutional bulwark in favor of personal security and private rights"; if that were not enough, the First Congress later added the Fifth Amendment to the Constitution, forbidding that anyone "be deprived of life, liberty, or property, without due process of law."[17]

What Congress could not do directly through bills of attainder it also could not do indirectly through the impeachment power. Thus, the Constitution in Section 3 of Article I specifies that "Judgment in Cases of Impeachment shall not extend further than to removal from Office, and disqualification to hold and enjoy any Office of honor, Trust or Profit under the United States." If an impeached individual had committed criminal offenses, then that individual was also "liable and subject to Indictment, Trial, Judgment, and Punishment, according to Law" in ordinary courts separate from the impeachment process.

The effect of such constitutional restrictions was to leave Congress with only a political tool for addressing political offenses. We demand that the government meet a high standard before depriving private individuals of their life, liberty or property. The process due to an individual accused of a criminal offense and facing possible imprisonment is appropriately cumbersome. We force criminal prosecutors to jump through some serious hoops before we judge a criminal defendant guilty.

But how much process is due before a government official can be deprived of office? In most circumstances, we would say no process at all. What does it mean to give a fair hearing to federal officers who exercise political power before deciding to dismiss them from public service? If the voters are unhappy with an elected representative, we do not demand that the electorate hear the representative out before making a change. If the president is dissatisfied with the performance of a cabinet secretary, we do not require that the president hold a hearing before saying "you're fired." For public officials exercising policymaking power, we do not recognize those individuals as having any private right to their job and thus nothing is owed to them before turning them out from that job.

When we choose to insulate public officials and government employees from such ready removal, we do so because we think it is in the public interest that they not be so easily removed rather than because of any consideration of their private interests and whatever entitlements they might like to have to their position. And, indeed, that is the calculation that the constitutional framers made when deciding to entrust an impeachment power to Congress but not a power to remove officers by address. Removal by simple majority vote risked turning the executive and judicial branches into little more than playthings of the legislative branch. The more onerous requirements of the impeachment process were constitutionally useful not because that process was owed to the officeholder but because that process would be more useful to maintaining the independence of the three branches of government and ensuring that Congress did not act impulsively. Congress owes an executive or judicial officer nothing, but Congress owes the American people cool deliberation rather than heated passion before intruding itself into the workings of the other branches of government.

If we think the process that is due for political misdeeds should be determined by the needs of the people rather than the needs of the officeholder, two considerations are probably paramount. First, Congress has a responsibility to be accurate and well informed before removing a potentially meritorious and useful public officer. Presumptively, the individuals occupying public office are competently performing their public duties. If Congress had carte blanche to throw those individuals out on a whim, the people would be no better off (assuming the new officer is equally competent and the disruption is minimal) and might be worse off (if the new officer is less skilled or the disruption to activities of the government from an impeachment is more substantial). Congress owes a duty to the people not to go off half-cocked and exercise the impeachment power inadvisably or for ignoble purposes. Congress therefore has a constitutional responsibility to make use of impeachment procedures that help ensure its actions are sober and well informed. How much and what kind of impeachment process is necessary to satisfy that responsibility will vary depending on the circumstances. There is no single framework that Congress simply must adopt in order to act in a constitutionally proper fashion.

Second, Congress has a greater burden to bear depending on the position held by the officer who is accused of impeachable offenses. The vast majority of federal impeachments have targeted lower-court judges, particularly trial court judges. As important as those officers are, their responsibilities are limited and their contributions to the commonweal are not unique. The stakes of removing an individual district court judge from office are simply lower than those of removing someone from a more elevated office. The institutional repercussions of pursuing such an impeachment are more circumscribed, and the costs of making a mistake are more modest. Cutting some procedural corners in such cases is more tolerable, if not desirable. The situation is unavoidably different when the individual accused of committing impeachable offenses is a Supreme Court justice, a cabinet secretary, or a president. Any impeachment aimed at those officers will inevitably be more sensationalistic and disruptive. The political challenge to the coordinate branches will be more substantial and threatening when an impeachment targets an officer of substantial stature and responsibility. In the case of a president or vice president, Congress faces the further complication that such individuals ascended to their office through popular election and might well face an electoral check in the future. Congress will be imposing itself on the people's choice to hold those offices. If the legislature feels justified in displacing such an officer, it had better be prepared to show its work. The people should rightly expect Congress to take more care in such situations.

This, of course, suggests that there is no single process Congress must follow to fulfill its constitutional responsibilities when exercising the impeachment power. Circumstances matter, and political judgment is necessary to determine what process should be followed to accomplish the particular political objectives of a given impeachment effort. The process that is due for responding to political misdeeds is far short of the process due in a criminal proceeding. The principle that should guide Congress in deciding how to proceed with an impeachment is less one of doing justice to the impeached official than one of providing a justification to the citizenry at large for the actions Congress is taking. The process of impeachment should support the purpose of an impeachment and build public confidence in what Congress is doing.

The constitutional impeachment process is not a single operation. The House and the Senate have distinct constitutional duties to fulfill. The procedures that they should, and do, follow are distinct as well.

What Process Is Due from the House?

The Constitution says essentially nothing about the impeachment process in the House. It simply directs that the House of Representatives possesses the sole power to impeach. What does that even mean, and what does the House need to do in order to exercise that sole power to impeach?

Ultimately, if the House wants to impeach someone, it needs to muster a simple majority in support of articles of impeachment that can be presented to the Senate. How the House gets there is entirely up to the chamber itself to determine. Across its history, the House has adopted an array of different procedures for advancing impeachments, generally reflecting changes in how the House has conducted its general business.

The fairness, or lack thereof, of impeachment inquiries in the House has not historically been of much concern, but President Donald Trump made it a central feature of his defense during the course of his first impeachment in 2019. Senator Lindsey Graham, for example, advanced a resolution that attracted the support of most Republican senators demanding that the House "provide President Trump with fundamental constitutional protections." Citing the process adopted when President Richard Nixon and President Bill Clinton were impeached, the senators insisted that the full House debate and vote on whether to authorize an impeachment inquiry in the first place and then provide the president with the procedural rights that he might enjoy in a criminal proceeding in an ordinary court.[18] White House counsel Pat Cipollone went further, denouncing the impeachment inquiry as "constitutionally invalid." Because the House impeachment inquiry "violates fundamental fairness and constitutionally mandated due process," the president refused to cooperate with the investigation.[19] House minority leader Kevin McCarthy likewise wrote to House Speaker Nancy Pelosi demanding that the impeachment inquiry be suspended "until transparent and equitable rules and procedures are established" with "an eye towards fairness, objectivity, and impartiality." McCarthy argued that nothing less would do, "given the enormity of the question at hand—the removal of a duly-elected sitting President."[20]

The concerns with the House impeachment process have revolved around two particular issues: how the House launches the impeachment process and how the House investigates impeachable offenses. In assessing such concerns, our focus should not be on whether an impeached officer gets a fair hearing. Any procedures we think the House should adopt in its exercise of the impeachment power are not for the benefit of the accused but for the benefit of the republic. The procedures adopted should serve the purposes for which the sole power to impeach was entrusted to the House and the political goals that a particular impeachment is attempting to accomplish.

Let us start with how impeachments are launched. Is it constitutionally acceptable for the House Speaker to initiate an impeachment "by means of nothing more than a press conference," as the White House counsel complained? In short, yes.

There is no constitutional requirement that the House take two successful votes on impeachment—one to authorize some kind of inquiry and one to ratify whatever emerges from that inquiry. An impeachment inquiry is not "invalid" because there has been no vote to formally launch it, and any eventual impeachment would not be "invalid" because the process that led to it did not feature a floor vote authorizing a specific inquiry.

Of course, the House's own rules might require such a vote, and the House must follow its own rules until it chooses to change them. But there is no rule requiring such an authorizing vote. The House has changed its internal procedures dramatically over time. At one point, the House did not rely on standing committees but instead created select committees to handle many legislative tasks. Through much of its history, the House has limited the investigatory powers of its standing committees and required that those committees go to the floor to receive special authorization to issue subpoenas or spend substantial resources on staff. It no longer does so; therefore, it no longer needs to take such votes to specially authorize particular investigations. The House might want a select committee to pursue an impeachment inquiry, but it could also choose to rely on its standing committees to do the job with their preexisting jurisdiction and resources—and that is how the Democratic leadership decided to approach the first Trump impeachment inquiry. It is not up to the target of an impeachment to determine who will compose the committee that will draft the articles of impeachment or who will chair that committee. Such matters are in the hands of the House majority and its leadership.

Cipollone's letter suggests that only an authorization vote would make the House "democratically accountable" for its actions. But it is not obvious why that should be. To actually impeach an officer, the House members do have to record a vote and be individually accountable for whether or not they took that step. Why should they have to separately go on record merely to authorize an inquiry? If the inquiry results in an impeachment vote, there will be a record of each member's position. If the inquiry does not turn up sufficiently serious impeachable offenses, then the process dies. Arguably, it was once the case that the House believed that members should go on record authorizing particular investigations, but it is not clear that those votes were ever about holding the members democratically accountable to their constituents. Historically more important was the desire of the House floor majority to keep a tight leash on individual committees and committee chairs. In any case, the House does not now expect that each member must go on record before a committee launches an investigation, for example, into what happened in Benghazi or how a president might be profiting from foreign guests in his hotels. As a practical matter, the voters increasingly cast partisan votes for House members and are perfectly capable of holding them accountable for how the House majority spends its time, whether or not an individual member ever goes on record authorizing particular investigations.

It is not obvious that a separate vote to authorize an impeachment inquiry serves any purpose other than delay and obfuscation. Requiring an authorization vote creates another procedural hurdle to be cleared that could drag out an inquiry, including in cases where time is of the essence. Such a requirement could also create uncertainty and redundancy when committees already have standing authority to conduct investigations. A committee investigating potential misconduct in the executive branch, for example, could be stymied in an ordinary oversight investigation on the grounds that the investigation is a mere stalking horse for an impeachment inquiry. Any work such a committee completes might have to be replicated once an impeachment inquiry is specifically authorized.

Worse, a vote to authorize an impeachment necessarily has to take place before a great deal of relevant information has been collected or made public. If a vote authorizing an impeachment is seen by some citizens as indistinguishable from a vote to impeach, then House members in swing districts might well prefer to know how strong the case for impeachment actually is before they have to go on record effectively supporting an impeachment of a sitting president. In a perfect world, voters would be able to distinguish support for an impeachment inquiry from support for an impeachment—but in our imperfect world, the House leadership is expected to protect caucus members from unnecessary politically damaging votes. As a matter of institutional design, Congress's ability to inquire into misconduct should not be held hostage by such electoral calculations. Rather, the system should allow for a process that investigates allegations of misconduct and uncovers the facts, and that forces politicians to take responsibility for how they respond to those facts. A system that instead puts a thumb on the scale with the intent of hiding potential misconduct is hardly in the public interest, even if it might serve the immediate personal or partisan interests of those who fear that their conduct might come under scrutiny. Americans should be reluctant to build into constitutional practice such a bias toward obstructing investigations. The constitutional framers did not themselves build in that kind of bias.

Let us turn now to the second issue—that of how an authorized impeachment investigation should be conducted. What process is due in a House impeachment inquiry? Generally speaking, not much; but here there may be circumstances that would justify the use of more robust procedural protections for the accused.

Does the House need to hear from the target of an impeachment before deciding whether to impeach? In the case of the Trump impeachment, the president and his defenders insisted that he should be able to present evidence to the House, object to the admittance of evidence, and cross-examine and recommend witnesses. They wanted something like a trial before an impeachment vote. Of course, the Constitution specifies that an impeached officer is entitled to a trial—in the Senate after a successful impeachment vote. The Constitution imposes no such procedural burdens or fact-finding requirements on the House, and it does not guarantee a federal officer the right to such procedures before being impeached.

Impeachment by the House is the beginning of a constitutional process, not the end. If a democratically elected president is to be displaced from office, it will only be as a result of a bipartisan supermajority of senators voting to do so after a trial. If the House could by itself and by majority vote oust a president, then there would be good reason to demand a robust process before reaching that decision. If a single political party held it within their power to remove a sitting president of the opposite party, then there would be good reason to object to a partisan process that did not give a fair hearing to the other side. But the power of the House is quite limited.

Impeachment has frequently been analogized to a grand jury indictment, and the analogy is informative here. The House is a prosecutorial body in an impeachment context. The House members must decide what steps they think are necessary to satisfy themselves that a particular impeachment is warranted and to prepare a credible case that can be argued in the Senate, where the defense will have an opportunity to poke holes in it. It might be prudent for the House to create a more robust adversarial proceeding in order to help the House members themselves assess the strength of the case, but any such process is for the benefit of informing the House, not for protecting the accused from a possible impeachment. A federal officer has no particular right not to be impeached, and the bar for impeachment is consequently set low. We want more procedural protections when the consequences of mistakes are high. Before we imprison an accused individual, we want to be confident that the defendant is actually guilty of a crime. But the stakes in the House are not that high, and impeached officers will still get their day in court. If the House has been impetuous in impeaching an officer, there will be an opportunity to recognize the mistake and correct it when the officer comes to trial.

The Senate trial provides an opportunity for accused officers to mount a robust defense, plead their case, and seek total vindication. The procedural bar for a Senate conviction is set high. There the House can have no expectation of a sympathetic hearing, and accused officers can make use of the fact that a bipartisan supermajority in the upper chamber is almost always necessary to remove them from office. It might not be possible to impeach a ham sandwich in the House, but the accused has no expectation of a fair or bipartisan hearing in the lower chamber.

The saga of Judge John Watrous tested the House's impeachment process and highlighted this concern for a fair hearing in which the accused might attempt to clear their name. Watrous was the first federal district judge appointed for the new state of Texas, but he soon found himself at odds with the state courts and the state legislature over the question of how disputed land titles tracing back before the Texas Revolution should be resolved. The legislature demanded that he resign from the federal bench, but he refused. He was the subject of repeated impeachment efforts in the House during the 1850s, though none succeeded. The second such at-

tempt resulted in a report by the House Judiciary Committee rec-
ommending impeachment. Critics of the committee complained
that the report was based entirely on documents supplied to the
committee by aggrieved Texans. Watrous had not been notified of
the committee's activities, and the judge had not been given an opportunity to present a defense. William Boyce of South Carolina
thought the "prudent course" was to give Watrous an opportunity
to respond before proceeding out of respect for "the importance of
preserving the independence of the judiciary, and the complex and
expensive nature of the proceedings on impeachment." By contrast, Lemuel Evans of Texas thought it had become untenable for
Watrous to continue in his seat "when the people of the State have
no confidence in his integrity." The only way for Judge Watrous to
restore public confidence was if he "be placed upon his trial, and
have an opportunity of acquitting himself before the Senate of the
United States if he be innocent"[21]

The House is a partisan political institution. It is inescapable
that impeachments, which require only a simple majority vote,
will sometimes be partisan in nature. A House majority must
anticipate what will happen in a Senate trial if it proceeds to an
impeachment on a largely partisan basis; House members must
anticipate how their own constituents will react if they cast a vote
for an impeachment along largely partisan lines; and the House
must consider what the consequences are for the nation if a high
constitutional officer, such as a president, is impeached along
those partisan lines. Such considerations might encourage the
House not to act if it cannot do so on a bipartisan basis. But if a
majority of the House becomes convinced that an impeachment
is necessary and useful, even if it can attract few members of the
other party to its cause, voters will have the option of considering
this when they next cast their ballots for their representatives.

Ultimately, this is where the demand for more process in the
House has some traction: on the political question of how the public will evaluate the impeachment process. The White House can
make its case to the voters that the House should make use of a

more elaborate process before voting on a presidential impeachment, or that a House majority has pursued impeachment with
unseemly zeal, or that an impeachment is not substantively justified and that the House majority is grasping at straws. Those are
political arguments that the voters can and should hear and that
the electorate can and should and undoubtedly will judge in a subsequent election. The citizenry at large may have little interest in
how fair the process was leading to an impeachment of a district
court judge, but at least a significant portion of the electorate is
likely to feel far more invested in how the House conducts its business if the future of the presidency is on the line. In that context,
the House has a responsibility to appear to play fair with the
president—not out of respect for the individual occupying the
office but out of respect for the voters who supported that president. In a high-profile impeachment, the House has a political
imperative to build confidence in the general public that it is doing
the right thing. The House could ask the voters to simply wait and
see the strength of the case as it is presented to the Senate, but it
is probably wiser not to test the patience of voters in that way. In
a political fight for public approval, the House majority would be
damaging its own case if it unnecessarily handed its opponents
credible talking points about the unfairness of the process and
allowed the accused officer to posture as an aggrieved victim of a
one-sided investigation.

Partisan opponents of a sitting president will always be the
loudest and most visible advocates of an impeachment, inviting
charges that agitation for an impeachment is just sour grapes
from sore losers. If a presidential impeachment is to be seen as
anything other than a partisan effort, it must strive to move beyond that history. That will certainly not be a sufficient condition
for convincing the Senate to convict a sitting president, but it is a
necessary condition. And it is critical to persuading the general
public that the House has done all that it can to justify asking the
Senate to take the dramatic step of removing a president before
the next election.

WHAT IS A FAIR IMPEACHMENT PROCESS? 59

The modern House leadership is used to taking a narrowly partisan approach to conducting its affairs. The House of Representatives is organized to empower even a narrow partisan majority and to conduct its business through simple majority votes. The partisan minority is given few procedural protections and has little influence over what the House does. A high-profile impeachment should not be conducted in such a single-mindedly partisan fashion. The House will eventually need to reach across the political aisle when it presents its case in the Senate. It would be well served by starting that process early, during the impeachment inquiry itself. The Democratic majority in both the Trump impeachments preferred to cut Republicans out of the process rather than look for common ground with potentially sympathetic Republicans. The witnesses called to testify at public hearings, the selection of managers who would prosecute the impeachment in the Senate trial, the drafting of the articles of impeachment—all of those decisions could have been made with an eye toward winning over open-minded skeptics; but they were instead made in 2019 and 2020 as if the purpose of the impeachment was primarily one of exciting their partisan base. If the purpose is something more than that, however, the House should strive to maximize its bipartisan appeal when it pursues high-profile impeachments.

What Process Is Due from the Senate?

The process that is due from the Senate in the impeachment process is far more substantial than the process that is due from the House. The text of the Constitution simply says that the House has the sole power to impeach. By contrast, the Constitution requires more of the Senate. The Constitution in Section 3 of Article I talks about the Senate's role in terms of a trial. It specifies that the Senate has the power "to try all impeachments." It requires that the senators take an oath when "sitting for that Purpose." It assigns the chief justice the role of presiding officer when the president is being tried on articles of impeachment. It speaks in terms of "Judgment in Cases of Impeachment." It is in the Senate that the accused is to be granted a hearing. It is the Senate that ultimately serves as the constitutional court of impeachment.

But what kind of court is the Senate when sitting for the purpose of trying an impeachment, and how must it behave? It is certainly not an ordinary court. When sitting as a court of impeachment, the senators are sometimes compared to jurors, but this is an error. The senators are not jurors in a legal trial. They are political actors charged with the task of inquiring into an officer's alleged misconduct and taking whatever action might be necessary to secure the public interest (constrained by the constitutional limit of removal and disqualification from office—no beheadings allowed). This responsibility has implications for how the senators should conduct themselves.

We might begin with an extreme case: Must the Senate conduct a trial at all? Should a constitutionally conscientious senator ever agree to table or significantly delay an impeachment trial? The text of the Constitution does create some space for that kind of constitutional hardball.[22] The Constitution says that the Senate "shall have the sole Power to try all Impeachments" and provides some directions on what should happen when the Senate is "sitting for that Purpose"; but the Senate is *empowered* to have a trial, not *mandated* to have a trial.

There are circumstances in which it might make sense for the Senate to cut the process short. The Senate has always had the power to adjourn without voting on every article of impeachment presented by the House. When President Andrew Johnson was impeached, the House approved eleven articles of impeachment. After the trial, the Senate voted on only three of them—the three that the proponents of removal thought were the strongest. The House fell one vote short of winning conviction on each charge, and the implications were obvious. The Senate then resolved to adjourn without voting on the remaining articles. In the very first impeachment case, the Senate resolved that it did not have jurisdiction to hold a trial on impeachment charges because Senator

William Blount was not an officer subject to impeachment. When Judge George English resigned before his Senate trial in 1926, the House resolved that it did not wish to proceed with the prosecution, and the Senate voted to dismiss the charges.

The Senate could make quick work of a House impeachment effort. The Senate could entertain a motion to dismiss the charges at the outset of a trial on the grounds that the allegations do not meet the constitutional standard of impeachable offenses, and a majority of the Senate could send the House packing without ever hearing a witness or seeing evidence. If a majority of the senators thought the House was abusing the impeachment power by bringing frivolous charges, there is no reason why the Senate would have to pay obeisance to the House by going through the motions of a pointless trial. When President Bill Clinton was impeached by the House, a lame-duck Republican Senate recognized that an acquittal was inevitable and dragging out the process was not in anyone's political interest. The Republican Senate was ready to move on and eager to get the impeachment fight over with, so it adopted a highly truncated process. When President Donald Trump was impeached by the House, the Republican-controlled Senate similarly decided to hold only an abbreviated trial, though perhaps out of a different political calculation.

In the late stages of the John Tyler presidency in the 1840s, as the White House and the Senate were at complete loggerheads, the Senate had no interest in confirming the president's nominees for any office of significance. Describing the "want of concord" between the White House and the Senate, one senator later recorded that "nominations and rejections flew backwards and forwards as in a game of shuttlecock." Tyler would sometimes nominate the same individual after he had already been rejected, leading the Senate to reject him again "within the same hour."[23] If a president can sit in a Senate anteroom scribbling the same name over and over again on a scrap of paper only to have it repeatedly rejected, it is at least imaginable that a similarly stubborn House might repeatedly vote articles of impeachment against an officer even as the Senate refused to budge in its view that the officer was not guilty of any impeachable offense. If articles of impeachment were ever to fly backwards and forwards between the House and the Senate as in a game of shuttlecock, it is easy to imagine that the Senate would dispense with the necessity of holding a trial each time before informing the House that the charges had not been sustained by the necessary two-thirds majority.

The prosecution and defense do not stand on the same constitutional footing when going before the Senate for an impeachment trial. An impeached officer has a right to demand a trial before being convicted and removed, but the House has no claim on the Senate such that it could demand a trial before an officer is acquitted or charges are dismissed. If the House wants to use a Senate trial to embarrass a federal officer when there is no hope of conviction, the Senate has no obligation to give the House a platform to do that. The House has its own platform by which it can exercise its unilateral power to impeach and fully air its grievances in its own legislative chamber.

The Constitution is flexible enough to allow the Senate to peremptorily reject impeachment charges that the majority of the senators find baseless. Significantly, however, the historical practice and easily imagined examples that result in articles of impeachment being dismissed or set aside all involve a majority of senators going on record with their refusal to convict. If a majority of the senators cannot envision ever entering a guilty vote on an impeachment case, then the result of a trial is a foregone conclusion. That Senate majority might make their will clear rather promptly.

However, senators ought to be extraordinarily reluctant to acquit an officer on the basis of such minimal proceedings. The constitutional requirement that an officer can only be convicted after a trial recognizes that only an extensive procedure of hearing and evaluating evidence and arguments is adequate to determine the veracity of any charges. The textual requirement that senators take an "Oath or Affirmation" is indicative of the seriousness and deliberativeness with which the senators should take their duty to sit in judgment of articles of impeachment. Senators who refused to listen to any evidence or argument and chose to snooze through an impeachment trial would rightly be condemned for failing to take their constitutional oath and duties seriously. Likewise, senators who were content to hide behind a majority leader and neither sat for a trial nor recorded a vote would be failing to meet their constitutional responsibilities or to fulfill the office with which they had been entrusted by their constituents. Constitutionally conscientious senators, then, should approach an impeachment with an open mind, prepared to "do impartial justice," as their oath would have it, prepared to set aside prejudgments and weigh the arguments and evidence that are laid before them. The Constitution itself does not require the House to undertake an elaborate process before voting on articles of impeachment, and the House has not always done so. A Senate trial, by contrast, holds open the possibility of persuasion. Senators should not seek to close themselves off from that possibility.

There is a long history of the Senate refusing to take votes on nominations made by the White House and bills passed by the House of Representatives. Allowing such measures to expire through inaction is a recognized and accepted part of our constitutional practice, though it might frequently be frustrating to those who would prefer to see action taken. There is no such history of ignoring impeachments. Refusing to take action when presented with one would be a significant break from tradition and, as a consequence, a significant escalation of institutional and partisan conflict.

Although the Constitution creates a default expectation that individuals will retain their offices unless their opponents clear a high bar to justify their removal, the Senate would be doing more than simply preserving the status quo if it refused to hear charges against an impeached individual. The Senate would be ignoring a legislative chamber's considered judgment that the impeached officer presented such a danger to the republic that there was an urgent need for the officer's removal. Perhaps the House might behave in such a way that would justify a Senate's belief that the lower chamber no longer deserved a presumption of being taken seriously, but the Senate should not rush to take such a view or treat the House with such contempt.

A minimal presumption by the Senate of good faith on the part of its constitutional partners both facilitates the continued functioning of the government and nurtures the public legitimacy of all its components. If the Senate were to dismiss the House's concerns that the republic was endangered, solemnly expressed through a vote of impeachment, it would unavoidably subvert public confidence in the American constitutional system as a whole and stoke profound distrust in all governmental action. It would dramatically escalate partisan strife for minimal countervailing gain. The Senate need not be persuaded by the House's concerns, but it has an obligation as a responsible partner in government to give the House a hearing. The constitutional design of fragmented power does not assume that the various coordinated parts of government will always agree, but it does presume that those coordinate institutions will attempt to find points of agreement and will deliberate together in search of the common good. An institution that stops even trying to do so is broken nearly beyond repair and derelict in its duty to the people.

If the Senate does choose to conduct a trial when the House managers appear in the chamber to impeach a federal officer, what must they do to satisfy the constitutional requirement? That is, if a supermajority of the Senate does think conviction and removal is justified, what procedures should they follow before imposing that judgment?

If the refusal to conduct a trial sits at one extreme of the Senate's power to try an impeachment, then the other extreme might consist of the Senate rushing to render a guilty verdict. We have seen examples of the Senate cutting the trial short when acquittal is a foregone conclusion, but we have not seen a case in which the Senate has rushed through a trial in order to convict an officer. The possibility raises questions about the bare minimum that the

Senate must meet to satisfy its constitutional obligation to conduct a trial before convicting and removing an officer.

As with quick acquittals, one can imagine better and worse reasons for a quick conviction, but it is worth highlighting that there
might be good reasons for a fast process. A more ignoble reason is
likely to be purely political in the meanest sense. A partisan supermajority could attempt to take down an officer of the other
party with trumped-up impeachment charges in the House and a
kangaroo court in the Senate. The Senate might not bother to hold
a meaningful trial simply because the fix is in and any trial would
be nothing but a show trial. A lengthy trial would not only delay
the inevitable but might also expose just how weak the case for
impeachment actually is. Perhaps a serious trial would create an
opening for some wavering senators to get cold feet about voting
to convict or allow public opinion to turn in the defendant's favor.
Such a danger seems fairly remote, however. Not only is it hard to
assemble the kind of Senate supermajority necessary to execute
such a plan, but a coalition that confident in its powers is likely
able to afford going through the motions of a trial. The risk of a
Senate show trial is probably negligible, even if we may not have
great confidence that a partisan supermajority will reach the right
conclusion.

There are circumstances in which a quick conviction might
seem not only justifiable but commendable. The worst-case scenarios envisioned by the framers when contemplating the need for
an impeachment power are also scenarios in which speed is of the
essence. If a perfidious president is selling out the country to a
hostile foreign power, Congress may need to move with great urgency to replace the commander in chief. If a traitorous president
attempts to mount an insurrection to keep himself in power, Congress might be obliged to move as quickly as the emergency dictates. One might imagine circumstances in which the facts are not
in dispute and the only issue is whether the conduct in question
is impeachable. If the secretary of defense fiddles while the District of Columbia burns, it might not require much fact-finding to

understand the situation. The real question for the House and Senate to answer might simply be, What should be done about it? It might well require months for congressional investigators to determine whether an executive officer had conspired with seditious actors, but it might require no time at all to determine that an executive officer had been derelict in his duties in quelling a seditious riot. A well-chosen impeachment charge might obviate the necessity of a lengthy process even if Congress were performing its constitutional duty with proper due diligence.

The amount of procedure due in an impeachment process is not a fixed quantum. Although an impeachment trial might have great ramifications for the country, the procedural hoops that Congress must jump through in order to remove an officer may well depend on the political situation. If a district judge has been convicted in a criminal court of accepting bribes and now languishes in a federal prison, the case for impeachment and removal is obvious but is also not terribly pressing. Congress does not need to move at breakneck speed to address such a problem. If, however, the crisis is great and removal a dire necessity, then cutting some procedural corners might be entirely justifiable. Similarly, the Senate has no obligation to cater to every dilatory tactic that some individuals might deploy in order to extend their time in office. A cabinet officer who insists that witnesses and evidence essential to a proper defense will take many months to acquire need not be accommodated to the furthest degree. A president who refuses to comply with subpoenas for testimony and documents and looks to bog down congressional inquiries through extended litigation in the court system need not be countenanced. The obstruction might itself become a reason to impeach and remove, and an officer might be given an ultimatum that senators are inclined to convict unless the officer can promptly produce exculpatory evidence. The Supreme Court influentially argued, outside the impeachment context, that the "specific dictates of due process" depend on such factors as the private interests at stake, the risk of erroneous decision making, and the public interest involved.[24] The impeachment context is one in which the public interest is extremely significant and the private interest negligible. No officer is truly entitled to retain public office, and the public's interest is that Congress take as much care as possible to get a correct result while avoiding a possible calamity of leaving an unfit officer in place. Ironically, the more important the office, the less process might be due precisely because the public can better afford a mistaken rush to judgment than an extended process. There is no one way to conduct a Senate impeachment trial. As the court said in a different case, "due process is flexible, and calls for such procedural protections as the particular situation demands."[25]

What is the very least that a Senate must do to satisfy its constitutional obligation to provide an officer with a trial before convicting and removing? There is little reason to think that an officer is constitutionally entitled in an impeachment trial to all the accoutrements of a criminal trial. Articles of impeachment are not a criminal indictment, and the officer does not risk life or liberty when undertaking a defense in the well of the Senate. The defendant may well be heard in an ordinary court with more rigorous proceedings at a later date. At its most basic, the process required in any given situation is what might be necessary "to exclude everything that is arbitrary and capricious."[26] For the Senate to meet its constitutional obligation before convicting an officer, it may not "disregard the deep-rooted demands of fair play." At a minimum, fair play dictates that an individual must be given "notice of the case against him and opportunity to meet it."[27] "The hearing, moreover, must be a real one, not a sham or a pretense."[28] A Senate that convicts and removes an officer after a trial lasting but a single hour for the offense of shooting someone dead on live television in the middle of Fifth Avenue would be doing all that is necessary. A Senate that fails to notify an officer that the impeachment has taken place, or that refuses to hear from an impeached officer, or that renders a conviction on the basis of conduct that the officer could not have known might place them in jeopardy would fail to generate "the feeling, so important to popular government, that justice has been done."[29] What constitutes a Senate impeachment trial may be flexible, but it cannot ignore the demands of fundamental fairness.

A Senate impeachment trial is not like an ordinary judicial trial. Senators are understood to already be familiar with the case by the time it reaches their chamber. They are not shielded by the rules of evidence from hearing the kinds of testimony or seeing the kinds of documents that might be regarded as too prejudicial in an ordinary courtroom. They are not barred from drawing inferences from witnesses who refuse to answer questions on the basis of the Fifth Amendment privilege against self-incrimination. They need not assume the same burden of proof that prosecutors would need to meet in a criminal trial. They are not expected to be sequestered so as to avoid publicity regarding the case. They are not instructed to avoid discussing the case with others. Senators can expect to be relentlessly lobbied by their constituents, their colleagues, the media, and others up until the moment that they cast their final vote. The Senate took a recess during Andrew Johnson's trial so that the senators could attend the Republican National Convention, which nominated Ulysses S. Grant for the presidency and debated whether to endorse the impeachment and whether to condemn the Republican senators who would not vote to convict. The Republican senators who voted not to convict Andrew Johnson knew that the vote would have consequences for their later electoral viability, just as the Republican members of the House who voted to impeach Donald Trump knew that the vote would likely cost them their House seats. Politics "ain't bean bag," as Mr. Dooley once said, and an impeachment trial is still part of politics.[30]

Even so, an impeachment trial should not be politics as usual. The Senate might continue to conduct legislative business during the course of an impeachment trial, but in order to do so, it adjourns from the trial and gavels in as the ordinary Senate. To emphasize the separation, the Constitution requires that the senators take an oath. The current form of that oath, as contained in long-standing Senate rules, is that each senator affirms that "in all things appertaining to the trial of the impeachment of ____ now pending, I will do impartial justice according to the Constitution and laws."

What is required to live up to that oath is certainly different than what we would expect from jurors in an ordinary court. Before Trump's first impeachment trial, Republican senator Lindsey Graham told any member of the press who might be interested, "I'm not trying to pretend to be a fair juror here."[31] On the other side of the aisle, Democratic senator Elizabeth Warren had been declaring for months that she was ready to convict Trump.[32] As soon as impeachment talk got serious in the House, the press began to hound senators about how they would vote in a possible impeachment trial, and some senators were happy to oblige them—and the senators' voters and donors—with an answer. Some thought that such senators should be excluded from taking the oath or participating in the impeachment trial, but that was never going to happen. Neither the Senate as a body nor individual senators have ever believed that senators should be recused from the trial due to potential conflicts of interest.

We have seen worse conflicts of interest than senators publicly lobbying for an impeachment or for a result in an impeachment trial. When President Andrew Johnson was put on trial in the Senate in 1868, the senators who sat in judgment of him were not exactly disinterested parties. The Republican Congress had set up the impeachment by passing the Tenure of Office Act, over Johnson's veto, barring him from removing cabinet members without the consent of the Senate and including in its terms that any violation would be a "high misdemeanor." Republican senators gave instructions to Johnson's secretary of war as the president sought to fire him, and thus played a key role in the very event that was the basis of the president's impeachment. Ohio senator Benjamin Wade would assume the office of the president if Johnson were convicted (since the vice presidency was still vacant after Johnson had ascended to the presidency after the assassination of President

Abraham Lincoln). Tennessee senator David Patterson was the president's son-in-law. Both were allowed to participate in the trial. In his opening statement of the trial, House manager Benjamin Butler pointed out that "there is no right of challenge by either party to any of [the Senate's] members for favor, or malice, affinity, or interest." He observed that if such challenges were allowed, "no trial could go forward, because every intelligent senator could be objected to upon one side or the other."[33] The right of their constituents to have their representatives in Congress participate in the impeachment and trial of the president was understood to be far more important than the right of the president or the House to exclude senators who might be less than impartial judges. Legislators have sometimes asked to be excused from voting in such proceedings. North Carolina senator Thomas Blount, for example, excused himself from voting in the 1798 impeachment proceedings against his brother, Senator William Blount of Tennessee. No member of the House or Senate has ever been disqualified from participating in impeachment proceedings.[34]

The senators have a duty to do impartial justice according to the Constitution in the impeachment trial of the president. That surely means, among other things, that they have a duty to vote to acquit if they believe that the president has not committed an impeachable offense under the Constitution. It means that they have a duty to conduct a trial that provides both sides an adequate opportunity to present their case. They have a duty to consider the evidence and the legal arguments that are relevant to determining whether the president has committed an impeachable offense. They have a duty to vote to convict if they believe that removal is constitutionally justified.

That does not mean that they have to wait until the formal start of a trial to begin assessing whether an officer has committed impeachable offenses or limit their deliberations to the specific evidence and arguments that the House managers and the counsel for the president might present on the Senate floor. That does not mean that they have to sit for the impeachment trial with an open mind and no prejudgments on the merits of the case. That does not mean that they have to refrain from making public statements about an officer's conduct.

It is to be expected that, when attempting to impeach a high government official like the president, the House will spend substantial effort trying to develop its case in public before taking a vote to impeach, precisely to build political momentum behind the impeachment effort and establish a public justification for taking that grave step. No one expects the senators to be less informed about what the House is up to than the average voter back home. Indeed, the House should take into account that the Senate is an important audience member to how the impeachment inquiry proceeds. If the House rushes to impeach without gathering or displaying evidence, a majority of the senators might well conclude that the House has no business presenting its case for the first time on the Senate floor.

When the transcripts of the White House tapes were released, revealing the extent of President Richard Nixon's complicity in the cover-up of the Watergate break-in, senators did not hesitate to publicly express their belief that the president had engaged in serious misconduct. In the final days of the Watergate crisis, the president was visited by a group of Republican congressional leaders, including Senator Barry Goldwater and Senate minority leader Hugh Scott. They were there to deliver the bad news that Nixon's support in the Republican ranks in the House and Senate had collapsed. Nixon resigned shortly after Goldwater and Scott told him that he would not have enough votes in the Senate to win an acquittal.[35] No one thought the senators were failing to do their constitutional duty by not reserving judgment until a Senate impeachment trial. The senators could read the newspapers like everyone else and make up their own minds, and they had done so.

In recent years, the Senate has experimented with creating a special trial committee to hear evidence on the impeachment of lower-court judges. The full Senate was expected to familiarize itself with that trial record, but the ordinary business of the Senate would not be put on hold for a long impeachment trial before the full chamber for relatively low-level officers. Such a trial process raises real concerns about its adequacy to allow the senators to do impartial justice when the time comes to pass final judgment.[36] A trial committee would clearly be inappropriate in the case of high-ranking officials, such as the president of the United States. The stakes for the legitimacy of the constitutional system and the independence of the other branches of government are simply too high for the Senate not to demonstrate that it is fully committed to the deliberative process of a trial.

Is There Anything Wrong with Fast Impeachments?

Process takes time. That is true in ordinary courts, and it is true in impeachment proceedings as well. The more opportunities that the House offers to an accused officeholder to present evidence and to call and cross-examine witnesses, the longer the impeachment inquiry takes. The same is true in the Senate trial. The Senate has been willing to take shortcuts with the trial when an acquittal seems inevitable. But what if a conviction seems inevitable?

Is it equally acceptable for the House and Senate to speed through an impeachment process in order to convict and remove an officer as it is to cut the process short in order to acquit an officer? It is a familiar warning that we should not rush to judgment. Speed can create mistakes. Criminal defendants are constitutionally guaranteed "a speedy and public trial" so that their fate is not held in suspense as the government temporizes, but defendants are also entitled to reasonable time to develop and make their case. Excessive speed might undermine the fundamental commitment to providing a fair trial that is mostly likely to reach the truth.

There is a risk that cutting procedural corners makes it more difficult to determine what the truth of the matter is and thus increases the risk that the constitutional court of impeachment will make mistakes. Such concerns, however, must be counterbalanced by the looming political problem that the impeachment mechanism is designed to address in the first place. At least in some circumstances, it is dangerous to leave an officer in place to abuse or usurp the powers of government. There is no provision in the federal constitutional scheme for temporarily suspending such an officer. The president continues to exercise the powers of his office after his impeachment and right through his impeachment trial. If an impeachment effort is motivated by a fear that the president is acting in a tyrannical fashion, then time is of the essence for stripping that individual of the powers of the presidential office. There are occasions in which Congress must act with a sense of urgency.

It is readily imaginable that an officer might commit obviously impeachable offenses in broad daylight and plain sight of all the members of Congress. In such circumstances, the House might rush to impeach with no elaborate investigation, and the Senate might rush to convict with no extended deliberation. No one imagines that the senators do not know what everyone else knows. The president could be impeached, convicted, and removed from office in a day's time.

The House might simply move directly to a vote on proposed articles of impeachment without having ever authorized an inquiry, let alone provided some kind of formalized opportunity for the target of the impeachment to respond. Before the Democrats took control of the House after the 2018 elections, this model had already been tried out. Democratic representative Al Green introduced directly onto the House floor three different resolutions of impeachment against President Donald Trump. The core of those articles of impeachment focused on the president's public statements and how they had brought the office of the presidency into "contempt, ridicule, disgrace, and disrepute" and "sown seeds of discord among the people of the United States." There was no serious need for the House to inquire into whether the president made the statements that formed the factual basis of those articles of impeachment. The open question was simply whether the president's rhetoric amounted to impeachable offenses, and no formal inquiry was necessary for the members of the House to reach a conclusion on that issue (though perhaps hearings would have been useful for helping the House deliberate on that question).

In the case of Green's resolutions, there was nothing like a majority ready to pursue an impeachment, so the House quickly agreed to table the motions. Green was using the resolutions to try to build political support for general opposition to the president. But it is not hard to imagine circumstances in which a similar resolution was not just an attention-grabbing move but actually had the support of a House majority. Where Green's particular resolutions were quickly set aside, some similar measure might instead be adopted by a simple floor vote. A majority of the House could reasonably conclude that they knew all they needed to know to impeach an officer without any formal inquiry of their own, simply on the basis of press clippings, personal observation, a special counsel report, or a criminal trial record. The House does not constitutionally need to authorize an impeachment inquiry because it does not constitutionally even need to have an impeachment inquiry.

The Senate has a constitutional obligation to go through a more involved process than the House, but that does not mean that the Senate trial needs to be slow moving. The impeached officer must have an opportunity to respond to the charges and mount a defense, but that need not be a lengthy process. The Senate cannot take summary action and purport to convict and remove an officer without allowing the individual to offer a defense at all. Similarly, the Senate could not allow the House to present its case at a leisurely pace and then demand that the defense cut its argument short. The Senate need not tolerate impeached officers attempting to drag out the proceedings as they continue to abuse their office, but the Senate must give the officers a hearing and treat both the House and the defense fairly.

The impeachment power is available to Congress to address the possibility of a federal officer, particularly the president, posing an immediate threat to the safety of the country. This was a concern of some Republicans during the impeachment of President Andrew Johnson. Some of them feared that the president was intent on sparking a new civil war and using the powers of his office to aid the secessionists. Under such circumstances, every moment would count and Congress would have a responsibility to perform its constitutional duty without delay so as to render the president harmless. Johnson was able to calm such fears, so much so that Congress did not feel the need to hurry his impeachment and removal; in the end, a critical number of senators were persuaded that he could be trusted to serve out the rest of his term of office. But things could have gone differently.

President Donald Trump's second impeachment came closest to satisfying the conditions for such a fast impeachment and trial. On January 6, 2021, supporters of President Trump rioted on the steps of the Capitol and broke into the House and Senate chambers in order to prevent Congress from counting the electoral votes and certifying Joe Biden as the next president of the United States. Trump had given a speech to those very supporters, urging them to continue fighting on his behalf, and he watched in silence for hours as the rioters forced the members of Congress to flee for their lives and refused to answer the pleas of congressional Republicans that the president take action to stop the violence and secure the Capitol.

Some aspects of the president's actions after the 2020 election would require substantial investigation to uncover and make public, and the kind of lengthy process that the House select committee ultimately performed in order to investigate the events of January 6th would clearly have required an extended impeachment inquiry and trial. A fast impeachment and trial would have depended on a willingness to draw up carefully limited articles of impeachment that could command widespread assent across the partisan divide and that required no investigative work to reveal. It would require the political will to take such action and an assessment that the American public could be made to understand that such an extraordinary step was necessary. If the House and the Senate were convinced that the president posed an imminent threat to the safety of the republic even after the riot had been quelled late in the day of January 6th, they could have and should have moved immediately to disarm and safely isolate the president.

Instead, Congress dithered. Rather than remain in session after the electoral ballots were counted on January 6th, Congress adjourned and the members returned home. Rather than working with Republicans to craft articles of impeachment that might command broad bipartisan support, the House took days to draft a more partisan resolution. Rather than immediately presenting the articles of impeachment to the Senate and demanding that it return to begin a trial, the House waited until after Trump had left office before presenting the articles to the Senate. Rather than holding an impeachment trial on January 7th or 8th, the Senate did not judge the president until well after the inauguration of his successor. Rather than take charge of the situation, members of Congress publicly urged the cabinet to act in its stead under the Twenty-Fifth Amendment—an amendment designed to address the possibility that a sitting president had suffered a debilitating stroke or fallen into a coma. As in the case of Andrew Johnson, the congressional leadership contented itself with working behind the scenes to gain assurances that the president no longer presented a threat and did not need to be formally stripped of his powers as commander in chief. Congress was apparently satisfied that enough had been done when the leadership of Twitter took away Trump's bully pulpit by suspending his social media account.

Such informal actions are also part of the process by which Congress can attempt to remedy the political problem posed by a rogue federal officer. Just as presidential administrations before the adoption of the Twenty-Fifth Amendment cobbled together workarounds to deal with the problem of temporarily incapacitated presidents and the Supreme Court has carried on when terminally ill justices refuse or are unable to resign, so Congress and its allies can apply bandages to festering wounds in the body politic and hope that an impeachment does not prove necessary.

Congress must assess the threat and adopt the countermeasures that seem most necessary at the time. But Congress is not limited to relying on such half measures. If a competent and aggressive president attempted to incite an insurrection, disband Congress and the courts, or orchestrate an *autogolpe*, or self-coup, while in office, Congress need not say a prayer and hope things do not get too bad or wish that someone else take on the responsibility of countering the president. Congress could act swiftly to defend itself and the American republic. It does not lack the power. It needs only the will.

3

What Is the Impeachment
Power For?

IT HELPS to know why you are doing something. It is hard to think through the best means to adopt if we do not know the end that we seek. It is difficult to make adjustments when plans go awry if we do not know what we were trying to accomplish with the initial plan. It is challenging to weigh the costs against the benefits when contemplating a proposed action if we are uncertain about the objective. We cannot choose the right tool for the job if we do not know what the job is.

The former professional football coach and sports announcer John Madden is often credited with saying, "Usually the team that scores the most points wins the game." The observation may not be profound, but it can be useful. It is surprisingly easy to lose sight of the ultimate objective while focusing on the details of what should only be means to that end. It is sometimes tempting to think of a task as the end in itself rather than one possible means to an end. It can be agreeable to train your sights on easily measured and achievable objectives and lose sight of larger purposes.

The use of the impeachment power can similarly fall victim to such hazy thinking. The end goal of an impeachment is too often taken for granted. This is not surprising since the goal of an impeachment is usually quite clear—to remove a government official from office. But removal is not always the goal, and sometimes is politically unobtainable. If removal is the only possible goal of an impeachment, then an impeachment process that ends in an acquittal is necessarily a failure and an impeachment that moves forward when the odds of conviction are remote is surely misguided.

Assessing the broader uses of the impeachment process gives us a better appreciation of the nature of and possibilities for implementing the impeachment power. Getting beyond a simplistic understanding of how the impeachment power might be used can also clarify why legislators need to identify their ultimate objectives before beginning an impeachment inquiry. If legislators are confused or uncertain about what they are trying to accomplish with an impeachment, the entire venture will be jeopardized.

The Clinton impeachment, for example, was so unsatisfying in part because it seemed so constitutionally unimportant.[1] The heaviest artillery in the constitutional arsenal was called out to address a scandal of the meanest character. Despite a numbing amount of commentary on the scandal, there was surprisingly little effort to explain the constitutional value of an impeachment. Republicans seemed to assume that Clinton had defaulted on his presidency by lying under oath in a civil suit and could be removed from office on a technicality. The president and his defenders, of course, were in no position to advance a rich constitutional defense of his presidency, but they seemed content to exploit Republican weaknesses. With its foreordained outcome and sordid subject matter, the impeachment was a constitutional crisis only in its banality.

The House's rather reductionist approach to the constitutional text should not be surprising. Given the relative clarity of Clinton's offenses and the ambiguity of the Constitution's requirements, advocates of impeachment had immediate strategic reasons for minimizing discussions of the purposes of impeachment. But this thin deliberation on the meaning of Congress's constitutional responsibilities is also unsurprising given the historical and intellectual context of the Clinton impeachment—and the same could easily be said about the Trump impeachments. Our recent impeachment experience has emphasized relatively clear cases of criminal wrongdoing by public officials. The long drama of Watergate in the 1970s and the spectacle of criminally convicted and imprisoned federal judges in the 1980s were relatively easy cases that emphasized criminality as the sufficient condition for impeachment. The reliance on an independent counsel's grand jury investigation of presidential misconduct as a prelude to a congressional impeachment inquiry in the 1990s further highlighted the criminal, and essentially private, dimensions of the probe. It was predictable, therefore, that the House would approach impeachment in a highly formalistic manner—a mechanical matter of comparing discovered facts to an implicit list of "impeachable offenses." As the public disinterest, if not active disapproval, of the Clinton impeachment suggests, this formalistic emphasis is not enough.

Asking what constitutes an impeachable offense is not quite the same as asking why Congress must impeach. The listing of impeachable offenses involves an abstraction that quickly loses significance in the context of an actual impeachment investigation. "Crimes" that seem real and significant in the abstract may seem trivial in a given political context, even as actions that seem innocent in the abstract may take on a more ominous cast within a given political situation. The mantra of "obstruction of justice" had a rather different meaning in the context of Watergate than in the context of "Zippergate." The Reconstruction-era Republicans who mounted the only previous impeachment of a sitting president in the case of Andrew Johnson in 1868 recognized that their political and constitutional task was to explain why Johnson's actions threatened the health of the republic, not to minutely examine the phrase *high crimes and misdemeanors*.

Simply providing a definition of impeachable offenses is unlikely to be satisfactory to those who must determine whether to act on them. Democratic witnesses in the House hearings in the Clinton impeachment were quick to reassure worried members of

Congress that the House had discretion on whether to impeach, even upon the presentation of clear evidence of an unambiguously impeachable offense. But the concept of discretion does not capture the considerations at stake in an impeachment inquiry. Although it emphasizes that impeachments are not mechanical acts set in motion upon discovery of evidence that one of a predetermined set of crimes has been committed, the idea of discretion also seems to imply that congressional representatives may simply ignore what they regard as impeachable actions by the president and that the decision to initiate an impeachment turns on considerations unrelated to the Constitution. "Discretion" implies, for example, that Congress could recognize that a president has committed an impeachable act, but still choose not to impeach because the president is of the same party as the majority of Congress and doing so would be politically damaging to legislative careers. "Discretion" suggests that the scope of impeachable crimes is fixed and clear, but that the prosecution of those crimes is optional. It reinforces the assumption that we already know what high crimes are, and that in any given case we must merely decide whether they have been committed and whether to punish them.

In fact, the rationale for impeachments must often be constructed through the impeachment process itself. That is especially true in the case of an impeachment targeting such a high-ranking officer as the president of the United States. Impeachments require judgment. They are not the mechanical application of constitutional law. They are products of the constitutional judgment of high political officials. There is not simply a single moment of decision in which members of Congress lay the requirements of the Constitution against the actions of a government official and observe whether the acts are covered by the law. The entire decision-making process of impeachment is suffused with constitutional considerations. In the case of the Johnson impeachment, congressional Republicans well understood this aspect of their political task. For them, constitutional sensibilities, policy preferences, and partisan calculations were conjoined and provided the motivation and justification for the impeachment. More recent presidential impeachments were never placed within a compelling constitutional context, even when it would have been possible to do so. Republicans in 1998 allowed independent counsel Kenneth Starr to explain what President Clinton had done, and they were unprepared to explain why it mattered. Without an explanation of the constitutional significance of Clinton's actions, the congressional reaction seemed out of proportion with the underlying facts. The same could easily be said of the first impeachment of President Donald Trump in 2019. If those presidents had shown bad judgment, many voters thought Congress had shown bad judgment as well in seeking to truncate their regular terms of office. As congressional majorities were unable or unwilling to frame their efforts in constitutional terms, the impeachments were easily framed in familiar partisan terms. The members of Congress needed to engage in a debate about the principles behind the impeachment power and explain why an impeachment was substantively justified in those cases. As partisan pressures broke down any consensus over the scope of impeachable offenses, the critics of the president in each case needed to rebuild those constitutional foundations and not simply try to interpret and apply putatively settled law.

Impeachments are a political exercise, in that the impeachment power rests in a menu of options that legislators might pursue. The choice facing legislators is not simply a binary one of choosing whether or not to impeach, but a more multifaceted one of choosing whether to impeach or to do something else. Legislators must think about the comparative advantage of making use of the impeachment power in a world in which other options are on the table.

Democracy depends on the art of persuasion. To get things done in politics, we must persuade our fellow citizens to take action. Elected representatives recognize that they will be called upon to explain their actions, and their ability to provide persuasive justifications to skeptical constituents, colleagues, and interest groups shapes their behavior.[2] We lose sight of an important aspect of the impeachment process if we forget that it is inescapably a political undertaking by political actors before a political audience. The political task of justifying an impeachment is made much harder if legislators do not understand the goals they are attempting to accomplish.

Because the impeachment power is inevitably political, we should also recognize the temptation that politicians might have to use the power for the most ignoble of political ends. Impeachments might come to be seen as an available partisan weapon. The lesson that many politicians took from the experience of the Clinton impeachment was that impeachments could be more politically costly for Congress than for the president. Clinton's favorability rating with the public only increased with the impeachment, and Republicans in Congress found their political brand damaged. That lesson might make congressional leaders gun-shy and reluctant to pursue a necessary impeachment, but it also might deter abuses of the impeachment power.

The political calculus depends on the political environment, and the political environment has changed. At least for the moment, representatives are rewarded for playing to their base. In an intensely partisan environment, members of Congress are most concerned with the preferences of their supporters. Successful political careers are now built through the kind of media attention that can be translated into political campaign contributions from small-dollar donors who themselves often have political preferences that are both intense and extreme. From a purely partisan perspective, an impeachment effort can be used to try to rough up an incumbent president heading into a reelection campaign. The incentives that drive congressional behavior in the early twenty-first century might drive members of Congress into talking up the possibility of impeachment for the sake of media hits, viral videos, and fund-raising solicitations. Such incentives might encourage impeachment efforts even when there is little justification for them. Short-term political gains can be a purpose for which impeachments are pursued, but they are not what the impeachment power is for. We should at least recognize that politicians will sometimes use political tools for unworthy ends, and we must be vigilant against the abuse of the impeachment power.

A Possible Remedy for a Political Problem

There is a tendency to think of impeachable offenses like landmines. If the president or some other government official accidentally or purposefully steps on one, then it explodes and they must suffer the consequences. Constitutional lawyers might find this line of thinking particularly attractive because it allows them to identify a finite set of actions as "high crimes and misdemeanors" and to set Congress about the business of determining whether the official has actually committed such offenses—or, if Congress so prefers, to outsource that investigative work to a special counsel, who could effectively make the impeachment process itself a mere formality.

This is the wrong way to think about impeachments. Impeachment is a powerful political tool for addressing a class of important and distinctly political problems, but it is not always the right tool for the job. Borrowing from James Madison, a recent writer has characterized the impeachment as an "indispensable remedy" built into the constitutional design.[3] The impeachment power was indispensable, Madison thought, because "some provision should be made for defending the Community against the incapacity, negligence, or perfidy of the chief Magistrate." It was a remedy because "some mode of displacing an unfit magistrate" might be needed in an extreme situation.[4] To be sure, the impeachment power was not the only safeguard against an unfit magistrate, but it was a power that might be necessary, and the drafters recognized that the Constitution should not be deficient if such a situation arose.

If impeachment can be used to address political offenses, that does not by itself establish that it is particularly effective at addressing every political offense. When some members of the

House of Representatives became agitated over the surprise veto of a key policy initiative of the Whigs by the newly elevated President John Tyler, Isaac Jones of Maryland rose to the floor to try to make some sense of the debate in 1841. If the president's veto message had led any members of the House to "change our opinions of the bill," then it was "our constitutional duty" to debate the merits of the bill and the president's veto. If the president had acted "corruptly in the discharge of his duty" in vetoing the bill, then "the Constitution has provided the remedy of impeachment." But if "portions of his veto message are extra constitutional" and "written in a style" that does not comport "with the rules of rhetoric" or had cast aspersions on the House, then "the debate today, has, I think, repaid him, principal and interest."[5] A president who offends the House can be repaid in kind, but the impeachment power should be saved for other types of injuries.

When the House was contemplating whether to impeach federal district judge Charles Swayne early in the twentieth century, one of the potential charges focused on Swayne's having jailed an attorney for contempt of court. One of the leaders of the impeachment effort emphasized to his colleagues that the parties in question "undertook to appeal their case to the higher courts, but they found that they could get no relief." Not even the Supreme Court could take jurisdiction over the case. A majority of the House was ultimately persuaded that "where a judge of a court of general jurisdiction abuses his power in this matter of contempt there is but one remedy, and that is the remedy of impeachment."[6] When citizens who had been abused by a federal officer had nowhere else to turn, the constitutional court of impeachment had to be prepared to fill the gap. (The Senate, however, was ultimately not convinced that Swayne should be convicted and removed for such an offense.)

Those who would seek to persuade members of the House, the Senate, and ultimately the public that impeachment is the right remedy for the problems confronting the nation would have to do more than show that a president has done something that might be classified as an impeachable offense. They would need to demonstrate that an individual's continued occupation of the White House had become unendurable and that leaving such an individual to face the electorate again or to serve out the remainder of the designated term of office posed unacceptable risks to the nation.

Removal of a Misbehaving Individual

The most obvious, and most frequent, use of the impeachment power is to remove a misbehaving individual from office. Under American constitutions, legislatures do not have the power to dispense criminal penalties to individuals. The impeachment power cannot be used as a device for convicting individuals of crimes and meting out punishments. It has a more limited political purpose in America, and removal from office is the only penalty that necessarily follows from a conviction in an impeachment trial. The constitutional text mandates that civil officers "shall be removed from Office on Impeachment for, and Conviction of, Treason, Bribery and other high Crimes and Misdemeanors." They *shall be removed* upon conviction.

The moment the Senate pronounces guilt in an impeachment trial, the convicted individual immediately loses his office. Whether the officer is removed is not discretionary. The Senate does not take a separate vote after a conviction to determine whether removal should follow. The most recent guilty verdict in an impeachment trial came against U.S. district judge G. Thomas Porteous, Jr., in 2010. Porteous had been charged with corruption, and the Senate found him guilty on all four articles of impeachment. Upon concluding the roll call on the fourth and final article of impeachment, the presiding officer directed "judgement to be entered" in the Senate journal, to wit "two-thirds of the Senate present having found him guilty of the charges contained in articles I, II, III, and IV, it is therefore ordered and adjudged that said G. Thomas Porteous, Jr., be and is hereby removed from office."[7]

It is clear that the most pressing reason for the constitutional drafters to include an impeachment power in the constitutional text was to make it possible to remove a misbehaving officer. Some thought that an impeachment power was "proper to secure good behavior" when officers held life tenure. Perhaps it was fit for a country with a monarch but unnecessary in a democracy, "the periodical responsibility to the electors being an equivalent security." As the debate progressed, a majority of the delegates at the Philadelphia Convention were persuaded "of the necessity of impeachments, if the Executive was to continue for any time in office." The nation should not be powerless until the next election if the president succumbs to "treachery" or schemes to "corrupt his electors."[8] Circumstances might arise when an individual needed to be stripped of the authority of public office and time was of the essence.

The constitutional drafters were especially focused on the possibility of impeaching and removing the "chief Magistrate," the president, even though they knew that the president would only be elected to a limited term of office. But they themselves had created an office in which an individual "held his place for life" and would not be held to account by the voters. Federal judges were to enjoy life tenure because it was essential that they be independent from outside influence if they were to be free to do equal justice under the law in the cases that came before them. Across American history, there have been nearly four thousand federal judges, but fewer than fifty presidents. With no other means to remove them from office when they misbehave, it is perhaps not surprising that in practice the impeachment power has most often been used to strip judges of their office.

Things might have played out differently. There have been occasional suggestions that federal judges, who "shall hold their Offices during good Behavior," could be ousted by something less than an impeachment trial. Congress might have been persuaded, for example, that a committee of judges could be empowered to determine that "the behavior of the judge has been other than good behavior within the meaning of the Constitution" and to remove a colleague from the bench.[9] With such an arrangement in place, federal impeachments might have become quite rare indeed. Alternatively, when the First Congress was establishing executive offices to aid the president in executing the law, the representatives might have been persuaded by the idiosyncratic theory offered by one member that impeachment was the *only* constitutional means for removing misbehaving officers. Once appointed, federal officers, ranging from the secretary of state to the local postmaster, could not be removed except by Congress exercising its impeachment power. "Once in office, he must remain there until convicted upon impeachment."[10] (James Madison was quick to leap to his feet to declare that "he did not concur with the gentleman in his interpretation of the constitution," for if that interpretation were correct, then there was "a fatal error interwoven in the system, and one that would ultimately prove its destruction."[11]) If there were no other means for firing an incompetent, ineffective, or misbehaving executive officer, then Congress might have found itself routinely using the impeachment power to clear out the dead wood.

We did not go down those paths. Instead, judges were understood to hold their office until they died, voluntarily resigned, or were removed by impeachment. Executive officers, on the other hand, were understood to be removable by the president. Stubborn judges who have refused to step down when they have tarnished their office have forced Congress to go through the impeachment process. Cabinet officers who found themselves mired in scandal have either resigned or been given their walking papers by the president. They have very rarely hung on long enough for Congress to start thinking about impeaching them. In the vast majority of cases, getting rid of problematic officers has not required the use of the impeachment power, and it should be no surprise that the history of federal impeachments is primarily a history of impeaching judges.

A more difficult case could arise if the president refused to re-move an executive officer who had engaged in egregious miscon-duct. Officials suffering through a personal scandal weigh down a presidential administration, and there are ample incentives for a president to cut such individuals loose. Political appointees who are abusing their office in their zeal to advance the president's own political and policy agenda, however, are more likely to be sheltered by the White House. Impeachment by Congress is a fallback solu-tion for stripping such individuals of their public authority when the president neglects or refuses to act. Such an impeachment of a cabinet officer or even a subcabinet officer would clearly implicate the presidency itself. A president who neglects to remove an abu-sive executive officer is thereby engaging in presidential miscon-duct. A president who more positively endorses the officer's actions and refuses to remove the officer from a position of public author-ity would be guilty of an even more serious offense. Mounting an impeachment of such an executive officer would quickly become a proxy battle with the president, and the partisan battle that would ensue would be quite similar to what would happen if the president were the one in the dock. Congress has the authority to remove executive officers when the president refuses to do so, but the chal-lenge of gathering the political will for such a task is a formidable one. Beginning an impeachment campaign with the president's underling might help isolate or politically weaken the president, and might even reduce the necessity of contemplating a presiden-tial impeachment, but the stakes are necessarily high for those sit-ting at both ends of Pennsylvania Avenue.

The clearest reason for pursuing an impeachment in order to remove an individual from office is because that person poses an immediate danger to the republic. The impeachment power pro-vides a safety valve in case presidential incompetence or malevo-lence becomes so great that we cannot as a nation afford to wait until the next election for removal to take place. The two impeach-able offenses that the founders identified in the constitutional text—treason and bribery—tend to fall into this category. If the commander in chief refused to call the army into the field to resist an invasion by a foreign power, such inaction would necessitate removal at once. If a president absconded to a foreign shore and refused to perform the duties of the presidency, an impeachment would be necessary to provide a new head of state. If a president stood by while members of the cabinet colluded with domestic insurrectionists, Congress would have to step in and do what the president was unwilling to do and strip those officials of public authority. If the president ordered federal employees to violate the rights of individuals and promised to pardon them for their actions, Congress would need to restore the rule of law by deposing a lawless chief executive.

Actual cases in which government officials have posed such an immediate danger to the nation are hard to identify, but a few individuals may fall into this category. The Federalist trial judge John Pickering was slowly descending into madness and alcoholism, resulting in increasingly incoherent decisions on the bench, forcing the Jeffersonians to remove him by impeachment (after his family and Federalist politicians refused to encourage him to resign voluntarily). Justice Samuel Chase's intemperate and partisan rant in seating a grand jury could plausibly have been interpreted as a precursor to more vigorous efforts by the justice to frustrate federal policy or even disrupt the workings of the government. Judge West Humphreys of Tennessee refused to resign from the bench even though he had joined the Confederate government at the outbreak of the Civil War and was no longer carrying out his judicial duties—at least not for the Union. He was removed from office by a unanimous vote in 1862. President Andrew Johnson's executive efforts to block congressional Reconstruction and his vocal encouragement to Southerners disposed to resist Reconstruction could have been construed as posing an immediate threat to the continued well-being of the nation, especially in a capital filled with rumors of a renewed outbreak of hostilities or even a coup d'état. President Donald Trump's encouragement of means both fair and foul to overturn the results of the 2020 presidential election could easily have led to the conclusion that his replacement by Vice President Mike Pence would be a necessary condition to securing the peaceful transfer of power to the rightful winner of the election.

Fortunately, few government officials and few individual actions can really pose that kind of threat to the nation. The nation is strong enough to survive most acts of misconduct and incompetence until the next election, and most officials have had the good sense to resign when their continued presence in office threatens to paralyze the government. Other solutions are generally available for addressing the problems that a government official might be creating. A district court judge might issue an astonishingly bad opinion, but the appellate courts stand ready to remedy such wrongs. An executive branch official might prove unworthy of an office of trust or honor, but the president can resolve the situation with a phone call. A president might embark on a path that would bring the nation to ruin, but Congress and the courts have many tools at their disposal to check even presidential abuses and try to set the ship of state aright.

In some cases, the continued presence of an individual in public office might be intolerable, even if not so cataclysmic. Such impeachments are consequential for the individual, but they may not be particularly consequential for the political system as a whole. The impeachments may be necessary, but their resonance is limited.

Most of the impeachments pursued by the House have been of this character. Judges who are unwilling to resign from office despite being incapacitated or incarcerated force the hand of Congress. Judges who can no longer be trusted to act appropriately in conducting trials or who face imminent jail sentences for their own criminal behavior must be removed from the bench. An official who cannot be effectively checked by other means might have to be removed in order to put a stop to a string of abuses. Arguably, individual officeholders who have egregiously violated well-established political, legal, or constitutional norms might need to be removed because their mere presence is no longer consistent with the nature and terms of their office. When West Humphreys abandoned his judicial post in Tennessee in order to join the secessionist cause, the House was compelled to act to declare his seat officially vacant. When Harry Claiborne refused to give up his seat on the district court after his conviction for tax evasion in 1984, the House could not easily ignore the situation. When Samuel Kent announced in 2009 that he would retire from the bench due to disability after pleading guilty to obstructing an investigation into his possible sexual abuse of court employees, the House proceeded with an impeachment until he submitted a letter of resignation. Judges arrested for domestic violence or investigated for sexual harassment, exposed as patrons of strip clubs and escort services, or charged with leaking information to the targets of criminal investigations could only stave off impeachment and removal by voluntarily resigning from office.

In such circumstances, the threat of impeachment is often enough to achieve the intended goal of vacating the office. The allegations in such a case might be contested as untrue, but the conduct they allege would be widely recognized as an egregious violation of the public trust. Bipartisan support for the officer's removal would be evident, and conviction and removal by the Senate seemingly assured. Precisely because Senate conviction seems inevitable, the formality of going through the process is often unnecessary.

Removing Individuals from Public Life

Sometimes removing individuals from office is not enough. They must be removed from public life.

The Constitution empowers the Senate to try all impeachments, but it limits the penalties that the Senate can impose when it convicts. "Judgement in Cases of Impeachment shall not extend further than to removal from Office, and disqualification to hold and enjoy any Office of honor, Trust or Profit under the United

States." Impeachment addresses political offenses and consequently can only result in political punishments. Permanent disqualification from future office is the most substantial political punishment that can be imposed.

In practice, the House has very rarely asked that the Senate not only remove an individual from office but also disqualify that person, and the Senate has very rarely imposed that additional penalty. In only three instances has the Senate followed up a conviction with a disqualification. Judge West Humphreys was the first federal officer to ever be disqualified, and he was charged with joining an insurrection against the federal government. The two other cases likewise involved federal judges, Robert Archbald and Thomas Porteous, but they were merely charged with corruption. Perhaps the House and Senate thought Archbald and Porteous were distinct from other officers charged with corruption in that their offenses extended across stints in multiple offices, and in Porteous's case included lying to investigators during his confirmation process. Congress could not hold out hope of rehabilitation for such repeat offenders.

It is easy to imagine that Congress would not generally think that disqualification from future office is the purpose of an impeachment effort. If an individual has been convicted of impeachable offenses, one might assume that this would be sufficient to place a stain on their public reputation and keep them out of office in the future. The president would be unlikely to nominate and the Senate unlikely to confirm someone who previously had to be involuntarily removed from office. If an individual's reputation had been sufficiently rehabilitated such that a future president and Senate would be willing to bestow an office of trust on him, then perhaps that judgment should be made by those future officeholders who would have the benefit of viewing the entire record of a lifetime. Why would the Senate need to tie the hands of future presidents and senators?

Pursuing an impeachment in order to disqualify targeted individuals from future office might well be a reason to proceed precisely if Congress were concerned that such individuals might make a political comeback. The circumstances in which this would make sense are extremely narrow but imaginable. Section 3 of the Fourteenth Amendment is instructive in this regard. Until recently, this provision of the Fourteenth Amendment seemed of merely historical interest. It imposes a disqualification of its own: no person who had taken an oath to support the Constitution and subsequently "engaged in insurrection or rebellion" is eligible to serve in Congress or hold office in either state or federal government. In drafting this amendment, the Reconstruction Congress clearly feared that the former secessionists would return to political power in the South. Those oath-breakers might have been marginalized when the Fourteenth Amendment was ratified in the summer of 1868, but who could say whether they would not come storming back into political prominence when martial law was finally lifted in the South? Even in those extreme circumstances, however, the Fourteenth Amendment left open the possibility that the disqualification could be removed by a two-thirds vote of each house. No one was completely beyond redemption.

A similar dynamic could be in play in an impeachment context. A current Congress might well worry that an individual who richly deserved impeachment and removal now might nonetheless regain political influence in the future and seek to foreclose that possibility. The House of Representatives was clearly worried about just such a possibility when it impeached Donald Trump in the aftermath of the storming of the Capitol on January 6, 2021. The single article of impeachment adopted by a majority of the House after that event concluded as follows:

> Wherefore, Donald Trump, by such conduct, has demonstrated that he will remain a threat to national security, democracy, and the Constitution if allowed to remain in office, and has acted in a manner grossly incompatible with self-government and the rule of law. Donald John Trump thus warrants impeachment and trial, removal from office, and disqualification to hold and

enjoy any office of honor, trust, or profit under the United States.[12]

In the judgment of the House, Donald Trump not only was a threat to the republic at that moment but would also present such a threat in the future; and it was at least plausible, if left to his own devices, that he could rebuild his political support and ascend to high office, where he would once again be a threat to democracy. Of course, the Senate disagreed with that assessment and would not even vote to convict the former president, let alone disqualify him from future office. Even so, the desire to bar an individual from future office can be its own independent justification for impeachment.

Notably, a desire to disqualify an individual from future office might still be relevant even when removing an individual from office has become a moot point. By the time Donald Trump was brought to trial in the Senate for a second time, he had already completed his term of office and Joe Biden had been inaugurated as president. The Senate had no opportunity to remove the former president from office in that impeachment trial, but it did have the opportunity to impose a prospective punishment by disqualifying Trump from holding office in the future. Knowing that the House had already allowed the president to remain in office for weeks after the events of January 6th and anticipating that the Senate was unlikely to achieve the two-thirds majority needed to convict the former president, disqualification might no longer have been a reasonable purpose for continuing to trial. If the House had moved with celerity in the hours after the riot, it might more plausibly have argued that it feared how the president might use the powers of his office if he were not immediately removed and by extension how he might use political power in the future if not disqualified. Likewise, in the immediate aftermath of the siege, the House managers might credibly have thought that they could secure the necessary two-thirds of the Senate to convict Trump of an appropriately drafted article of impeachment. The actual behavior of the

House undermined disqualification as the justification for an impeachment. The House majority seemed more focused on punishment than incapacitation.

There have been many cases in which officers have escaped impeachment by resigning. Congress has generally let a resignation be the end of the matter, since removing the individual from office was the whole point of the impeachment effort. But Congress might instead think that resignation is not enough. It might be thought necessary that the full gravity of an officer's offense be made public and that the individual be banished from public life through a conviction and disqualification. If disqualification had been an important goal of more impeachment efforts, Congress might have regularly continued its impeachment proceedings even after an individual had resigned. Former officers could be disqualified from future office as readily as incumbent officers.

The power of the Senate to disqualify convicted individuals might come with an important caveat. The constitutional text empowers the Senate to disqualify a convicted individual from holding any "Office of honor, Trust or Profit under the United States," but what is such an office? The scope of disqualification is obviously limited to federal office (offices "under the United States"). But an individual convicted and disqualified in the Senate could still go on to hold office in a state government. Perhaps more significantly, but also more controversially, an "Office of honor, Trust or Profit" might only include appointed offices. Elected federal offices—the presidency or a seat in Congress—might well be outside the scope of the impeachment disqualification clause. Even if the House and Senate hope to exclude an impeached officer from future political life, they quite likely cannot prevent such individuals from mounting an electoral campaign and persuading the people to vote for them. Attempting to bar a sitting president from regaining the White House in the future is probably not a viable reason for pursuing an impeachment.[13]

There is another prospective goal that might keep the impeachment power relevant even after an individual steps down from office, but it is statutory rather than constitutional. The Constitution lists only two possible punishments that might follow from a conviction in the Senate: removal and disqualification. Congress has created pensions and other benefits for former federal officials; however, individuals who have lost their office through impeachment and conviction in the Senate might be excluded from such statutory arrangements. Further, the Former Presidents Act provides various benefits to former presidents but excludes individuals who have left the presidency due to a Senate conviction.[14] Likewise, impeachment proceedings have been held over the heads of judges to convince them to resign rather than retire so that they would not qualify for pensions. Therefore, the desire to deny statutory benefits to an officer might provide an independent reason to pursue an impeachment.

A final caveat to the Senate's power to punish should be noted. The Senate can do no more than prohibit an impeached and convicted officer from holding future federal office. It cannot effectively remove that individual from public life as a whole. The Senate does not possess the ancient power of sending a disgraced official into exile. Donald Trump cannot be banished to live out his days at the Trump International Golf Club in Dubai. Likewise, the Senate cannot prevent an impeached and convicted individual from occupying a prominent place in public life. Such an individual could still launch a social media company, anchor a television talk show, or tour the country holding rallies. In the American republic, even scoundrels are allowed to mount the public stage and try to shape public opinion.

Conducting a Grand Inquest

On January 4, 1804, the House of Representatives heard from a committee appointed to examine the precedents and prepare the necessary forms to embark on an impeachment of a federal district judge. The House then resolved to proceed, and a delegation marched from the House chamber to that of the Senate and announced that "they were the managers instructed by the House of Representatives to exhibit certain articles of impeachment." The managers were asked to take their seats, and the Senate sergeant-at-arms proclaimed their arrival:

> Oyez! Oyez! Oyez! All persons are commanded to keep silence on pain of imprisonment, while the grand inquest of the nation is exhibiting to the Senate of the United States, sitting as a Court of Impeachment, articles of impeachment against John Pickering, judge of the district court of the district of New Hampshire.[15]

Pickering became the first judge to be impeached by the House and the first federal officer to be convicted and removed by the Senate.

The Senate organized itself as the court of impeachment, and the House styled itself as the "grand inquest of the nation." That appellation was borrowed from British practice, and it carried with it significant weight. Part of that weight had ostensibly been shed as the impeachment power was reimagined in the American republic. The English Parliament exercised extensive judicial powers, and the "Commons of England in Parliament are supposed to be a greater and a wiser body than a Grand-jury of any one county." The House of Commons was the "greatest and wisest inquest in England."[16] Some Americans therefore objected to borrowing the British nomenclature. The House of Representatives was constrained in ways that the Commons was not. The Commons "has the awful power of originating bills of pains and penalties, and also bills of attainder, which go to life, liberty and property, which happily this house has not." The constitutionally limited House of Representatives "can in no proper sense be called the grand inquest of the nation." There was perhaps some danger in the House claiming for itself "a term not found . . . in the Federal Constitution."[17]

But most were perfectly content to domesticate the grand inquest, like the impeachment power itself, so that it was more suitable to a federal republic as well. It was as the grand inquest of the nation that the House had the responsibility to examine the conduct of the officers of the federal government, identify errors and abuse, and call officers to account for their activities. "All gentlemen admitted, that the House had the superintendence over the officers of the Government, as the grand inquest of the nation." It was that responsibility that gave the House "a right to demand a sight of those papers, that should throw light upon their conduct."[18] The "character of this House as the grand inquest of the Nation" lodged in it a duty "not only to impeach those who perpetrate offence, but to watch and give the alarm for the prevention of such attempts."[19] "As the Grand Inquest of the Nation," the House of Representatives had a "power to impeach all civil officers, from the President down," and as a consequence had the authority to inquire into how those officers had been conducting themselves while holding the public trust.[20]

The impeachment power gave the House the ability to hold public officials responsible for their misconduct, but in order to perform those duties, the House was consequently entrusted with the power to peer into the workings of all parts of the federal government. To safeguard the public welfare and address the grievances of the people, the House could demand answers from government officers and access to the records of government operations. The impeachment power made the House, on behalf of the people, the ultimate supervisor of government affairs.

One purpose of the impeachment power is to investigate government operations and illuminate how they function. Such investigations might well vindicate a federal officer and serve to wash away the stench of scandal. They might reveal that the problems can be resolved by means short of the trial and removal of an officer, or they might demonstrate that the government must be purged of some of its officers. Impeachment inquiries need not always lead to impeachments, and the House does not need the agreement of the Senate to achieve its goals if what it primarily wants is to lay bare the conduct of federal officers.

This purpose of the impeachment power has slipped from the consciousness of modern legislators. Congressional oversight of the executive branch has become routinized in the work of congressional committees, and the constitutional justification for such oversight has been pinned less on the impeachment power than on the legislative and budgeting authorities of Congress. But the authority of the House extends beyond drafting statutes and appropriating funds. Congress can investigate how well the president has fulfilled the duty to take care that the laws are faithfully executed and to inquire into whether the president's subordinates in the executive branch are assisting or frustrating that task.

As the First Congress was debating how to establish the great departments of the executive branch, James Madison reminded his colleagues that the president is "responsible to the public for the conduct of the person he has nominated and appointed to aid him in the administration of his department. But if the President shall join in a collusion with the officer, and continue the bad man in office, the case of impeachment will reach the culprit, and drag him forth to punishment." The president should be "answerable for the conduct of the officer," but it was not the responsibility of the president alone to secure the good behavior of those charged with administering the government.[21]

The inquiry by the Select Committee to Investigate the January 6th Attack on the United States Capitol was properly the work of the House under its impeachment power. It was an instance of the House acting as the grand inquirer of the nation to discover what had transpired in the executive branch, and more particularly in the White House, in the weeks between the presidential election in November 2020 and the assembly of Congress to count the electoral ballots on January 6, 2021. The House has no authority to investigate crimes as such and cannot mete out punishments for violations of criminal law. The House has ample authority, however, to inquire into how executive branch officials up to and including the president conducted themselves while in office. The legislative function of the House is to look ahead and determine what policies should be adopted to best serve the common good in the future. The inquisitorial function of the House is to look back and determine whether misconduct has taken place.

In addition to detaching committee investigations of executive branch activities from the impeachment power, the modern Congress has also preferred to leave many questions that could have been the basis of impeachment inquiries in the hands of judicial or quasi-judicial bodies. In some cases, such alternative investigative bodies might be more expert in doing the necessary work or more trusted to produce results that would be broadly viewed as legitimate. But relying on prosecutors and lawsuits to uncover the facts surrounding potential executive or judicial misconduct has the unfortunate feature of steering the inquiry toward questions of the violation of the law. Perhaps the most prominent recent example of this dynamic is the appointment by the attorney general of special counsel Robert Mueller to investigate potential illegal activities surrounding Russian interference in the 2016 presidential election. As a former director of the Federal Bureau of Investigation with bipartisan credentials, Mueller was potentially well suited to doing the work that might otherwise have been done by the Department of Justice if not for the potential conflict of interest with President Donald Trump. To the extent to which there were crimes to be investigated, such an appointment was all to the good. But Mueller was ill suited and could not be expected to perform the political task that a congressional impeachment inquiry would have performed. A congressional inquiry would not have been limited to asking whether criminal laws were broken during the run-up to the 2016 election. Moreover, when Mueller was handed an additional task of investigating whether the president had committed criminal obstruction of justice, he was given an impossible task. Not only was the Department of Justice barred as a matter of policy from indicting a sitting president for any federal criminal offenses, but the alleged misconduct involved Trump's exercise of the powers of the presidency, which by its nature would have strained any theory of criminal liability. The questions of greatest interest surrounding

Donald Trump were not questions of criminal law but questions of constitutional malfeasance. In principle, these were questions that should have been asked and investigated by the House of Representatives, not an appointed officer of the Department of Justice. Whether the president should be cleared or censured for his conduct during the election and the subsequent investigation were ultimately political questions that required a political process to determine. The House of Representatives, however, was disinclined to do that work itself and was not generally trusted to be able to perform that task in a manner that would create public confidence in the results.

Notably, if impeachments are a grand inquest into the conduct of public officials, then there is no reason why that inquest should be cut off by an officer's departure from office. If impeachments are to deter public officers from gross misconduct, then leaving the door open to a legislature scrutinizing the conduct of former officers is potentially useful. The House of Commons had not limited itself to impeaching incumbent officers, and state legislatures in America have sometimes done the same. The House should lay bare misconduct in the government whenever it has reason to believe that such misconduct has occurred.

The impeachment power gives the first, most democratic branch of the government the ability to scrutinize the actions of individuals in the other branches of government and call them to account for their actions. As the Massachusetts Constitution of 1780 stated for its own state assembly, "The house of representatives shall be the grand inquest of this commonwealth; and all impeachments made by them shall be heard and tried in the senate."[22] The House investigates and exposes, and if necessary, goes to the Senate to impeach. The investigation and exposure are in themselves valuable activities and independent rationales for exercising the impeachment power of the House. An excessive focus on conviction and removal as the only goal of an impeachment inquiry forecloses the kind of congressional oversight of the conduct of federal officers that the Constitution contemplates in a system of separated powers. It likewise emboldens presidents to advance claims of executive privilege and other doctrines so as to shield their conduct or the conduct of their subordinates from congressional scrutiny. In articulating the idea of executive privilege at its inception, President George Washington recognized that such a privilege should not throw a veil over executive misconduct that the House had proper constitutional authority to scrutinize.

Sending a Message to Future Officeholders

The offenses committed by an individual officer might not be so severe in and of themselves. If the standard for impeachable offenses is raised high enough, then relatively few instances of misconduct would be worthy of an impeachment inquiry.

Whether consciously or not, we tend to think that way about presidential misconduct. The libertarian scholar Gene Healy believes that this is a mistake. He wryly observes, "We've somehow managed to convince ourselves that the *one job* in America where you have to commit a felony to get fired is the one where you actually get nuclear weapons."[23] How much better off would we have been if we had been willing to impeach—or at least threaten to impeach—our worst presidents? But Healy is unusual in his desire to knock the presidency off his pedestal. In our current political culture, impeaching a president is perceived to be a particularly fateful step that would threaten to create financial and security uncertainty that would ripple across the globe. That might change. If impeachment inquiries were to become more frequent, we would likely adjust to a new reality and observe them with greater equanimity. The spectacle of a president being impeached twice in a single term of office might have shifted our perception of the impeachment power at least a little bit. Perhaps in the near future the possibility of an impeachment will feel less like an "emergency measure" and a bit more like a part of ordinary politics.[24] Even if impeaching a president does begin to feel like a less momentous occasion, the political incentives pushing senators to rally around an embattled president of the same party make it exceedingly difficult to convict and remove a sitting president. The political stakes of removing a president are high enough that they necessarily raise the bar on what may be regarded as a serious impeachable offense when it comes to the occupant of the White House.

By contrast, the nation does not quake at the thought of removing a cabinet secretary or a district court judge. The political stakes are lower when it comes to such offices, and the partisan pressures to support incumbents in such positions are more tempered. The meaning of high crimes and misdemeanors may be the same across the offices encompassed within the impeachment power, but the type of conduct that is deemed incompatible with an office necessarily depends on the particulars of the office; and the political reality of what members of Congress can be mobilized to do can never be ignored within an impeachment context.

An impeachment might be particularly consequential for the individual who is placed in the dock, but it matters for the larger political system as well. Impeachments have an audience, and Congress sends a message to other current and future officeholders by how it addresses misconduct in an individual case. The bad behavior of a single, relatively minor public official might not be very consequential in and of itself, and thus might not seem to warrant the time and effort necessary to pursue an impeachment. Such behavior might be far more troubling if it becomes widespread, however, and one purpose of an impeachment is to nip such a possibility in the bud. If Congress shows that it is willing to tolerate misconduct by federal officers, then that has systemic implications that magnify the significance of such incidents. Congress should concern itself not merely with an instance of misconduct but with the type of misconduct that is revealed in a particular case. An impeachment sends a message that such conduct will not be tolerated, and in so doing deters other officers from following such bad examples.

Sometimes Congress just needs to use the impeachment power to emphasize the stability of the norms that are already in place and widely accepted. An impeachment in that context can be norm-reinforcing. Unpunished violations of norms of behavior subvert the norms themselves. Allowing a judge to stay in office after egregiously bad behavior has been exposed and sanctioned in other venues might send the wrong message to the larger judiciary that such behavior is not so bad. An impeachment can put an exclamation point on the political and legal system's judgment that some actions should not be tolerated. The question to be asked in such circumstances is whether the established norms really require reinforcement by these means.

Establishing Norms of Acceptable Political Behavior

Impeachments can be used for even more ambitious purposes. Rather than reinforcing well-settled norms of political behavior, an impeachment might attempt to construct a new norm that will shape political behavior in the future. The impeachment power can be an effective tool for articulating, establishing, preserving, and protecting constitutional norms.

The Constitution necessarily assigns discretionary power to designated government officials. The discretion of government officials is circumscribed to some degree by a system of constitutional rules. We tell government officials that there are some things they may not do, and we often reinforce those rules by making them judicially enforceable. We also circumscribe political discretion with evolving expectations of how political power is to be properly used. The preservation of the constitutional system may well require that political behavior within the constitutional rules be further constrained by precepts that help preserve those rules. Questions of constitutional propriety arise within the boundaries of constitutional law. Thomas Cooley, a leading

American jurist of the latter half of the nineteenth century, pointed out that a more "complete and accurate" definition of a constitution would be "that body of rules and maxims in accordance with which powers of sovereignty are habitually exercised."[25] His near contemporary in England, A. V. Dicey, made a similar observation. Such norms—what Dicey called "conventions"—were if anything even more important in the English context, where there was no written constitution with judicially enforceable rules to limit political discretion. They were the "conventions, understandings, habits, or practices which, though they may regulate the conduct of the several members of the sovereign power . . . are not in reality laws at all since they are not enforced by the Courts."[26] Critical features of the modern British constitutional order, such as the fact that the king may not veto laws passed by Parliament, are a matter of informal understanding and political practice. Some norms might be relatively unimportant, but others might be indispensable. They are all put in place and maintained through political action. Partisanship and self-interest can generate significant political pressures that inherited constitutional norms might struggle to contain. When political elites are no longer willing to defend constitutional norms and are unable or unwilling to punish those who violate them, the norms eventually collapse.

Impeachments serve a larger constitutional function when the norms at issue are not particularly clear or well accepted. The impeachment itself becomes a vehicle for trying to establish the new normative commitments. The fate of the individual being impeached is less important than the message being sent. The officer in the docks is held up as an object lesson. The impeachment is primarily educative and forward-looking, not punitive and backward-looking. The critical audience for the impeachment is the other current and future federal officers who are being instructed on the proper bounds of acceptable political behavior. The actual removal of the impeached official is almost beside the point. The impeachment is the message. Once the message has been sent and received, the mission has been accomplished.

Such norm-creating use of the impeachment power had been part of the British experience as Parliament struggled to wrest greater authority from the king, and it has been part of the American experience as well. When Associate Justice Samuel Chase was impeached for his judicial conduct in the run-up to the 1800 elections, the Jeffersonians hoped to set some clear ground rules for the federal judiciary in the new constitutional system. Federal judges could not understand themselves to be partisan actors on the political stage and expect to keep their offices. When President Andrew Johnson was impeached in the midst of Reconstruction, Republicans in Congress wanted assurances that the president would not use all the tools at his disposal to obstruct congressional policy and undermine the political base of the members of Congress. Johnson was spared conviction in the Senate when he apparently satisfied enough swing members that he would relent in his battle with Congress and serve out the rest of his term quietly.[27]

That said, there are risks involved in using the impeachment power as a tool for supporting constitutional norms. An impeachment might divide rather than unify the country around those norms and, as a consequence, might leave the norms in a weaker state than they otherwise would have been. The overall message of an impeachment might be misread if the Senate refuses to convict, leaving friends of the impeached officer to argue that the target of the impeachment was in fact vindicated by the Senate's action. An impeachment is a high-stakes confrontation, and advocates of impeachment should consider the consequences of losing as well as the potential benefits of winning. If the goal of an impeachment is to bolster constitutional norms, then the fight over the legacy of the impeachment will be as important as the battle over the impeachment itself.

It is always worth considering whether alternative tools can accomplish the desired goals just as well or better than the tool of impeachment. If the goal is to bolster political norms, then a resolution of censure or even a simple electoral victory might be equally or more effective in conveying to other ambitious political operatives that a particular officer's example is not one worth following. It is possible to cheapen the coin of impeachment by spending it too often and too meanly. If the impeachment tool comes to be seen as mere partisan showboating, then it will be worse than useless. Officers must fear impeachments as politically costly and reputationally damaging, even if they are survivable.

An impeachment that only seems to redound to the political benefit of the impeached official is more likely to subvert norms than reinforce them, and more likely to embolden norm breakers than chastise them. Impeachment campaigns may be moments of high drama, but the protagonists must take care not to unwittingly cast themselves in the role of the villain rather than the hero. Being clear about why an impeachment should be pursued, and what it should be understood to mean, is essential to convey the right moral of the story.

Congress and Constitutional Checks and Balances

The system of separation of powers created by the drafters of American constitutions at both the state and federal level is famously one of checks and balances. The constitutional drafters of the early republic had come to believe that free government could only be preserved if political power were divided and spread across many hands. If that system were to collapse, the power that had been distributed could be consolidated under one banner. A dictator could wrest power from where it properly belonged in the constitutional system and exercise it unilaterally. The risks of that happening were myriad. The revolutionaries who drafted state constitutions in 1776 were especially fearful that governors would become miniature kings, so they wrote constitutions that often created an enfeebled executive branch. The Federalists who argued for constitutional reform a decade later thought those early constitutional drafters had tilted too far in one direction. James Madison was among those who looked at the experience of the states and thought that, in a democratic political system, the greatest danger was not from the executive but from the legislative branch, which "is everywhere extending the sphere of its activity, and drawing all power into its impetuous vortex."[28] The Federalists hoped to find an equilibrium in which each of the branches of government would balance one another rather than swallow everything into its ravenous maw.

In order to keep the branches of government in balance, each branch would need to possess an arsenal of weapons by which it could defend its own turf and check the actions of the other branches. The president was given a qualified veto power over legislation, not just to potentially improve the quality of the policy proposals enacted into law but also to defend the office of the presidency against the potential incursions of an aggressive legislature. Legislatures in England and America had been learning how to effectively check aggressive executives, so Congress was given various means to defend its interests and protect itself from being kneecapped by an ambitious president. The impeachment power is perhaps the greatest of those checks. Only the elected legislature is empowered to remove members of the other branches from office.

If we think about the impeachment power as part of a system of checks and balances, we should readily see that one purpose of using the impeachment power is to defend congressional prerogatives against executive and judicial overreach. One type of high crime and misdemeanor is overstepping the bounds of a limited constitutional office and encroaching on the jurisdiction and authority of a coordinate branch of government.

The mostly neglected second article of impeachment against President Donald Trump in his first impeachment in 2020 is an example of Congress using the impeachment power to defend its own prerogatives. That article focused on how President Trump had responded to the congressional inquiry into his actions relative to the government of Ukraine in 2019. As the article of impeachment put it, President Trump "without lawful cause or excuse ... directed Executive Branch agencies, offices, and officials not to comply" with congressional subpoenas. In doing so, he had, according to the House majority, "sought to arrogate to himself the right to determine the propriety, scope, and nature of an impeachment inquiry into his own conduct."[29] Obstruction of an impeachment inquiry was itself an impeachable offense.

The Constitution does not vest Congress with an explicit power of oversight or investigation, except in the form of the impeachment power itself. Nonetheless, judges and politicians have long understood legislatures to have the authority to do some investigative work even outside the impeachment context. Congress must be able to investigate if it is to identify public policy problems and design effective solutions in its legislative capacity. When the Senate is called upon to ratify a treaty or confirm a nominee for an office, it must gather information to help it determine whether it should accede to the president's wishes. When Congress considers whether it should authorize the use of military force against another nation, it must take steps to determine whether such military action is warranted or advisable. When the House contemplates whether it should exercise its sole power of impeachment, it must inquire into the conduct of government officers to determine whether anything is amiss, and whether impeachment and removal are the proper remedies.

Presidential administrations are often the targets of such investigations, and presidents are not always eager to cooperate with them. Claims of executive privilege have been a common basis on which presidents have asserted limits on how far they should cooperate with congressional investigations. Like congressional oversight, executive privilege is not mentioned in the Constitution, but has instead been inferred from it as a necessary implication of the president's constitutional responsibilities and the effective functioning of the separate branches of government.

When the House of Representatives balked at passing a statute needed to help implement the controversial Jay Treaty of 1795, it asked the president to supply all the communications relating to the negotiation of the treaty to inform its deliberations about whether to adopt the legislation the president wanted. George Washington responded that it was his "constant endeavor to harmonize with the other branches" of the government, but that some of the requested documents were sensitive. The House had no proper right to such documents, and the president had no duty to provide them. James Madison, then serving in the House, responded to Washington's message by insisting that the president could only appropriately assess the executive branch's own interest in those papers, but he "ought not to refuse them as irrelative to the objects of the House," which was something that the House alone could properly judge. Washington admitted that the House had the constitutional authority to inspect the executive's papers if it were part of an impeachment investigation, but such a purpose had not been "expressed." Madison countered that the House had no obligation to state that it wanted access to documents for purposes of an impeachment inquiry, and in many cases it might even be "evidently improper to state that to be the object of information."[30] In the end, they compromised, and the House passed the desired bill.

The first president and the Fourth Congress were grappling with some basic constitutional and political problems that continued to bedevil the 45th president and the 116th Congress. George Washington was confronting the emergence of the first divided government, in which the House majority was in organized opposition to his own administration, a situation that Washington came to regard as threatening to the very foundations of the republic. An opposing party is particularly motivated to make unpleasant demands on the presidential administration and to scrutinize its every action with great skepticism, and presidents are often inclined to think that an opposing party is behaving unscrupulously and unfairly. At the same time, presidents can often rely on their partisan friends to go easy on them and not be too aggressive in exposing the administration's problems.

Washington and Madison were also confronting a fundamental question in the American constitutional system about who should be able to judge the constitutional rights and responsibilities of the various branches of the government and what tools Congress had available to it to compel a reluctant executive to cooperate with its inquiries. They left those questions unresolved, and they remain unresolved today. Both the House and the president insisted on their own authority to judge their own constitutional responsibilities, but both denied the authority of others to judge those responsibilities. The president could reasonably assert executive privilege, but he could not reasonably tell the House what information it did or did not need to perform its own duties. The president had control over the information that the House wanted to examine, but the president needed the House's cooperation to advance the policies he desired. And as Washington seemed to recognize, the House had the ultimate power to impeach the president and could demand whatever information it might deem relevant to that inquiry or let the president face the consequences if he refused to satisfy their concerns.

The system has worked through give-and-take. Both branches of government have recognized that they should not push things too far and that there are deals to be made to overcome impasses. Madison in the House understood that some information did in fact need to be kept confidential if the president were to be able to perform his constitutional functions on behalf of the nation. Washington in the White House understood that interbranch cooperation and concessions would be necessary to keep the government functioning and that, as a practical matter, there were things he needed from the House, so he had to find ways to satisfy its members.

White House counsel Pat Cipollone's letter to the House regarding the impeachment inquiry of Donald Trump could not have been more distant from Washington's letter to the House in tone, substance, and attitude. Trump's White House counsel responded to the House's "numerous, legally unsupported decisions made as part of what you have labeled—contrary to the Constitution of the United States and all past bipartisan precedent—as an 'impeachment inquiry.'" In the eyes of the White House, the inquiry "violates fundamental fairness and constitutionally mandated due process." The House was simply seeking "to overturn the results of the 2016 election and deprive the American people of the President they have freely chosen." The "baseless, unconstitutional effort to overturn the democratic process" had "left the President with no choice" but to refuse to "participate in your partisan and unconstitutional inquiry." President Trump "cannot allow your constitutionally illegitimate proceedings to distract him and those in the Executive Branch from their work on behalf of the American people." The President "has a country to lead," and the executive branch would simply ignore the so-called "impeachment inquiry" in the House.[31]

Cipollone's letter reflected the intense partisan divide in contemporary politics and the distrust between the Democrats in Congress and the Trump White House. It also reflected a sense that the House and the administration had reached the endgame. James Madison's House had some leverage over the Washington administration because it had something that the administration wanted, and there was some realistic possibility of reaching an accommodation that could satisfy both sides. Nancy Pelosi's House seemed to have lost much of its leverage over the Trump administration. The president seemed to be assuming that he would inevitably be impeached and that there was no legislative policy agenda to be advanced, so he had nothing more to lose by refusing to cooperate further with the House. He was positioning himself for the Senate trial and the 2020 electoral campaign.

More than once after the Democrats captured the House of Representatives in the midterm elections of 2018, President Donald Trump had taken to Twitter to express his irritation at "presidential harassment!" Undoubtedly, he was not the first occupant of the Oval Office to feel that way, but his response had been different. The Trump administration had tended to adopt a posture of maximal presidential obstruction of congressional investigations into the conduct of the executive branch and the individuals surrounding it. That defiance culminated in Cipollone's letter to Speaker of the House Nancy Pelosi declaring that the administration would not cooperate in any way with an impeachment inquiry that it regarded as "illegitimate" and "constitutionally invalid."

Cipollone, on behalf of the president, had thrown down the gauntlet. The White House refused to offer documents or testimony to the House—even those that might have put the president's or the administration's conduct in a better light. The House could either choose to impeach the president based on what it already knew or could discover without the president's cooperation, or it could drop the impeachment effort and move on. The president had dared the House to impeach him, and he had then chosen to mount his defense against possible removal in the Senate and in the court of public opinion. Members of Congress of both parties should have understood the institutional stakes of such a challenge. If President Trump could simply issue a blanket refusal to cooperate with any congressional oversight of executive branch activities and still not be impeached, then Congress should expect that future presidents would try to build on that example.

Congress has some capacity to pressure an administration to comply with its subpoenas by turning to the courts or even using its inherent contempt power to detain an uncooperative witness, but its more substantial weapons have always been political.[32] Congress can refuse to adopt policies that an administration wants. The Senate can refuse to confirm nominees that the president wants to see seated. Congress can refuse to provide funding for White House priorities. At the extreme, the House can vote to impeach and the Senate can vote to remove officers who stonewall congressional investigations.

Congress is often reluctant to use those constitutional weapons, in part because there will be collateral damage. Congress also wants laws passed, the government funded, and vacant offices filled. The stakes of a particular dispute between the branches are not always high enough to make those costs worth bearing. The Trump administration could credibly threaten complete noncooperation with the House because it did not think there was much to be gained by cooperation; in those circumstances, Congress could lose an important part of its leverage over the White House. The challenge for the House is in demonstrating to a presidential administration that there are still things to lose, and perhaps still things to be won. And, ultimately, as Madison himself noted, if certain issues cannot "be adjusted by the departments themselves," then "there is no resource left but the will of the community."[33] The two sides can plead their case to the electorate and pray the voters can resolve the disagreement.

Advocates of an impeachment need to think about what they are hoping to accomplish. Other political actors who are being asked to lend their support to such efforts must similarly consider what is to be gained by making use of such a powerful constitutional weapon. Proponents of an impeachment need to be able to explain why it makes sense to use this last-resort option and why there are no better tools available for accomplishing their ultimate political objectives. There are times when an impeachment is necessary, but we should not want impeachments to become part of our normal political experience. It is an extraordinary remedy for extraordinary situations, and if we reach for that remedy, we should know why we are doing so and be prepared for the consequences.

4

What Are High Crimes
and Misdemeanors?

WHEN THE FEDERALISTS gathered at the Philadelphia Convention in 1787 to draft a new federal constitution, they had little doubt that liberty would be fleeting if powerful government officials were not watched over and potentially countered by others. In the heady days of the American Revolution, many Americans had assumed that a combination of democratic elections and weak government would do the job. After running that experiment for a decade, many Americans had concluded that those initial assumptions were mistaken. Government needed to be able to harness more power to advance public ends, and democratic elections were not enough to keep government officials in check. In criticizing the Virginia state constitution of 1776, Thomas Jefferson emphasized that democracy was but a means for achieving the real objective, which was liberty. Only a properly designed democracy would promote that goal:

> An *elective despotism* was not the government we fought for, but one which should not only be founded on free principles, but in which the powers of government should be so divided and balanced among several bodies of magistracy, as that no one could transcend their legal limits, without being effectually checked and restrained by the others.[1]

This was the lesson of English history and the most learned political science of the Enlightenment era. Alexander Hamilton boasted that, like "most other sciences," the "science of politics . . . has received great improvement" in modern times. The "efficacy of various principles is now well understood," including the need for "the introduction of legislative balances and checks." They were the "means, and powerful means, by which the excellence of republican government may be retained and its imperfections lessened or avoided." Of course, perhaps the most important check on abuse of power by government officials was the electoral one. When the people were unhappy with how they were being governed, they should have the ability to replace their governors. But few thought that would be sufficient. The "enlightened friends to liberty" recognized that populist urges could give rise to "a state of perpetual vibration between the extremes of tyranny and anarchy." Popular participation in the operation of the government was a necessary but not a sufficient condition for achieving a regime of ordered liberty.[2]

In his arguments during the convention and the subsequent ratification debates, James Madison hammered home this point. It was not enough simply to lay down in the constitutional text what the boundaries of government power should be. Constitutional drafters could list sacred rights that shall not be infringed and specify the limits of the powers of office that shall not be transgressed, but all those words would be no more than "parchment barriers" if ambitious politicians, perhaps backed by public approval, sought to tear through them. "Maintaining in practice the necessary partition of power" required giving the various parts of the government "the means of keeping each other in their proper places." "Ambition must be made to check ambition," which meant that the several offices of the government must be so divided and arranged such that "each may be a check on the other, that the private interest of every individual may be a sentinel over the public rights." Each branch would need "an equal power of self-defense" against encroachments by the others and a means of protecting the people from incipient despotism.³

The presidency was a particular point of concern. To be sure, many of the classically trained founders worried that the example of the "petty republics" of antiquity and the more recent history of the American states since the Revolution demonstrated the "amazing violence and turbulence of the democratic spirit." If Americans had shown too much of a willingness "to throw all power into the Legislative vortex," it was necessary to devise an "effectual check . . . for restraining the instability and encroachments" and "follies" of the popular branch. The revolutionary states had gone too far in enervating their governors so as to avoid any possibility of creating a monarchy on American shores, and the delegates in Philadelphia soon settled on vesting executive power in a single chief executive officer who would have the power and energy to defend the nation and administer the government. But that created a new set of problems. A president powerful enough to do what needed to be done was also powerful enough to cause a problem. The republic needed a president, but it was essential that the republic be made safe from that president.⁴

It is notable that just a few years removed from a successful revolutionary war fought for American independence that the constitutional framers in Philadelphia were thinking about the kind of institutional design and modes of political accountability that would make such violent action to stop abuse of political power unnecessary. One type of fear was the possibility that an unscrupulous chief executive, in particular, would corrupt the political process to keep himself in power and beyond the reach of justice. George Mason, author of Virginia's state constitution and Declaration of Rights, was among those who worried about conspiracies and corruption allowing someone to procure "his appointment in the first instance" and then "repeating his guilt" to remain ensconced in power. But another type of fear was of a tyrannical ruler, whether he had come to power by fair means or foul. Benjamin Franklin, the eldest member of the convention, must have had this in mind when he pointed out that the traditional remedy "where the chief Magistrate rendered himself obnoxious" was "assassination." Edmund Randolph, the sitting governor of Virginia, was more explicit in warning against the likelihood of "tumults & insurrections" if there was no alternative mode of dealing with a president who took advantage of his "great opportunitys of abusing his power." Although not wanting to make impeachments too easy, Elbridge Gerry of Massachusetts thought it important that a "bad" magistrate "ought to be kept in fear of them." Some thought periodic elections would be sufficient to avoid such problems, which were much more pressing in the case of an official who "held his place for life," but most did not think the prospect of electoral replacement would be adequate to cover the field.[5]

Deciding that the House of Representatives could launch an impeachment process against the president and other federal officers still left open the question of when they could do so. The Constitution lays down a substantive standard for what constitutes an impeachable offense. Article II specifies that officers can be impeached and removed for "Treason, Bribery, or other high Crimes and Misdemeanors." The offenses of treason and bribery are relatively straightforward to define, but have been of limited significance for how the impeachment power has actually been used over time. In practice, the most important set of impeachable offenses has also been the least clear: those that fall within the scope of "high Crimes and Misdemeanors." The history and purpose of the impeachment power demonstrate that the scope of impeachable offenses is broad and flexible in order to allow Congress to reach the unpredictable but potentially serious threats to the constitutional order that can arise from the misbehavior of federal officers.[6]

But let us consider the options.

The Inkblot Answer

The unfamiliarity of the phrase *high crimes and misdemeanors* and the relative rarity of impeachments have led some to embrace what might be called the "inkblot" theory of impeachable offenses.[7] During his contentious Senate confirmation hearings for an appointment to the Supreme Court, the conservative judge Robert Bork infamously characterized the Ninth Amendment as an "inkblot" with no practical meaning. The Ninth Amendment comes at the end of the Bill of Rights and simply says "the enumeration in the Constitution, of certain rights, shall not be construed to disparage others retained by the people." It addressed one concern about adding a Bill of Rights to the original constitutional text, which was that any list of rights would be incomplete and might leave the citizenry worse off than if no rights were enumerated at all.

The problem, from a judicial perspective, is that there was no guidance for identifying what those "other" rights might be, and in practice the courts have largely avoided relying on the Ninth Amendment when making judgments. Constitutional interpreters were left in the dark in trying to make sense of the substantive content and outer boundaries of the terms of the Ninth Amendment. In such circumstances, Bork thought, judges should defer to whatever elected officials had decided.

> I do not think you can use the ninth amendment unless you know something of what it means. For example, if you had an amendment that says "Congress shall make no" and then there is an ink blot and you cannot read the rest of it and that is the only copy you have, I do not think the court can make up what might be under the ink blot if you cannot read it.[8]

The inkblot problem of constitutional interpretation had very specific implications for judges, according to Bork. Legislators could be influenced by the Ninth Amendment to vote against a bill they thought would violate important, but unenumerated, rights. A court, on the other hand, "has exceeded its powers under the Con-

stitution" if it "makes up a new right for which there is not historical evidence."[9]

Other judges and scholars disagreed with Bork about whether
the Ninth Amendment is bereft of discoverable meaning and what
judges should do in such circumstances; but the important point
is that some provisions of the Constitution can be extremely hard
to interpret. And we might well think that the phrase *high crimes
and misdemeanors* is as difficult to understand as the Ninth Amendment. Perhaps modern lawmakers are left completely to their own
devices to make sense of the phrase. In effect, they are making it
up, and "high crimes and misdemeanors" could mean anything—
or nothing.

Like Bork's hypothetical court, we might think such a situation
is radically disempowering. If the impeachment clause just said
that officers could be impeached and convicted for "Treason,
Bribery, or" and the rest was hidden under an inkblot and lost to
history, should Congress refrain from ever impeaching an officer
except when the charges included treason and bribery? Perhaps
the proper implication of a government official encountering a
piece of constitutional text that cannot be read is to ignore it.
A constitutional provision with no clear meaning cannot authorize governmental action. The effective scope of the impeachment
clause shrinks to the listed offenses of treason and bribery.

Members of Congress who have found the phrase *high crimes
and misdemeanors* to be equally baffling have tended to imagine
themselves empowered rather than disempowered by that possibility. Impeachable offenses could mean anything at all. Then it
might follow, as the German philosopher Friedrich Nietzsche
once suggested, if "nothing is true, everything is permitted."[10]

House minority leader Gerald Ford infamously suggested this
approach when advocating for the impeachment of Justice William O. Douglas in 1970:

> What, then, is an impeachable offense? The only honest answer
> is that an impeachable offense is whatever a majority of the

House of Representatives considers it to be at any given moment in history.[11]

From this perspective, the impeachment clause is completely open-ended and simply empowers members of Congress to use their best judgment on whether an officer needs to be removed. If the meaning of high crimes is effectively an inkblot, then there is nothing holding members of Congress back from impeaching a troublesome officer.

The inkblot theory has few adherents, and for good reason. In one of the several efforts to impeach President Andrew Johnson during the fight over Reconstruction, the Iowa Republican James F. Wilson thought he detected among some of his colleagues a temptation to rely on something like Gerald Ford's position. Wilson had little sympathy for the president, and he later served as a House manager in Johnson's impeachment trial, but he would not tolerate the House embracing such an expansive theory of its power:

> Having the sole power to impeach, may the House of Representatives lawfully exercise it whenever and for whatever a majority of the body may determine? Is it a lawless power, controlled by no rules, guided by no reason, and made active only by the likes or dislikes of those to whom it is intrusted?[12]

He disregarded the view that impeachable offenses were "whatever this House may declare on its conscience to be an impeachable offense." Unlike his more fervent colleagues, "I prefer the Constitution to that conscience of this body which may be evidenced by a mere partisan majority. I would be willing to be judged by a Republican conscience and yet shrink from the conclusions of one directed by a Democratic majority."[13] Fortunately, neither the text nor the history of the impeachment power requires such a result. Rather than throwing up our hands and giving up on any effort to determine what the limiting principles constraining the scope of impeachable offenses might be, we can and should try to make sense of the history and logic of the impeachment clause.

The Ordinary Crimes Answer

At the other extreme from Ford, it is sometimes suggested that there are extremely few impeachable offenses. It is tempting, especially for those charged with an impeachable offense, to attempt to analogize high crimes to ordinary crimes. The Constitution lists two familiar sorts of criminal acts as impeachable, and the language of crimes, misdemeanors, trials, and convictions that permeates the impeachment process are resonant of the ordinary criminal justice system. Ordinary criminal offenses have the advantage of being well known, and thus both provide clear notice to officers that they should avoid committing such offenses and reduce the need for legislators to have to grapple with a broader but less conventional category of impeachable offenses. Legislators who prefer to outsource impeachment investigations to special counsels benefit from a list of impeachable offenses that is coterminous with the criminal code.

Alan Dershowitz has been the most prominent advocate of this view of late, but he is part of a long tradition of zealous defense attorneys who have sought to help their clients escape conviction in the Senate by arguing that the House had exceeded its constitutional authority. When Justice Samuel Chase faced an impeachment trial in the Senate in 1805, he presented his own defense brief to the senators and instructed them that "no civil officer of the United States can be impeached, except for some offence for which he may be indicted at law."[14] As impeachment threats swirled around President Donald Trump more than two centuries later, Dershowitz argued that Congress should understand the impeachment power as limited to statutory crimes comparable to the named offenses of treason and bribery. Anything else would open the door to politicized impeachments and threaten to make government officers more dependent on the good will of Congress in order to retain their offices. One way to maintain the independence of the executive and judicial branches from the legislative branch is to sharply limit the circumstances in which

Congress could legitimately attempt to remove individuals hold-ing office in the other two branches of government.[15] Impeachable offenses under the terms of the Constitution, Donald Trump's de-fense team argued in his first impeachment trial, are limited to "a violation of established law."[16] If a president is accused of mis-deeds that cannot be found in the statute books, then the House should not bring forward articles of impeachment and the Senate should refuse to convict in any impeachment trial.

This political point can be reinforced with a long-standing rule of thumb regarding statutory interpretation. The canon of *ejus-dem generis*, or "of the same kind," has been used by judges in the Anglo-American tradition for centuries to guide them when they encounter a list of specific words in a legal document followed by a more general term. Thus, "apples, bananas, and other foods," might best be understood to mean, "apples, bananas, and other fruits" so that "other foods" is construed to be limited to items that most closely resemble apples and bananas. Similarly, we might think "high crimes and misdemeanors" to be limited to acts that closely resemble treason and bribery, which at the very least are ordinary crimes and perhaps even part of a more limited sub-set of all the offenses that could be prosecuted in a criminal court. James F. Wilson thought as much, insisting that the only way to prevent officers from being impeached for offenses "created by the fancy of the members of the House" was by taking our bear-ings from the "fact that the framers of the Constitution selected by name two indictable crimes as causes of impeachment" and by implication "all other offenses for which impeachment will lie must also be indictable."[17]

Notably, the "violation of established law" standard offered by the Trump defense team skirts the issue of whether the impeach-able offenses must be indictable under ordinary criminal law. This leaves open the possibility that Congress might write legislation classifying a whole range of presidential or judicial conduct as "high misdemeanors," and thus within the realm of "established law" even though not within the realm of ordinary criminal law.

The scope of impeachable offenses could still be very broad under this standard, but it requires Congress to plan ahead and anticipate presidential acts in statutes. If the president were to do something that Congress had not already anticipated in legislation, then the established law standard would let him off the hook no matter how appalling it might be.

It is no accident that President Andrew Johnson preferred to require the House to point to "indictable crimes" and that President Donald Trump preferred to require the House to point to offenses in "established law." Congress passed the Tenure of Office Act of 1867 over President Johnson's veto. Under the terms of that statute, the Senate had to agree before any Senate-confirmed official in the executive branch could be removed or a replacement could exercise the powers of the office. The legislation specified that any violation of its terms was a "high misdemeanor." When Johnson violated the act by attempting to fire his secretary of war, the House could argue that the president had violated an established law, even though the violation of the statute was not a criminal offense that could be prosecuted in an ordinary court. Johnson had violated an "established law" but had not committed an indictable crime. In his first impeachment trial, Trump had done neither. The established law standard allowed the Trump team to concede the legitimacy of the Johnson impeachment without having to concede that Trump himself was impeachable. If Congress had passed a statute that made it a high misdemeanor for a president to spend more than four days out of a calendar year playing golf, his defense team would likely have found the established law standard inadequate and developed a strange new respect for the indictable crimes standard.

Neither scholars nor Congress have been very persuaded by such claims. Justice Joseph Story warned long ago against the instinct that Dershowitz represents of attempting to constrain the impeachment power by tying it to a finite list of impeachable offenses. Among the most respected justices to ever serve on the Supreme Court, an influential scholar, and among the earliest professors of Harvard Law School, Story was hardly an uncritical observer of legislatures, but he thought the impeachment power could not be read so narrowly. Story worried in part that if the Dershowitz standard for high crimes and misdemeanors were to be accepted in the nineteenth century, then even "many most flagrant offences" would not be impeachable because of the limited scope of federal criminal law. In such circumstances, he thought it obvious that "the silence of the statute-book" would make "the power of impeachment, except as to the two expressed cases . . . a complete nullity; and the party . . . wholly dispunishable, however enormous may be his corruption or criminality."[18] Perhaps we have less reason to fear that problem given the proliferation of federal criminal offenses over the past few decades, but Story still would not have been satisfied. As he noted:

> Again, there are many offences, purely political, which have been held to be within the reach of parliamentary impeachments, not one of which is in the slightest manner alluded to in our statute-book. And, indeed, political offences are of so various and complex a character, so utterly incapable of being defined, or classified, that the task of positive legislation would be impracticable, if it were not almost absurd to attempt it. . . . No one has yet been bold enough to assert, that the power of impeachment is limited to offences positively defined in the statute-book of the union, as impeachable high crimes and misdemeanors.[19]

Story suggested that the common law was an appropriate source for fleshing out the meaning of high crimes and misdemeanors, but it is clear that he was thinking about the peculiar common law of parliamentary practice rather than that of ordinary courts. To understand the scope of impeachable offenses, he looked to "the parliamentary history of impeachments" and found "many offences, not easily definable by law, and many of a purely political character [that] have been deemed high crimes and misdemeanors worthy of this extraordinary remedy." There was a reason the framers entrusted the impeachment power not to "common tribunals of justice" but "to a tribunal capable of understanding, and reforming, and scrutinizing the polity of the state, and of sufficient dignity to maintain the independence and reputation of worthy public officers."[20]

Wilson took little comfort in Story's invocation of "political offenses." What is a political offense, he asked his colleagues on the floor of the House in 1867. "Is it the doing of something that the dominant political party in the country do not like?" That would hardly be satisfactory. President Johnson "has done many acts of political littleness, meanness, and treachery," but "disaster alone" could result from the House impeaching presidents for political meanness. Such offenses were to be "tried by the suffrages of the people, and not on impeachment before the Senate."[21]

Wilson was certainly right that the impeachment power should not properly be used to resolve ordinary political disagreements. He was wrong, however, in thinking that the type of "political offenses" Story had in mind were of that sort.

The Political Offenses Answer

Most of the historic and scholarly debate over the meaning of high crimes has taken place in the space between those narrow and broad readings. High crimes are neither just a subset of the criminal code nor anything that Congress might desire. So what are they? Egregious misconduct, even if not criminal, can justify taking the extraordinary step of impeaching and removing a sitting federal officer.

In the impeachment trial of Judge Charles Swayne at the beginning of the twentieth century, House manager Henry W. Palmer submitted an extended brief on the scope of the impeachment power. He began by observing that the constitutional drafters did not "invent the remedy by impeachment, but adopted a well-known and frequently used method of getting rid of objectionable public officers, modifying it to suit the conditions of a new country." The impeachment power had sometimes been abused in England, but that did not undermine its utility. The "same necessity existed here as in England for the remedy of impeachment," for America too could suffer from objectionable public officers. The founders had thrown safeguards around the impeachment power to make its abuse less likely, but the "Constitution should be construed so as to be equal to every occasion which might call for its exercise and adequate to accomplish the purposes of its framers."[22]

Joseph Story's emphasis on an unidentifiable class of offenses "of a purely political character" as central to high crimes and misdemeanors is consistent with the problem motivating the inclusion of the impeachment power in the constitutional text in the first place. The impeachment power in England might have been used, in part, as a vehicle for holding aristocratic lords to account for violations of the law before a jury of their peers. Men "whose elevated situation placed them above the reach of complaint from private individuals" might only be held to account through a trial in the House of Lords. But in the new American republic, there was not much need for a legislative upper house to hear criminal cases and deal with scoundrels who enjoyed the "highest rank and favour with the Crown."[23] In America, no one would stand beyond the reach of ordinary courts. A republic still had the need for an impeachment power, however. An elected legislature could usefully employ the impeachment power as "a republican mechanism" for keeping government officials in check.[24]

Even in a system of government characterized by regular elections, there would be a need to quickly address the problems caused by abusive public officials who would not be facing an electoral check anytime soon. This was most obviously true in the case of the new office of the presidency. The president envisioned by the framers of the U.S. Constitution would be a powerful officer with a fairly extended term of office. It was easily imaginable that things could go wrong. The scope of the impeachment power was not limited to the president, but the chief executive officer highlighted the need for the possibility of an unscheduled removal. The impeachment power was the most obvious check on such abusive officers that the framers could readily imagine.

The constitutional framers were familiar with the impeachment device from English history, and after independence, it was quickly incorporated into American state constitutions. In English parliamentary practice, impeachment was a tool for checking the monarch and the ministers appointed by the monarchy, and the term *high crimes and misdemeanors* developed within that practice to refer to misconduct by public officers.[25] The influential English jurist William Blackstone noted at the time of the American Revolution that "oppression and tyrannical partiality . . . in the administration and under the colour of their office" could often escape ordinary justice and was therefore accountable "by impeachment in parliament."[26] Famously, more than a century before the American Revolution, the House of Commons had impeached the Earl of Strafford for attempting "to subvert the fundamental laws and government of the realms . . . and instead thereof to introduce arbitrary and tyrannical government."[27] The British imperial officer Warren Hastings was embroiled in an impeachment scandal at the time of the Philadelphia Convention, and the House of Commons eventually charged him with "arbitrary, illegal, unjust, and tyrannical Acts" that rendered him "guilty of High Crimes and Misdemeanors."[28]

The early state constitutions included their own impeachment provisions based on the English practice. For example, the Delaware constitution of 1776 empowered the assembly to impeach those "offending against the State, either by maladministration, corruption, or other means, by which the safety of the Commonwealth may be endangered."[29] The New York constitution vested in the "representatives of the people in assembly" the "power of impeaching all officers of the State, for mal and corrupt conduct in their respective offices."[30] The Massachusetts constitution of 1780 established an impeachment process for officers charged with "misconduct and maladministration in their offices."[31] Likewise, the officers of Virginia were impeachable for "offending against the State, either by maladministration, corruption, or other means, by which the safety of the State may be endangered."[32]

As the framers in Philadelphia contemplated creating a powerful and independent chief executive subject only to quadrennial elections, they agreed overwhelmingly that some ability to truncate the term of office of a misbehaving president would be necessary. When Alexander Hamilton boldly proposed an executive appointed "for life," he held out the promise that such an executive, along with the other federal officers, would "be liable to impeachment for mal- and corrupt conduct."[33] As the framers got serious about the details of the presidency in the new constitution, they resolved that he would have "to be impeachable whilst in office." A president constrained only by the need to win reelection would "spare no efforts or means whatever to get himself reelected." Subjecting him to a power of impeachment was "an essential security for the good behavior of the Executive." George Mason worried that a president who could not be impeached would practice "corruption" to secure his continued election to office. James Madison thought it was "indispensable that some provision should be made for defending the Community against the incapacity, negligence or perfidy of the chief Magistrate." In the months after his inauguration, the president might "lose his capacity," or "pervert his administration into a scheme of peculation or oppression," or even "betray his trust to foreign powers." Edmund Randolph declared the impeachment power to be "a favorite principle with him" given the "great opportunity of abusing his power" that the proposed chief executive would have. The initially skeptical Gouverneur Morris came around over the course of the debate to recognize that an impeachment power was a "necessity . . . if the Executive was to continue for any time in office." There were just too many possibilities for something to go wrong—anything from "treachery" to "incapacity."[34]

The delegates to the Philadelphia Convention struggled less with the necessity of a power of impeachment to remove a dangerous executive than with the details of how such a power should be constituted. They wrestled with where such a power could be safely lodged, but eventually settled on the House and Senate jointly exercising the power of impeachment and removal despite the risks it might pose to the independence of the other two branches of government. The proper scope of the impeachment power was the other thorny problem. The initial language of authorizing impeachments in cases of "malpractice or neglect of duty" certainly captured the range of concerns in the room. When a draft of the constitution came back from a committee on detail with the impeachment power reframed for cases only of "Treason & bribery," George Mason immediately moved that the scope of the power be opened back up to address the kinds of concerns that had driven the delegates to include an impeachment power in the first place. Too many "great and dangerous offences" would be left untouched by such a narrow basis of executive accountability. Mason's own suggestion of "maladministration" seemed unsatisfactory in making the executive too dependent on the good graces of the legislature, but his alternative formulation of "high crimes and misdemeanors" proved generally acceptable.[35] The president was too dangerous to be left in place without the means to remove him if things went wrong. "High crimes" seemed to capture the range of potential dangers that concerned Madison and others, without leaving the president vulnerable to impeachment over routine political and policy disagreements.

Such worries drove the discussion outside the Philadelphia Convention as well. Most famously, Alexander Hamilton devoted an essay to the impeachment power, where he contended that the jurisdiction of the court of impeachment extended to "those offenses which proceed from the misconduct of public men, or, in other words, from the abuse or violation of some public trust." They were political offenses, which "relate chiefly to injuries done immediately to society itself."[36] Charles Pinckney argued in the South Carolina ratification convention that "abuse of power was more effectually checked" under the proposed Constitution than under the Articles of Confederation, and the primary evidence he offered was the existence of an impeachment power by which "those who behave amiss, or betray their public trust" could be called to account by elected representatives of the people.[37]

In response to anti-Federalists worried that the Constitution invested too much power in federal officials, Federalists like South Carolina's Edward Rutledge responded that the "very idea of power included the possibility of doing harm" and to "argue against the use of a thing from the abuse of it, had long since been exploded by all sensible people." Federalists argued that it was better to adequately empower federal officers to do good, and then take care that if they "abused their trust, they were liable to impeachment and punishment." In North Carolina, Archibald Maclaine pointed out that it was "certainly necessary" that some "mode of punishment" be established so that federal officers "should be kept within proper bounds." Future Supreme Court justice James Iredell observed that the impeachment power was "calculated to bring [great offenders] to punishment for crime which it is not easy to describe, but which every one must be convinced is a high crime and misdemeanor against the government." When there is a "great injury to the community," the elected representatives of the people are the ones best positioned to assess its nature and cause and to take action against the offender, even when the offenses are of a nature that they "cannot be easily reached by an ordinary tribunal" or cannot "be punishable" by ordinary law.[38]

The anti-Federalist Patrick Henry was less impressed by the security offered by the impeachment power. Though critics of the Constitution were assured that officers who did "any thing derogatory to the honor or interest of their country" could be impeached and removed, Henry pointed out that those holding federal power would "try themselves" under the impeachment clause. He thought there could be no "security where offenders mutually try one another."[39] In more modern populist parlance, Henry questioned whether the creatures of the Capitol swamp could be trusted to try and convict one of their own. The Federalists tried to assuage such concerns by emphasizing that the power of impeachment would be exercised by the people's duly elected representatives to address the possible malfeasance of less electorally accountable federal officers. Henry did not question the adequacy of the high crimes standard to reaching presidential misconduct. He simply doubted whether a federal Congress could be trusted to act against federal officers when action was needed.

In contrast to Patrick Henry, George Nicholas told his fellow Virginia delegates that he expected the impeachment power, held in the hands of representatives who were accountable "to the people at large," to be an effective deterrent to "mal-administration" or abuse of the pardoning power by the president. Shortly after those ratification debates, Nicholas would move to Kentucky and draft that state's first constitution, including within it a power to impeach state officers "for any misdemeanor in office." Edmund Randolph even suggested that the president could be impeached if he were "dishonest" in abusing the power to adjourn the two houses of Congress or for accepting an emolument from a foreign power.[40]

Early commentators on the Constitution continued to emphasize this broad scope of the federal impeachment power. The framers had indeed drafted a limited power of impeachment, but that limitation did not narrow the scope of impeachable offenses to ordinary crimes. Supreme Court justice James Wilson pointed out in his law lectures at the University of Pennsylvania that the impeachment power in America was "confined to political characters, to political crimes and misdemeanors, and to political punishments," unlike the practice in England in which Parliament sometimes judged accusations of ordinary crimes committed by "offenders who were thought to be out of the reach of the ordinary power of the law."[41] The Senate was to be a constitutional court, not a criminal court. St. George Tucker, one of the first law professors at the College of William & Mary and an influential state supreme court judge, simply noted that "all officers of the government, including the president, are impeachable for misconduct in office."[42] In his overview of the Constitution, Justice Joseph Story concluded that "crimes of a strictly legal character" did fall within the impeachment power but that it would be "ordinarily applied" as a remedy to offenses "of a political character" that grew out of "personal misconduct, or gross neglect, or usurpation, or habitual disregard of the public interests, in the discharge of the duties of political office."[43] William Rawle, a prominent Philadelphia attorney who wrote one of the first treatises on the Constitution, concluded that the impeachment power was carried over into the United States because, though "the firmness and integrity of the ordinary tribunals" would be adequate to hold to account any American—no matter how exalted—only a court of impeachment could remove a current officeholder and thereby prevent the "injury sustained by the nation" from being "renewed or increased, if the executive authority were perverse, tyrannical, or corrupt." The "offenses which may be committed equally by a private person as a public officer" were not generally the proper subject of an impeachment but could instead be "left to the ordinary course of judicial proceeding." The impeachment power was needed to check "men whose treachery to their country might be productive of the most serious disasters."[44] With a century's worth of perspective, the great constitutional commentator of the late nineteenth century and influential chief justice of the Michigan supreme court, Thomas Cooley, concluded as follows:

> It is often found that offences of a very serious nature by high officers are not offences against the criminal code, but consist in abuses or betrayals of trust, or inexcusable neglects of duty, which are dangerous and criminal because of the immense interests involved and the greatness of the trust which has not been kept. Such cases must be left to be dealt with on their own facts, and judged according to their apparent deserts.[45]

Across its history, the U.S. House of Representatives has approved only a small number of impeachments, and yet it has not confined itself to cases involving violations of the criminal code.

The House's own practice manual concludes from the precedents that impeachable offenses consist of "misconduct incompatible with the official position of the office holder." Its assessment of presidential impeachments concludes that they have generally involved charges of "abusing or exceeding the law powers of the office." Many other impeachments involved nonfelonious behavior that was nonetheless judged to be "grossly incompatible with the office," ranging from officers "appearing on the bench during the trial in a state of intoxication" or "permitting his partisan views to influence his conduct in certain trials" to committing "sexual misconduct with court employees" or preventing, obstructing, or impeding the administration of justice. "Less than one-third of all the articles the House has adopted have explicitly charged the violation of a criminal statute or used the word 'criminal' or 'crime' to describe the conduct alleged."[46]

It is widely accepted that the scope of impeachable offenses should not be construed so broadly as to encompass ordinary political and policy disagreements. The constitutional drafters' rejection of "maladministration" in favor "high crimes and misdemeanors" marked an effort to tighten the standard for impeachable offenses from one that was common in some of the early state constitutions and to ensure that the president was more independent of the Congress than the governors frequently were of the state legislatures.[47] Maladministration could imply mere errors in judgment. High crimes and misdemeanors implied misconduct. Congress was not to remove a president simply because it disagreed with the president's policies or how the executive branch was administered. Ordinary political disagreements were to be resolved through ordinary political means. The heavy constitutional weaponry of the impeachment power was to be reserved for extraordinary occasions. Around the time of the impeachment of President Andrew Johnson, John Norton Pomeroy, former dean of the law school of New York University, argued that "very many breaches of public duty" were within the scope of the impeachment power, but not "a mere mistake in the exercise of [an officer's] discretion."[48] As John Randolph Tucker, the former chair of the House Judiciary Committee and former president of the American Bar Association, observed at the end of the nineteenth century, the "obvious purpose of the Constitution" was to empower Congress "to deprive of office those who by any act of omission or commission showed clear and flagrant disqualification to hold it." Failures of duty that were "due to mistake, inadvertence or misjudgment" were to be addressed by other means, but "a purposed defiance of official duty" or "flagrant misbehavior" were within the scope of this constitutional tool to deal with the dangers of a "wicked executive."[49]

It is a challenge for the House to distinguish between the "flagrant misbehavior" of a "wicked executive" and an instance of a mere "mistake, inadvertence or misjudgment." Federal officers will not always make it easy to know on which side of that line they are operating, and in a polarized political environment, it is only natural to jump to conclusions. One check on that tendency is to incorporate the target of the impeachment inquiry into the process at an early stage so as to give the officer an opportunity to craft a defense or to explicitly forgo the opportunity to do so. If a president can provide an appropriate rationale for the conduct in question and dispel the suspicion of simply being a "wicked executive," then the president may peel away votes in the House during the impeachment inquiry and at least create reasonable doubt in the public and in the legislature as to whether the actions under scrutiny merit immediate removal from office.

Advocates for impeachment can further substantiate their own instincts by self-consciously reaching across the political aisle. The supermajority requirement in the Senate provides an effective restraint on what Thomas Jefferson worried would become "the most formidable weapon for the purposes of a dominant faction that ever was contrived."[50] It has turned out to be very rare that a single party controls enough seats in the Senate to be able to convict and remove officers on a pure party-line vote. A partisan House majority might be able to impeach an officer, but if it wants to remove an officer, it needs to win over some votes from the other party. That process of stress-testing the case of impeachment should begin early. If impeachment advocates are only appealing to their partisan base, they will not only fail to mount a credible prosecution that has a chance of reaching the two-thirds threshold in the Senate, but they will also too easily delude themselves into believing that ordinary policy disagreements are something more nefarious. A House that does not bother to curb its partisan instincts risks abusing its own constitutional authority by rushing headlong into an impeachment that does not meet the constitutional standard of high crimes and misdemeanors.

A classic basis for distinguishing maladministration from misconduct is to focus on the motives of the officer. Early state constitutions frequently listed corruption as an instance of an impeachable offense.[51] The federal Constitution did not repeat that language, but the discussions surrounding the adoption of the Constitution made it plain that such considerations were still part of the founding-era thinking about the purpose of the impeachment power. Subsequent usage has frequently targeted corrupt behavior by federal officers, clarifying through the course of legislative precedent that corrupt acts are within the scope of the impeachment power. Determining whether any particular action of an officer is properly, or best, attributed to corrupt motives may require difficult judgments, but an important line of inquiry in attempting to ascertain whether an action is best characterized as misconduct is exploring the explanations for the action and evaluating the credibility of the proffered justifications for it.

The founding generation's concern when designing constitutions, and particularly when establishing an impeachment power, was a basic one. They thought it essential to create offices that enjoyed some independence from the momentary whims of the people and that could stand up to a reckless and self-aggrandizing legislature, but they feared the possibility of a tyrant. Although they tried to take care to create mechanisms that would elevate virtuous citizens into public office and encourage them to behave responsibly when there, they knew that no such mechanism could ever be foolproof. When Mason introduced the language *malad-ministration* to the list of impeachable offenses, his goal was to "reach many great and dangerous offences" that fell outside the scope of treason and bribery. If the framers were unhappy with his proposed language, they were in agreement with his goal.

Broadly speaking, the need for a constitutional mechanism to reach the "great and dangerous offences" that might be committed by public officers continues to animate discussions of the impeachment power. The impeachment power has been characterized as "an emergency measure meant to save the democratic foundation on which all other politics unfold," a fail-safe when "waiting until the next election might not be an option."[52] It is an "indispensable remedy" for coming to the "defense of the political community."[53] It is one of the "safeguards in the event that things went badly wrong"; a "last resort for holding high-ranking officials accountable for serious misconduct when other mechanisms fail or are not available."[54]

Break Glass in Case of Emergency

But when is it appropriate for Congress to break glass in case of emergency and pull out the impeachment power? When is waiting until the next election no longer an option? Ordinary policy differences and routine misjudgments should not be sufficient to justify trying to remove a president, executive officer, or a judge, but perhaps the emphasis here should be on *ordinary* and *routine*. At the extremes, the quality of an officer's judgment can come into question through the impeachment process.

Dereliction of duty, regardless of the motives or cause, would justify the need to remove an officer and designate a successor. If the president really did become incapacitated after being inaugurated, then impeachable offenses would rack up and allow for congressional intervention, even without the availability of the Twenty-Fifth Amendment. If the president "were to move to Saudi

Arabia so he could have four wives, and were to propose to conduct the office of the presidency by mail and wire from there," as Yale law professor Charles Black once imagined, there would be a case for impeachment and removal.[55] If a president were likewise to abscond to Palm Beach for a busy life of golfing, television watching, and tweeting and left the boring business of governing to subordinate staffers, Congress would not need to wait until the next election before sending that individual into retirement. If a judge were to abandon a judgeship in order to accept a position in a foreign government or were overcome with dementia and incapable of hearing cases, Congress could declare the seat open by impeaching and removing its incumbent. If a secretary of defense spent most days in a drunken stupor, Congress would not have to rely on the president to order the individual's removal. If an attorney general were to announce, with the apparent approval of the president, that no federal criminal prosecutions would be filed during their tenure, Congress could take action to see that the laws were faithfully executed by a new attorney general—and perhaps by a new president as well. We would not want to settle on an understanding of impeachable offenses that ruled out the possibility of congressional action to remedy the situation in such extreme cases.

Government officials must exercise good judgment about how they conduct themselves while in office, and Congress might give teeth to that expectation by impeaching those who egregiously violate it. What kind of behavior might be "grossly incompatible" with high office? The possibilities are endless—and highly contextual. We expect different behavior from a federal judge than from an elected official. The norms of political decorum are different in the twenty-first century than they were in the nineteenth. Impeachment might not be our first choice about how best to address matters of political decorum, but it should not be off the table.

Take the example of political speech. We quite rightly have an expansive view of the freedom of speech of ordinary citizens. We allow the government to suppress or punish citizen speech only in the most limited of circumstances. At the same time, we are perfectly capable of recognizing that speech can be grossly inappropriate even when it is not legally prohibited. It would no doubt be controversial to use the impeachment power to remove an officer for things the individual said, but we should be hesitant to rule out such a possibility. Imagine that a sitting federal judge told flagrant public lies about the fairness and outcome of a federal election or made false statements that could foreseeably lead to mob violence. Is there any doubt that such a judge could be impeached and removed from office? It would not matter if a judge made such pronouncements from the bench or on social media or at a lectern. They would be grossly incompatible with the office of a judge. Imagine a sitting federal judge who said in a television interview that the Republican Party is a seditious conspiracy and deserves to be wiped out and its members jailed or shot. There is no doubt that such a judge could no longer be trusted to faithfully perform the duties of a judgeship in the public trust. Imagine a sitting judge accompanying the incumbent president on the campaign trail and delivering speeches urging voters to reelect the president and to vote against all the members of the opposition party. Such a judge would be subject to impeachment and removal. The fact that such speech is protected by the First Amendment and not subject to criminal penalty would be no defense. Such actions are impeachable, and the Senate could appropriately conclude that such a judge deserved condemnation and conviction and removal in an impeachment trial.

It is not hard to imagine examples of speech that would be constitutionally protected if uttered by a private citizen but that could and should be grounds for impeachment and removal if uttered by the president of the United States. Speech that is divisive, intolerant, reckless, or dangerous, even if perfectly lawful, could become the foundation for an impeachment effort. Imagine if a sitting president were to appear in the White House press briefing room in blackface and perform a minstrel show. Imagine if President Trump had responded to the Charlottesville riots in

2017 not with a series of ambiguous and contradictory statements but with an impassioned speech in defense of white nationalists and the need for street justice against left-wing protestors. Imagine if the president invited leaders of white nationalist groups to join him on stage at a rally and gave his own version of Confederate vice president Alexander Stephens's cornerstone speech declaring that the American government is founded "upon the great truth that the negro is not equal to the white man; that slavery, subordination to the superior race is his natural and normal condition." Imagine if the president had borrowed a page from socialist leader Eugene Debs and proclaimed to a crowd of supporters that some of them would "lack the fiber to endure the revolutionary test," but that they should be willing to "fight for them; go to jail or to hell for them," and "shed their heroic blood" to lay "the foundation of the first real democracy that ever drew the breath of life in the world." Imagine if a president spoke from the Resolute Desk in the Oval Office to inform a television audience that the members of the opposition party are "vermin" and should be "eradicated" by patriotic citizens and to celebrate the fact that the members of the president's own party had more "rough guys" who were well armed and could "play it tough." Imagine a president traveling to the United States Military Academy to deliver a tirade to the assembled cadets declaring that Congress was full of traitors who were destroying America and that the time was coming when something would need to be done about it. Such a president should be hastily impeached and removed precisely because such a president would be engaged in behavior fundamentally incompatible with that high office and subversive of the ideals and functioning of the American republic. One would not need to demonstrate that such speech had led to violence to conclude that it would be intolerable for a sitting president to engage in such speech—that such speech is, in the most fundamental possible sense, unpresidential; that such speech is, in and of itself, an assault on the constitutional order when uttered by a sitting president.

Even the use of the lawful powers of the presidency might come to be viewed as a "scheme of peculation or oppression" that justified immediate removal. Suppose, as Charles Black once did, "a president were to announce and follow a policy of granting full pardons, in advance of indictment or trial, to all federal agents or police who killed anybody in the line of duty, in the District of Columbia, whatever the circumstances and however unnecessary the killing."[56] Such actions might not be criminal, but surely they would be impeachable. If the president were to have a sudden conversion to pacifism and ordered the American military to immediately lay down its arms and abandon their posts, Congress need not stand idly by. If a president were to call agents of enemy foreign powers into the Oval Office to share with them lists of the names of all covert American operatives, along with their local informants and assets, removal of the president by Congress might be necessary to shore up national security. If a president were to launch an unprovoked invasion of Canada and Mexico in a bid to "expand the American empire," Congress would not need to defer to the commander in chief.

We might try to construct additional barriers against the wanton use of the impeachment power, but one suspects those would be mere parchment barriers, to use Madison's phrase. One such barrier is the possibility of a good-faith exception to high crimes. Suppose a president has done things that the opposition party thinks are flagrantly unconstitutional. The president's critics start to argue that the president has violated the presidential oath of office by failing to take care that the laws—the real and true laws—are faithfully executed. If those critics were to succeed in capturing enough seats in Congress, would they be justified in moving ahead with an impeachment? If we view "high crimes" as analogous to ordinary crimes, then "we must assess a president's state of mind" to determine whether he intended to do something "evil" that he knew, or should have known, was wrong.[57]

A good-faith exception is one way to try to get out of the problem of criminalizing ordinary political disputes or, in this case, converting substantive constitutional and policy disagreements into impeachable offenses. If the president has a "good-faith argument that his orders are lawful," then he may be wrong but not impeachable.[58] Samuel Chase and Andrew Johnson made much the same argument when they found themselves in the congressional crosshairs for exercising power in ways that their critics thought was beyond the pale. If enough legislators listened to the critics of George W. Bush and Barack Obama and contemplated impeachment, those presidents would have leaned on the same legal reasoning. If there is an Office of Legal Counsel opinion that says you can do it, then it must not be an impeachable offense. A majority of congressional Republicans did not buy that argument when Chase and Johnson made it (though just enough senators did to win an acquittal), and a future impeachment target would likely find it to be a tough sell as well.

One could imagine another angle for arguing that an impeachment target acted with an innocent state of mind. Judge John Pickering's family argued that the mentally diminished judge could not form the state of mind needed to commit an impeachable offense, but Congress in 1803 reasonably concluded that it mattered less whether Pickering understood that he was behaving in inappropriate ways than whether a judge who could not be trusted to act in a manner consistent with the dignity of his office should continue hearing cases. Suppose a political naif were to be elected to the presidency. Suppose further that this individual's understanding of the expectations of the office of the presidency and the requirements of the Constitution is notoriously weak, and thus the individual's defenders have frequently made some version of the argument that the president should not be taken too seriously when saying or doing things that violate accepted understandings of how the president or the government should operate. Even if such a defense accurately described the situation at hand, it does not provide a strong reason for allowing someone who has demonstrated an inability or unwillingness to live up to the expectations of the office to continue to occupy it. Historically, we have not wanted to make gross incompetence in itself an impeachable offense, but a defense that an officer grossly misbehaved due to incompetence rather than malice does not seem very compelling.

There might be circumstances in which even good-faith disagreements are intolerable. Judge West Humphreys might have believed in good faith that Tennessee had a constitutional right to secede from the Union and that as a loyal citizen of Tennessee he had a duty to follow. That kind of argument might well have significance at a treason trial or in assessing whether to extend a pardon, but it was unlikely to make much difference for his impeachment. We should be cautious about ignoring good-faith disagreements about constitutional meaning or policy preferences, because such disagreements are the ordinary circumstances of politics.[59] We need to find ways to peacefully make collective decisions despite such disagreements, rather than invent new ways to ostracize and sanction those who are on the other side of the divide from us. Impeachments in such circumstances would be a way of trying to shut down political disagreement rather than work through it. But, as the staunch Jeffersonians or the Radical Republicans might have said, sometimes the necessary political act is to mark out the boundaries of acceptable political disagreement. However, if a president were to declare in his inaugural address that he was a loyal member of the Patriot Front and planned to govern in accord with its white nationalist commitments, and proclaimed that "the damage done to this nation and its people will not be fixed if every issue requires the approval and blessing from the dysfunctional system which remains American in name only," Congress could take steps to purge the government of this menace and establish that some political disagreements are not merely ordinary.[60]

A more important question is less whether there is a good-faith exception for constitutional abuses than whether impeachment is the best remedy when we are confronted with acts that we think violate the Constitution but that the relevant government official does not. The existence of good-faith disagreements might be helpful because, for example, it makes it more likely that the dispute can be successfully resolved through judicial review and the willingness of all sides to abide by the judgment of an independent judiciary. A president acting out of bad faith might be less inclined to care whether a gaggle of judges adds their legal opinion to the pile of opinions saying the president is wrong. Presidents acting in bad faith might be less willing to care if their legal advisers say they lack the power to do the things they want to do, and such individuals might be inclined to go searching throughout the far reaches of the executive branch or the streets of Washington, D.C., for an attorney willing to sign off on their dubious plans. Such impetuous chief executives may force us to take more drastic measures to neuter them in order to avoid more abusive behavior in the future.

Another possible barrier to promiscuous use of the impeachment power is that impeachable offenses can only involve abuses of public power. It is evident that the possibility of otherwise unchecked abuse of government power is the primary rationale for having the impeachment power. It is precisely in those sorts of cases that we would most easily be persuaded that the emergency has arrived and that we must turn to the constitutional fail-safe. If the president proclaimed to be the *dictator perpetuo* and subsequently canceled the upcoming elections, then one would hope that Congress would at least rouse itself to charge the president with committing a high crime.[61]

But we have never understood the impeachment power to be limited to such abuses of public power, and it seems implausible that we would want to take private misdeeds completely off the table. The case of Bill Clinton hovers over such arguments. The easiest way to get Clinton off the hook is to argue that high crimes do not extend to private misdeeds, even private criminal misdeeds. No one really wants their president to be guilty of perjury or obstruction of justice, but if the things being covered up are purely private failings, then perhaps Congress could see its way clear to letting this go.

There are likely two issues here that need to be separated in order to assess private misdeeds. One issue is the gravity of the misdeed. Charles Black posed a hypothetical of a president violating the Mann Act by transporting a woman across state lines for immoral purposes.[62] The president in such a case might have committed a crime, but it is not a sufficiently serious crime to warrant an impeachment. That does not imply that the president is "above the law," but simply implies that a president should be held accountable to the law in a manner consistent with his serving out his term of office. But as the private misdeeds become more serious, they are harder to overlook. If it were discovered that the president had committed a murder before entering the White House, we would hope that even the president's fellow partisans would think that the president had besmirched the office in a way that demanded impeachment proceedings. As Cass Sunstein comments, "The Constitution would not make a lot of sense if it did not permit the nation to remove murderers from the highest office in the land."[63] Private misconduct might be grossly incompatible with continuing to hold office.

A second issue might involve the nature of the private misconduct, which might be entirely separate from its gravity. Again, we can borrow an example from Charles Black, who imagined a president actively assisting a young White House intern in concealing the latter's possession of three ounces of marijuana—and thereby becoming guilty of "obstruction of justice." Black thinks it "preposterous" that this would be an impeachable offense.[64] Cass Sunstein agrees that this would be "absurd," and Sunstein clarifies why he thinks that is the case. "A cover-up of activity that does not amount to a high crime or misdemeanor may not itself amount to a high crime or misdemeanor."[65] Here we have to ask not only whether the underlying misdeed is a serious one, but also how it relates to the nature of the office that an individual holds. If the impeachment power is in part a tool for constructing and enforcing norms of expected behavior by public officers and reserving the stature and dignity of public offices, and by extension of the government itself, then a wide array of private misdeeds might fall within the ambit of high crimes. There are improprieties that might be tolerable if committed by a private citizen—and that might even be tolerable if kept hidden from public view—but that would be intolerable if they became publicly associated with certain federal officials. What is taken to be "grossly incompatible with the office" might well vary depending on the historical context or the office. Presidents and judges might be held to a different standard of behavior than a minor functionary within an executive department. Behavior that might have been condoned, or even rewarded, in the nineteenth century might properly be viewed as appalling if repeated in the twenty-first century. Legislators might reasonably regard it as particularly perverse and norm-eroding for the chief executive officer to engage in perjury and obstruction of justice, even if the crimes being investigated are trivial ones. If it became known, for example, that the commissioner of the Internal Revenue Service had never filed a tax return or that the director of Immigration and Customs Enforcement knowingly employed an undocumented immigrant with no work visa, we would expect those officials to resign or be fired. Such a revelation might not expose extremely serious misdeeds, but those particular misdeeds are of a nature that are at odds with the office being held. If those executive officers refused to resign and were not fired, then Congress might well feel obliged to take up the task of ejecting them. Similarly, in the case of the president, the cover-up itself might be more important than the crime. In fact, the president might engage in obstruction of justice by hindering an investigation into an act that turned out not to be criminal. The investigation might have been a case of smoke with no fire, but a president caught in the act of shredding the very documents a prosecutor was seeking might well be understood to have done something "grossly incompatible with the office" of the president. If the president had simply turned over the documents, no one would have thought an impeachable offense had been committed. But when the president converted the Oval Office into a "shred room," an impeachable offense was in fact committed where previously there was none.

The example of a president with a literal skeleton in their closet highlights another potential barrier to the use of the impeachment power, and that is whether the acts were committed before the individual assumed office. The House has been reluctant to impeach officers on the basis of prior bad acts, and this seems generally reasonable if the goal of an impeachment is to address a danger that the officer is currently posing to the nation. But, again, there are likely to be exceptions. If the voters were reasonably aware of a candidate's failings and nonetheless elected that person to be president, it would be very difficult for Congress to justify second-guessing that decision and removing the president for acts grossly incompatible with the office. If the voters are willing to overlook a candidate's history of murder, then perhaps they are the final judge of the expectations of the office. In the context of a state statute declaring that no officer shall be "removed from office for any act he may have committed prior to his election to office," the Texas Court of Criminal Appeals blanched at such a possibility. "To hold that a person running for office might commit murder, burglary, theft, robbery, rape or any of those offenses and thereafter be elected to office would be relieved from punishment is the most monstrous proposition that the writer of this opinion has ever heard advanced in justification of any such offenses."[66] The judges thought that statute had to be construed narrowly to avoid such heinous results. Congress might well feel the same about the impeachment power. Even if the voters were willing to forgive a popular candidate for public office of the gravest of offenses, Congress through the impeachment power might get a second bite at that apple. Certainly, if the president's murder spree during his misspent youth did not come to light until after he had already ascended to the White House, then it would be even harder for Congress to ignore those revelations and treat it as water under the bridge. Moreover, if those prior bad acts contributed to how the president won the White House, that would take us very close to the kinds of concerns that motivated the founders to include an impeachment power in the Constitution in the first place.

Ultimately, there is no escaping the need for political judgment in assessing high crimes. Many of us yearn for clear answers to the question of when to impeach. Constitutional lawyers are inclined to want to provide a legal answer to the question of what constitutes a high crime and misdemeanor. The hardest questions surrounding the use of the impeachment power are political questions in the broadest sense. How grave are an officer's offenses? What remedies are available to address them? How risky is it to leave an officer in place in light of what the individual has already done? How risky is it to forcibly remove a populist president from power on a largely partisan basis? The constitutional impeachment power forces Congress to confront such questions. Partisans will reach different answers on such questions, but even reasonable people not blinded by partisan passions are likely to differ in assessing them. Foes of a president and advocates of impeachment bear a burden to make a genuine effort to construct arguments that can find broad appeal and help persuade the skeptical and uncommitted. Allies of an embattled president and opponents of impeachment have a duty to listen to such arguments and take them seriously. Foes of the president have the obligation to demonstrate that impeachment is the last resort and that all other remedies have been tried and proven insufficient to the task. Allies have the obligation to take steps to walk the president out of impeachment territory by designing remedies that can be effective at mitigating the genuine damage that their fellow citizens see being done and not to simply try to sweep offenses under the rug. The impeachment process stirs passions, but the constitutional system only works if we are willing to deliberate in good faith with those with whom we disagree and look beyond our most immediate interests and inclinations. If impeachments come to be perceived as nothing but a formidable weapon of faction, then we will have taken a major step toward destabilizing our constitutional order, and we will have tarnished a necessary constitutional tool.

5

When Does Abuse of Power Justify Impeachment?

IT IS THE ETERNAL DILEMMA of politics that the very power that is entrusted to officeholders to accomplish public aims can be abused to do harm. This problem was at the forefront of political debates in the Anglo-American world in the seventeenth and eighteenth centuries. The growing tensions between the British Parliament and the king culminating in the Glorious Revolution of 1688 were accompanied by a robust Whig literature of political history and theory that would almost a century later become foundational to the political thinking of the American revolutionaries. For Whig writers, the overthrow of the Catholic King James II was a triumph of liberal constitutionalism over the powers of royalist absolutism. The conservative Whig Edmund Burke, who sympathized with the American revolutionaries, drew a sharp contrast between what the English had done in the 1680s and what the French were doing in the 1780s. The English revolution, he insisted, "was made to preserve our ancient indisputable laws and liberties" against the usurpations of an overly ambitious king. It sought to preserve the old ways, not to invent an entirely new form of government based on nothing but untried theories.[1] Many Americans celebrated the Glorious Revolution for similar reasons. It was restorative of limited government and dealt a blow to the forces of unchecked power. The Americans could not, and did not,

wish to copy the English example by raising up a new king to replace King George III, but they too insisted that their revolution
was being fought against those who were willing to cast aside ancient liberties and arrogate for themselves untrammeled political
power.

The lessons that filtered down to the American revolutionaries
emphasized that all political power had to be limited and carefully
guarded, but entrusting political power somewhere was an un-
avoidable necessity. Among the works that those revolutionary
leaders kept close at hand was Thomas Gordon's translation of and
commentaries on the Roman historian Tacitus. Tacitus recounted
the history of the early Roman empire and its often tyrannical
emperors. As Gordon summarized that history for his English
readers, "unlimited oppression generally follows unlimited power,
as all power that can be abused will be abused," and thus only a
madman or a wicked man "will desire unaccountable dominion."[2]
The French writer Montesquieu echoed that view, while also offering a solution that American constitutional drafters like James
Madison took as gospel. "Constant experience shows us," Montesquieu said, "that every man invested with power is apt to abuse it,
and to carry his authority as far as it will go." Liberty could only
flourish where there is "no abuse of power." Since power was a
necessary evil, it was impossible to rid society of power that could
be abused. The goal instead was to construct a "moderate government" where abuse was less likely. Abuse of power could only be
prevented if "power should be a check to power."[3]

Constitution making and political statesmanship did not deal
in certainties. Constitutional drafters and statesmen instead had
to calculate probabilities and balance competing concerns. One
bit of proverbial political wisdom that came to guide them by the
time of the American founding addressed the problem of abuse of
political power. If a power were certain to be abused, that might
be a good reason not to entrust someone with that power in the
first place. But the mere possibility that a power might be abused
could not be a good reason for withholding the power. As one

British parliamentarian observed a century before the drafting of the Constitution, "If all Power must be abolished, which is possible to be abused, there must be no Power left to the King, or Lords, or Commons."[4] All power might be abused. Sometimes it was necessary to risk the possibility of abuse.

Constructing a system of checks and balances could—hopefully—make the abuse of power less likely and could provide remedies when powers were abused. Judges and presidents could abuse their office, and the impeachment power was a potent check on that possibility. Judges and presidents could be deterred from wrongdoing by the knowledge that an impeachment inquiry might reveal and address that wrongdoing. When the mere threat of impeachment was not enough to deter misconduct, the actual use of the impeachment power could help set things right. The constitutional framers were not blind to the fact that Congress too could abuse its power, including the impeachment power itself. That was a risk worth taking nonetheless. Ultimately, trust had to repose somewhere, and they thought the most trustworthy officeholders would be the ones who had to repeatedly face the electorate and who had to persuade their colleagues in order to take any action. Those eager to impeach in the House would first need to persuade a majority of its members to do so and then persuade two-thirds of the senators that such an action was warranted; and then they would have to defend those actions to the people themselves at the next election. The impeachment power could be abused, but not easily.

A Question of Most Effective Remedies

Politics is inescapably at the heart of any impeachment, particularly a presidential impeachment. It is not just the case that political calculations inevitably affect how members of the House and the Senate exercise their constitutional responsibilities, though that is certainly true. It is also the case that impeachments require both the political act of persuasion to convince partisans that the dramatic step of impeaching and removing a high government official is warranted and the political act of judgment to determine whether impeachment and removal is necessary or advisable in any particular situation.

Election, a limited term of office, and a host of checks and balances would not necessarily be enough to protect the republic from an unhinged or villainous president. The Constitution needed a fail-safe to backstop its other protections against the abuse of power.

This raises the question of when the use of this particular remedy might be warranted. It is surely not the case that it is warranted whenever something that might be labeled a high crime or misdemeanor has been committed. Justice Joseph Story emphasized that "an impeachment is a proceeding purely of a political nature. It is not so much designed to punish an offender, as to secure the state against gross official misdemeanors." Unlike in the ordinary courts, the proceeding against an officer in the constitutional court of impeachment "touches neither his person, nor his property." It cannot punish the accused. A conviction in an impeachment "simply divests him of his political capacity." The "remedy of impeachment" addresses only "the political part" of any offense, and the application of that remedy is properly entrusted to "a political body," which "from its superior information in regard to executive functions" is "far better qualified to judge, how far the public weal might be promoted" by applying that remedy.[5]

The "remedy of impeachment" is appropriate in some circumstances and not in others. If it is a fail-safe, then it is presumably a last resort, to be deployed when all else has failed. If it is a mechanism for securing the state against serious threats to the system of government, then it presumably needs to be demonstrated that the state needs to be secured against such a threat. If it primarily offers an avenue for removing an officer who needs to be immediately removed, then the key question for members of Congress to ask is whether this officer in fact needs to be immediately removed. Are there other political remedies that could be applied that would be equally or more effective at addressing the nation's political ills? Answering that question necessarily requires contestable political judgment, but explaining how that question should be answered is a necessary part of the political task of persuading the nation that impeachment is appropriate.[6]

Impeachments are a matter of constitutional politics, not legalities. The impeachment power is entrusted to Congress as a potential remedy to a severe political problem, but the impeachment power is the heaviest artillery in the congressional arsenal and should not be used if other, less dramatic, remedies are available and can get the job done. This provides both opportunities for accused officials to explain why the remedy of impeachment is not necessary under the circumstances and obligations for legislators to explain why an impeachment is the only or best way to fix the political problem at hand.

If an impeachment is politically inevitable, whether because the misconduct is demonstrable and grave or because any misconduct has been "exaggerated by party spirit," as Story expected it sometimes would be, the accused may have no better course of action than to dig in, obstruct any investigations, deny wrongdoing, and defend themselves as aggressively as possible.[7] If impeachments are about nothing more than punishing wrongdoing, then there is little more to discuss than whether an offense covered by the Constitution has been committed.

If impeachments are understood to be a remedy for a particular kind of political problem, there are more options on the table for both the accused officeholder and for the members of Congress who must reckon with the officeholder. In many cases, that might mean that the best approach for the officeholder is to get all the cards on the table. Ignoring scandals or interfering with investigations just feeds suspicion that there are worse things to be found and encourages even more demands for more investigations down the road. Confidently laying out the facts before a friendly audience promises to set up whatever mea culpas and reforms are necessary while deflating the opposition's source of indignation and cutting off the steady drumbeat of uncontrolled revelations. Optimally, a president should want to clear their name, with all deliberate speed, in a friendly forum and be in a position to declare that a judgment has been reached and that it is time to move on.

If problematic behavior is uncovered, it becomes essential to take effective steps to be able to credibly claim that those mistakes are in the past and will not be repeated. Those steps might require changes in personnel, changes in operational practices, changes in institutional arrangements, or new resolves regarding personal behavior. The goal of all such reforms is to create effective remedies to the apparent political problem and contain any offenses safely in the past. Impeachments are driven by the need to solve a political problem of intolerable bad behavior. The force behind an impeachment effort can be dissipated if the political problem can be resolved by other less drastic means. If there are concerns that an investigation is being improperly obstructed, then steps should be taken to demonstrate that in fact all necessary investigations are speeding ahead unhampered. If there are concerns that classified intelligence is not being properly handled, then steps should be taken to demonstrate that any errors were isolated incidents with no prospect of recurrence. If impeachment threats are treated as political responses to perceived political problems, then a wide array of possibilities become available for addressing and ameliorating those problems. Admitting that there is a problem, however, is the first step toward a solution.

Once the facts are in evidence, it is possible to make a reasoned argument about whether anything that has happened rises to the level of an impeachable offense. All such assessments, however, are deeply contextual and political. Actions that may have been normal or perhaps scandalous in some contexts can seem far more threatening in other contexts. An officeholder can potentially insist that no actions have been taken that can be properly addressed by the impeachment power, or failing that, can insist that nothing has happened that warrants the use of the impeachment power. If, for example, members of Congress are concerned that the president is not sufficiently scrupulous in respecting the professional independence of investigations of those close to the president, then the available responses are either to double down on the presidential prerogative and insist that those members are wrong about the appropriate constitutional norm or to concede the value of the norm of investigatory independence and insist that everything possible is being done to respect that norm, even if some errors have been made in the past. Offenses might have occurred, but they should not be regarded as necessitating an impeachment. If the backdrop is a concern that the president is generally unfit for the responsibilities of the office, then the most compelling response is to demonstrate that such worries are unfounded. Mistakes of inexperience are of a very different character than mistakes of malice or indifference, and the president must work to characterize any offenses committed as innocent and amenable to correction.

Importantly, these arguments are all fundamentally political, not legal. The standard for impeachable offenses is ultimately political, requiring contextual political judgments about the nature and severity of the offenses rather than a legal judgment about whether they meet some predetermined criteria. Moreover, the audience for these arguments is also ultimately political. The president and the president's defenders must persuade the members of the House and Senate, and beyond them the American people, that no unforgivable sins have been committed. That is not primarily a lawyerly task but a political task. If the president loses the battle for public opinion, then the legislative conclusion that the offenses are in fact impeachable will follow.

Even if the revealed misconduct is in principle impeachable, it might still be the case that an impeachment is not an appropriate or necessary remedy to the problem. Although it is conceivable that behavior revealed by a thorough investigation would make it impossible to tolerate the president finishing out the term of office, that is generally unlikely. Impeachment should be the last option rather than the first option for addressing problems in the executive branch. Ongoing abuses that cannot be otherwise controlled might justify impeachment and removal, as would offenses so grave that they render an individual unsuitable for the continued responsibilities of holding office. The mere presence of an offense that might under some circumstances warrant an impeachment does not by itself establish whether an impeachment is necessary in these circumstances.

There is a reason that most federal impeachments have involved judges and have attracted bipartisan support in Congress. The combination of bad behavior, life tenure, and judicial independence means that impeachment and removal is the only adequate method for assuring citizens that they can have faith in the impartiality and fairness of their judicial system and for emphasizing to judges that they can and will be held accountable if they go astray. Presidents are not similarly situated. They are held accountable at the voting booth. Their tenure is limited. They are subject to a multitude of checks on their behavior. Individual citizens are not directly affected by failures of presidential temperament and virtue. The presidential task in the face of an impeachment threat is to reassure legislators and the public that they can be trusted to go forth and sin no more. If administrative or statutory reforms are made, a president might be able to persuasively claim that mistakes were made but that solutions have been found to prevent those mistakes from recurring. Impeachment at that point would accomplish nothing, while distracting the government from conducting the people's business.

Because the decision to impeach and then to convict is a political one, the challenge for presidents under scrutiny is to show that there is no political advantage to pursuing an impeachment. It should be easier for presidents to persuade members of their own party that this is true, and thus far better for the question to be fully mooted and resolved while their party is in a position of relative strength, rather than having to make that argument to a hostile congressional majority. Presidents are well positioned to work their way out of impeachment territory, but doing so requires confronting the political problems directly and reducing the threat from one of constitutional import to one of normal politics to be resolved by ordinary political means. If presidents instead resist any efforts to change operational practices and institutional arrangements in ways that might help reduce their proclivity to cause self-inflicted wounds, or if their allies prefer to look the other way rather than confront the problems, then those wounds are left to fester and may instead strengthen the case for impeachment and removal by demonstrating an unwillingness or inability to change course.

In order to think through when impeachment is warranted, when the impeachment process is the right tool for remedying a political problem, we have to understand what problems it might effectively remedy and what alternative remedies might be available. It is not enough to know whether a given incident is impeachable, though that is an essential starting point. We also need to consider the comparative advantage of pursuing an impeachment rather than attempting to use other political tools. The choice is rarely between impeaching and doing nothing—though sometimes it is! The choice is often between impeaching and doing something else. Legislators faced with a troublesome officeholder should at least diagnose the nature of the problem that they are facing and think through their options.

The *House Practice Manual* usefully summarizes and characterizes the precedents built up through congressional practice across our history. Looking across that history, it observes that impeachment "is a constitutional remedy to address serious offenses against the system of government" and help "maintain constitutional government." It offers a reasonable synthesis of how the House has actually used the impeachment power over the course of its history:

Impeachments have commonly involved charges of misconduct incompatible with the official position of the office holder. This conduct falls into three broad categories: (1) abusing or exceeding the lawful powers of the office; (2) behaving in a manner grossly incompatible with the office; and (3) using the power of the office for an improper purpose or for personal gain.[8]

The House has proceeded on the assumption that officers can be removed for a wide range of offenses that subvert the proper functioning of their offices. Individual impeachable offenses may not themselves threaten to topple constitutional government, and arguably no federal officer has ever posed such a fundamental threat to the continuity of the republic, but an individual who engages in unchecked abuses of office may impose intolerable costs on the country.

It is useful to focus on that first category of impeachable conduct: when a federal officeholder abuses or exceeds the lawful powers of the office. Distinguishing between situations in which officeholders attempt to exercise powers that they do not lawfully possess and situations in which they abuse powers that they concededly do possess can highlight the kinds of threats to the constitutional order that might arise, the kinds of problems that the impeachment power can appropriately address, and the array of political tools we routinely use to address such problems.

Abuse of Power

Late in his life, James Madison was increasingly worried about the possibility that the union of states might come apart. He particularly wanted to caution his colleagues not to overreact to what they thought were appalling political events, whether the congressional adoption of protectionist tariffs or presidential interference with the safekeeping of governmental funds. "No Constitution," he advised, "could be lasting without a habitual distinction between an abuse of legitimate power and the exercise of a usurped one." He thought the usurpation of power—the improper assumption of a power that a government official did not constitutionally possess—was particularly threatening to the constitutional order and might justify extreme measures to counter the willingness of the government to overleap its constitutional bounds. He thought the stakes were lower when government officials abused a power that they legitimately possessed, even if their actions were "unwarrantable" and "culpable." That is not to say that such abuses should be tolerated. Indeed, abuses might be "so enormous," so "unlimited or excessive," that they might be "at war with the Constitution" and the "foundation of the social compact itself." But, he thought, those who abused their power should be held "responsible under the forms of the Constitution," including in some cases by impeachment, rather than through such revolutionary steps as secession.[9]

As an institutional draftsman, Madison was well aware that there was a "liability to abuse" with every grant of political power.[10] If the likelihood of abuse were too high, then perhaps the power should not be granted at all. But Madison was concerned to emphasize that the mere possibility of abuse, or even the observation of actual instances of abuse, was not a reason to deny the existence of otherwise legitimate constitutional powers or strip government officials of the discretionary authority they might need to advance the public good. "Abuse is inseparable from the proper use of every thing."[11] If you accepted a free press, you had to accept that the freedom would sometimes be abused by scurrilous journalists. The proper response, however, was neither to crush the freedom of the press nor to revel in its abuses.

If we are to preserve useful institutions, whether the press, the presidency, or the representative assembly, we must work to root out those abuses when they occur. A constitutionalism concerned only with a system of rules is likely to be unworkable and perverse. Not least, it encourages an ethos of testing, circumventing, and subverting the rules while in pursuit of short-term political gains. The constitutional rules will routinely be bent, if not broken, if we do not preserve a constitutional culture that emphasizes and values the importance of limits on political power. A constitutional culture that only recognizes rules erases the possibility of abuse of constitutional powers and the damage such abuses can cause.

We should be concerned not only with the boundaries of political power but also with the uses of that power. Even if political actors are willing to respect the rules established by the Constitution, their actions may still be damaging to the constitutional fabric and contrary to important constitutional values. As a matter of constitutional propriety, we should care about how presidents exercise the discretionary authority that they have within the statutory and constitutional rules and not just about whether presidents have stepped over the line and violated some particular rule. In the aftermath of the Whitewater investigation and eventual presidential impeachment, Judge Richard Posner once criticized President Bill Clinton for conducting virtual "guerrilla warfare against the third branch of the federal government, the federal court system."[12] The question is not simply whether the president had committed the crimes of obstruction of justice or perjury, but whether the president had behaved in a manner that was inappropriate to his constitutional responsibilities by inflaming public passions against the independent counsel's office and the courts and by manufacturing novel legal claims of executive privilege primarily to hamper and delay investigations into presidential conduct.

The charge should have resonance now as well. A constitutionally conscientious president cannot behave like any other private litigant. The enhanced power of the presidency imposes an ethical responsibility to refrain from using that power, for example, to heap scorn upon a legal adversary. The symbolic significance of the presidency precludes some litigation strategies that might be available and appropriate to a private citizen. A sitting president pursuing a maximal litigation strategy in an attempt to exhaust every possible legal remedy before conceding an election result or providing documents to a congressional committee hampers the functioning of the government and undermines trust in governmental institutions. Andrew Johnson appealed to his right to free speech when criticized for giving public speeches telling his supporters that the Republican leaders of Congress were as much traitors as the leaders of the Confederacy, but congressional Republicans unsurprisingly viewed such accusations from a sitting president as more dangerous than if they had been made by the average citizen.[13] The president bore a responsibility to conduct himself differently than he might have in private life.

Donald Trump spent his presidency insisting that he need not behave in a manner that might be traditionally viewed as "presidential." He broke norms large and small. When his own interests were threatened, he did not hesitate to do whatever seemed necessary to protect and advance them. His efforts to use his leverage over a foreign power to disadvantage his electoral rivals and enhance his own electoral fortunes gave rise to his first impeachment. His willingness to use the powers of his office to stonewall congressional investigations into what he had done provided the foundation for an additional article of impeachment. His extended effort to subvert confidence in the conduct and outcome of the presidential election, to seek avenues to overturn the legitimate election results, and to stoke passions that eventually gave rise to an attack on the Capitol to stop the counting and certification of presidential electoral votes led to an unprecedented second impeachment. Such behavior might not have been out of character had Trump still been a real estate developer fighting off creditors or a celebrity seeking to keep potential scandals out of the public view. Hyperaggressive actions to advance purely personal interests might be tolerable, if not laudable, in the private sphere. When undertaken by a sitting president in the public sphere, it can be corrupting of the constitutional order.

The constitutional rules vest discretion in government officials, but it is constitutionally relevant how those officials choose to exercise that discretion. The constitutional text specifies that the House has the "sole power of impeachment" and the Senate the sole power to try impeachments. It also specifies the preconditions for an impeachment (the commission of "treason, bribery, or other high crimes and misdemeanors") and what will happen if civil officers are impeached and convicted (they "shall be removed from office"). The Constitution lays out a procedure for impeaching a president and a rule to constrain the use of the impeachment power, but it does not impose a positive duty on the House to impeach or on the Senate to convict. The members of the House and Senate have discretion both over whether to pursue an impeachment and removal of a misbehaving officer and over how they pursue such an inquiry. It is not enough for House or Senate leaders to say that they are acting within the rules. They should also be able to explain why the choices that they are making within those rules are constitutionally appropriate ones that help sustain the American constitutional project rather than corrupt it. A House that chooses to ignore high crimes because a president is of the same political party as the majority or a Senate that chooses to convict an officer of impeachable offenses with only the barest semblance of a trial might be acting within the constitutional rules, but could hardly be said to be living up to their constitutional responsibilities.

James Madison seemed to think the impeachment power was particularly well suited to addressing abuses of office. One example came in an exchange of letters between the former president and Henry Clay, who had served as Speaker of the House during Madison's presidency. In the spring of 1833, Clay was poised to return to representing Kentucky in the Senate, having just lost his own bid for the White House to the incumbent Andrew Jackson. Jackson's use of the powers of the presidency was a frequent source of complaint among Clay and his allies, who formed an opposition party and called themselves the Whigs, after the antimonarchical faction in England. Jackson further irritated his critics when he exercised a "pocket veto"—holding onto a land bill until after Congress had adjourned and could not override his veto. Clay fumed this was an "unconstitutional act," and he begged Madison's "opinion upon that Constitutional question."[14] Madison wrote back that it was obvious that the Constitution meant to give the president adequate time to consider bills and the Congress adequate time to consider and override presidential objections. "A disregard on either side of what it owes to the other must be an abuse" of power. Indeed, "an abuse on the part of the President, with a view sufficiently manifest, in a case of sufficient magnitude to deprive Congress of the opportunity of overruling objections to their bills, might doubtless be a ground for impeachment." The Constitution plainly states that a bill shall not become law if "Congress by their Adjournment prevents" the president from returning the bill to Congress with his objections. Jackson asserted that the Constitution gave him ten days within which to return a bill to Congress, and if Congress adjourned before the ten days were up, then it had no right to complain. For their part, Clay and Madison thought that it was an "abuse" of the president's constitutional power if he had "sufficient time to prepare his objections" but "unnecessarily put it out of the power of Congress to decide on them" by running out the clock.[15] Deciding whether the president had "sufficient time" or was "unnecessarily" delaying in disregard of the respect he owed to Congress were necessarily context-specific, political judgments, and they were judgments about how the president exercised powers he concededly possessed.

The issue was moot in 1833. Andrew Jackson, not Henry Clay, enjoyed the benefit of a friendly majority in the House of Representatives, and the president's allies had no interest in initiating impeachment proceedings against him no matter how much Clay (or Madison) thought Jackson had disrespected the Congress and abused his authority as president. Jackson's innovative pocket veto was not effectively challenged by Congress.

Perhaps unsurprisingly, subsequent presidents built on Jackson's example. By the time Senator Edward Kennedy fulminated on the Senate floor in 1970 that an asserted pocket veto by President Richard Nixon "has raised extremely serious questions about the distribution of power under the Constitution between Congress and the executive branch in the enactment of Federal legislation," he was reduced to writing stinging letters to the attorney general and hoping that the Supreme Court might weigh in. Even though Kennedy asserted that Nixon had "challenged one of the most basic prerogatives of Congress," the senator did not so much as whisper of the possibility of an impeachment for abuse of power.[16]

Madison was worried that his contemporaries were conflating mere abuses with usurpations and, as a consequence, too quickly reaching for the heavy artillery to address the problem. We seem to have trouble with the distinction as well, but more because we lose sight of the possibility of constitutional abuses and only tend to recognize constitutional usurpations. It is entirely possible for government officials to abuse their discretionary authority in ways that go beyond simply making poor choices or in ways that do not simply reflect ordinary policy disagreements. Just because a court would not—and should not—strike down something as a violation of the Constitution does not mean that it is not open to criticism as constitutionally objectionable.

It is easier to think in terms of crimes and rule violations. It is harder to think in terms of abuse of power. Charges of abuse are always more uncertain and more controversial. But if political leaders do not bother to refrain from abusing power or even to consider what might be an abuse of power, then the constitutional system will be substantially less valuable and less durable in the long run.

Exercising Unlawful Power

Constitutions are meaningless if they cannot be effectively vindicated when they are violated. In the years after the American Revolution, James Madison worried that written constitutions were indeed proving to be meaningless in a republic. Writing down limits on government power was pointless if there were no consequences to legislatures riding roughshod over such "parchment barriers."[17] James Madison's strategy of checks and balances was designed to provide more effective tools for preserving limited government in a democratic political system. Chief Justice John Marshall offered a different solution to the same problem by treating a constitution as a judicially enforceable fundamental law.[18] Both Madison and

Marshall thought it was essential to be thinking not only about what substantive constraints on power we wanted to build but also how we would enforce those constraints. Identifying ways to hold government officials "responsible under the forms of the Constitution" was essential to avoiding the temptation to resort to extraconstitutional and extralegal remedies, and it was essential to diminishing the amount of abuse within the system.[19] Impeachment is a potential remedy for constitutional misconduct. Determining when impeachment is appropriate requires thinking comparatively about the range of available remedies as well as about the nature and seriousness of the constitutional problem.

When the *House Practice Manual* concluded that the U.S. House of Representatives has used the impeachment power to address official misconduct that includes "abusing or exceeding the lawful powers of the office," it offered several examples of misconduct and impeachments of that type. The proffered examples, however, might all fit more squarely into the category of "abusing" rather than "exceeding" the lawful powers of the office. The manual points to the impeachments of Senator William Blount and President Andrew Johnson as based primarily on allegations that each "had exceeded the power of his office"—in Blount's case by entering into a "conspiracy to compromise United States neutrality" and in Johnson's case by attempting to remove a member of his cabinet in contravention to the terms of a federal statute.

We might think of "exceeding the lawful powers of the office" as an example of what Madison called a usurpation. Madison held out the Alien and Sedition Acts of 1798 as a classic example of "acts of usurped power" precisely because they were, to his mind, instances of the federal Congress claiming to exercise a power that they could not properly be understood to possess.[20] Both acts violated the U.S. Constitution by exercising powers that had not been properly delegated to Congress among the enumerated powers and, in the case of the Sedition Act, by acting against the express prohibition in the First Amendment of congressional abridgement of the liberty of the press.[21] Such usurpations were particularly dangerous, for if government officials could overleap the constitutional limits on their power, then the entire constitutional enterprise of attempting to constrain political power was in jeopardy. If government officials could exercise powers they did not lawfully possess, then their power was no longer limited at all. They were, quite simply, despots.

Impeachment is one remedy for officers who exceed the powers of their office, but in practice it has not been the primary or even a frequent remedy. Because impeachment has not been frequently used for this purpose, it is worth emphasizing that it *can* be used in this way. It is also illuminating to consider why impeachment has not been a favored remedy for this kind of constitutional problem. It highlights the fact that a consideration of alternative remedies is always central to consideration of the use of the impeachment power. It also helps clarify that the relative paucity of impeachments does not necessarily mean that there have been few impeachable offenses. American history is replete with impeachable offenses, but we have not always turned to the impeachment power to address them.

Although we do not often impeach government officials for exceeding the powers of their office, it would be strange indeed if we did not think such misconduct is impeachable. For present purposes, let us focus on the presidency. Considering the case of a president exceeding the power of the office is complicated by the fact that we have come to understand presidential powers so broadly. On the one hand, we as a country have been fortunate that presidents rarely engage in obviously unconstitutional activity. On the other hand, presidential powers are sufficiently expansive that even credible counterfactuals of presidents exceeding their powers are contestable.

To imagine presidents exceeding their powers, it might not be helpful to think about Article II. Presidents across history have leveraged that slim text to authorize many controversial actions. It might be more fruitful to ponder government actions that the Supreme Court has identified as excluded by the rights provisions of the Constitution or cases that might fall in what Justice Robert Jackson characterized as the "lowest ebb" of presidential power, where "he can rely only upon his own constitutional powers minus any constitutional powers of Congress over the matter."[22]

The Constitution does lay down some clear prohibitions that the president could violate. Yale law professor Charles Black posited the hypothetical of a president announcing that he would not under any circumstances appoint a Roman Catholic to any office and faithfully adhering to that pledge by requiring every potential appointee to answer a series of questions about their religious beliefs in the Oval Office.[23] Such a president would be acting in contravention to the constitutional prohibition that "no religious Test shall ever be required as a Qualification to any Office or public Trust under the United States." Immediately after taking the oath of office, the president might make an announcement welcoming supplemental funding of the official presidential salary with emoluments from each of the fifty states and any foreign governments that might be interested, and then promptly receiving large bags of cash on the White House lawn from representatives of those governments, in contravention to the foreign and domestic emoluments clauses. A president might order that troops be quartered in private homes over the objections of the owners, in contravention to the Third Amendment, or order that the *Washington Post* be seized and shut down so as to prevent it from continuing to publish criticism of the administration on its opinion pages, in contravention to any plausible reading of the First Amendment. A president might simply order that all domestic political enemies be rounded up and held in secret prisons.

Alternatively, we might imagine a president exceeding the power of the office by attempting to exercise powers reserved to Congress. According to the Constitution, no money shall be drawn from the federal treasury except as authorized by congressional appropriation. In practice, Congress tends to leave the president with a great deal of discretion to move money around, but one can imagine a determined legislature specifically prohibiting a president from expending any public funds on a favored program and carefully curtailing the discretion to use already appropriated funds for that purpose. A president ordering the expenditure of funds in defiance of such clear congressional mandates would be acting unlawfully. The president might direct family members to show up at the port of a disfavored state and start exacting taxes from arriving and departing ships, without any authorization from Congress. The president might issue letters of marque and reprisal without congressional authorization to favored campaign donors to capture ships belonging to nations that have displeased the administration. A president might declare that the midterm congressional elections are canceled on the grounds that the president's partisan supporters are likely to lose their seats.

It would be perverse to think that presidents violating the Constitution in such egregious and obvious ways were not impeachable and removable for such actions, which clearly qualify as "misconduct incompatible with the official position of the office holder."[24] They would be the type of usurpations that Madison thought justified aggressive remedial actions.[25] They are among the "political offenses" that Story thought were at the heart of the constitutional standard of high crimes and misdemeanors.[26] But impeachment is not the only kind of remedial action we might take, and it has not been the one that politicians have generally preferred to use when confronted with presidential violations of the law.

The standard response when presidents are accused of exceeding their lawful powers has been to file a lawsuit rather than articles of impeachment. That response has developed not because a president acting unlawfully is beyond the reach of the impeachment power but because the impeachment power has not generally been regarded as the best available remedy for such constitutional violations. Judicial review of presidential action is not the only available option to presidential misdeeds, but it is often the more helpful option. Why might that be?

Judicial review has several potential advantages over impeachment, but those advantages are conditional. Significantly, courts have proven to be reasonably effective in enforcing constitutional limits. That was certainly no foregone conclusion. A judiciary appointed by the president might not have been inclined to call out presidential misdeeds. If judges were to systematically serve as allies of the president, then it might be pointless to seek their assistance against a misbehaving chief executive. By demonstrating some independence from sitting administrations, courts have encouraged those who have been wronged by the president to seek legal recourse. Without effective judicial independence from the executive, impeachment would become a more attractive alternative.

Courts need not only the willingness but also the capacity to rein in a wayward president if judicial review is to be a meaningful remedy to constitutional violations. As Alexander Hamilton famously noted, the judiciary is the least dangerous branch precisely because it does not possess the power of the purse or the sword.[27] All judges possess is the power of their judgment, which primarily means that they have the power to publicize constitutional violations and hope that others will react appropriately. For the revolutionary generation, it was easy to imagine that a constitutional usurper would not react appropriately to having violations identified. A president willing to exceed the limits on presidential power could not be trusted to stop doing so or to voluntarily retreat. It was with such worries in mind that Madison admitted that extreme actions might be necessary in the face of constitutional usurpations, potentially up to and including revolution and the dissolution of the union. If confronted with a threat like that, judicial review would be inadequate and the defenders of the constitutional order would need to take more drastic measures to remove the usurper from power. Judicial review, rather than revolution or assassination, has become the dominant response because presidents have shown that they will comply with judicial orders. A president willing to defy the courts when they call out illegal actions would have to be curbed by some other means.

In the political thought that informed the founding generation, the usurpation of power was a moment of extreme danger. In defending his own actions as governor of the Massachusetts Bay Colony, the long-serving John Winthrop emphasized that any failures of his were due merely to his limited "skill and ability," an all too human failing that could and should be forgiven. But if a government official had transgressed a rule "clear to common apprehension," then "the error is not in the skill, but in the evil of the will." If a governor had failed "in faithfulness" from such wicked motives, then "he must answer for" it.[28] "Usurpation and tyranny" went hand in hand, as the English theorist Algernon Sidney noted in emphasizing that all legitimate political power exercised over the people must come from the people.[29] John Locke characterized usurpation as a kind of "conquest" by which "one is got into the possession of what another has a right to." A usurper might well add "tyranny" by extending his power "beyond what of right belonged" even to the lawful governors.[30] The Scottish philosopher David Hume thought it a "maxim in politics, which we readily admit as undisputed and universal, that a power, however great, when granted by law to an eminent magistrate, is not so dangerous to liberty, as an authority, however inconsiderable, which he acquires from violence and usurpation." Lawful power could always be limited and was by its nature in "the harmony of the constitution," but unlawful power "assumed without law" could only grow and become more ruinous.[31] The Virginia jurist St. George Tucker warned that "governments, free in their institution, have been overturned by the usurpations, or contrivances, of those to whom the administration of them hath been committed."[32]

The founders imagined that such constitutional violations would be willful, extraordinary, and dangerous, and that strong medicine would be needed to effectively address such a situation. We have instead discovered that constitutional violations are routine features of even a healthy constitutional system, and that they can likewise generally be remedied through more mundane instruments. If government officials exceed the limits of their constitutional powers, it is not necessarily a sign that the republic is teetering on the brink of a dictatorship. A judiciary with sufficient public standing can call out constitutional violations with the expectation that the offenders will back down.[33] Under such circumstances, it is less disruptive to let the judiciary do its job and save the impeachment power for a more dire situation.

Judicial review also has the advantage of being targeted. Judges assess discrete actions, and the remedy that they offer in the case of constitutional violations is to order an end to those violations. Impeachment, by comparison, is a clumsy tool. Congress cannot use the impeachment power to enjoin a president from continuing constitutional violations or to direct the president to take remedial actions to walk back the violation. Congress only has the options of removal from office or leaving the president in place. The removal option is appropriate and fine if the violations are sufficiently threatening or pervasive such that the officeholder's continuation in office promises only further infractions. If the constitutional violation at hand is simply an intimation of the constitutional violations to come, then the prompt removal of the offender is a necessary step. If, however, the constitutional violation in question is merely an isolated incident and not an indication of an officer likely to offend in the future, then a more targeted solution can address the constitutional violation without losing the services of an otherwise useful officer.

A crucial consideration then becomes what a particular usurpation says about the faithfulness of the officer. Does a particular instance of an officer exceeding the lawful powers of the position signal that the officer can no longer be entrusted with the responsibilities of high office, or is it merely evidence of a mistake? Isolated mistakes can be corrected, if mechanisms like judicial review are available to do so. If the character, fundamental judgment, and trustworthiness of the officer are called into doubt, however, then a targeted response only leaves the nation vulnerable to future lawlessness. Expeditious removal of such an individual from public power would be the only safe recourse.

Courts also potentially have the virtue of offering technical expertise. If our concern is with identifying and remedying constitutional violations, then we need a mechanism that is reasonably good at identifying violations when they occur. A body that is uninterested or incompetent can hardly be relied upon to make the right call when an officer has exceeded the constitutional powers of the office. The judiciary might be able to provide the specialized capacity that is well suited to calling misbehaving officers to account. To the extent that the constitutional rules are complicated or esoteric, judges might have the skills, training, and experience to best interpret those rules and identify possible violations.[34] Of course, the more transparent and political we think our constitutional commitments are, the less helpful a bench of specialized experts is for identifying and enforcing them. If judges bring no special knowledge to the table when considering whether an officer has exceeded the powers of office, then there is less reason to prioritize or defer to a judicial resolution of such constitutional questions.[35]

Even if the constitutional rules are readily accessible to politicians as well as to judges, however, judges might still have something to offer if they are more inclined to interpret those rules fairly. If we worry that legislators, on average, are buffeted by political forces that make them less than steadfast in safeguarding the constitutional rules, there might be an advantage to relying on more politically insulated judges who are more likely to see their primary mission as faithful adherence to the rules. Judicial review becomes a preferable remedy for constitutional usurpations when legislators cannot be trusted to reliably perform their own constitutional duty.

We turn to courts to remedy constitutional violations not because we have to but because we can. If American courts were not able to exercise the power of judicial review, impeachments might have been more common as legislators picked up the slack and made use of the available remedy for addressing constitutional violations by executive officers. Significantly, if chief executives were to insulate their actions from judicial review, for example, so that no one had standing to bring their policies before a court, then impeachment becomes a more attractive option for addressing the alleged violations of the law. The more willing and able courts are to hear challenges to executive action, the less necessary impeachment inquiries might be.

Of course, impeachment was not the only mechanism that the constitutional framers made available for removing a troublesome president from office. Elections were, and are, the primary vehicle for doing so. The electoral mechanism for removing presidents is obviously more wide-ranging than the impeachment mechanism. The electorate is not limited to removing presidents for high crimes and misdemeanors. It need not find an incumbent president guilty of some wrongdoing. It is enough that the electorate prefers someone else to exercise the duties of the president.

But the electorate clearly *can* remove a president for exceeding the lawful powers of the presidency. Are there circumstances when electoral removal is more appropriate than impeachment and removal for remedying constitutional usurpation? Surely there are. A Congress confronted with a president who has violated the Constitution might refrain from pursuing an impeachment not because such a president has not committed impeachable offenses but because an electoral resolution is a preferable means for addressing the problem.

Timing is one obvious consideration. A constitutional violation that occurs in close proximity to an upcoming election highlights the question of most appropriate remedy. There might be situations in which a president exceeds presidential authority in ways that necessitate immediate removal even if an election is on the horizon, but the argumentative burden on Congress for doing so would be high.[36] It might not be possible to safely leave a president in office until the next election if that person is obstructing electoral mechanisms or jailing political opponents or actively committing treason. In such cases, an electoral mechanism that occurs at a fixed time would be ineffective if it is subverted or the crisis of constitutional violation is so severe and fast-moving that the election arrives too late to prevent irreparable harm to the republic. But many constitutional violations do not take that form. A sufficiently timely and functioning election can be at least as effective as an impeachment.

The clarity of the constitutional violation might also be relevant. Unfortunately, there are often disagreements about whether in fact a high government official like a president has exceeded the constitutional powers of the office. Moreover, those disagreements are likely to be caught up in preexisting partisan divisions. As James Madison long ago predicted, constitutional questions are better answered when it is possible to deliberate on them coolly before they are the subject of heated controversy and the government is "disturbed by faction."[37] If Congress were to preempt an electoral resolution in such circumstances, it might well deepen societal and political tensions rather than restore constitutional order.

Those who think that the president has engaged in the usurpation of powers might be better served in taking their case to the people and persuading the electorate of the correctness of their position and the need to remove the president. Such judgments are likely to be delicate and uncertain, but a Congress confronted with a president who it thinks is exceeding the powers of the office must consider the best path by which to heal the constitutional rift. Stopping the immediate constitutional violation may only be a part of what needs to be done. When Congress contemplates whether impeachment is a better remedy than an election, it must consider how the use of that remedy will be perceived and accepted by the public and what will come next.

Remedies for Abusing the Power of Office

The abuse of power and its remedies raise many of the same considerations that guided our discussion of government officials exceeding the powers of their offices. Impeachment and removal is one remedy for the problem of an abusive government official, but it is a remedy with both benefits and costs. A constitutionally conscientious legislator will want to consider the utility of impeachment as a tool for the problem immediately at hand, but will also want to consider the possible efficacy of alternative remedies that might be available. The decision to impeach and remove an officer includes, explicitly or implicitly, a calculation about whether impeachment is the most efficacious remedy.

One significant challenge to recognizing that impeachment can be used to remove public officials for abuse of office is the concern that it would open the door to frequent impeachments. In particular, we might worry that presidential abuse of office is so common that, if it were impeachable, then presidents would have been impeached all the time—and will be impeached all the time moving forward. This claim is properly thought of as raising two issues. First, is abuse of office within the scope of the impeachment power such that Congress has the option of pursuing it? Second, is abuse of office common or rare? If abuse of office is both impeachable and common, why have we not impeached more often—and should we worry that, if we bring abuse of power firmly within the scope of the impeachment power, presidential impeachments will become more common?

That abuse of power is within the scope of the impeachment power has long been the historical practice and the scholarly consensus. The impeachment and trial of former colonial governor Warren Hastings in the British Parliament was contemporaneous with the drafting of the federal Constitution and was very much on the minds of the founding generation. In the very opening of the Hastings trial, Edmund Burke, who was a manager for the case for the House of Commons, emphasized the importance of the impeachment power for reaching abuse of office:

> If the constitution should be deprived—I mean not in form, but virtually—of this resource, we should certainly be deprived of all its other valuable parts; because this is the cement which

binds it all together, this is the individuating principle that makes England what England is. This it is by which the magistracy and all other things are directed, and must be tried and controlled. It is by this tribunal that statesmen who abuse their power are tried before statesmen and by statesmen, upon solid principles of state morality. It is here that those who by an abuse of power have polluted the spirit of all laws can never hope for the least protection from any of its forms.[38]

Burke's emphasis on the ability of Parliament to address abuses of power through impeachments was taken for granted in the United States and was incorporated into the American practice as well. Towering figures, ranging from James Madison and Alexander Hamilton and St. George Tucker at the time of the founding to Joseph Story and John Randolph Tucker and Thomas Cooley in the nineteenth century to William Howard Taft and Edward Corwin in the twentieth century, all accepted the view that abuse of power was within the scope of the impeachment power.[39] That is the modern consensus as well. As Thomas Cooley concluded:

> It is often found that offences of a very serious nature by high officers are not offences against the criminal code, but consist in abuses or betrayals of trust, or inexcusable neglects of duty, which are dangerous and criminal because of the immense interests involved and the greatness of the trust which has not been kept. Such cases must be left to be dealt with on their own facts, and judged according to their apparent deserts.[40]

Around the time of the impeachment of President Andrew Johnson, John Norton Pomeroy, one of the leading constitutional scholars of the day, included an extensive discussion of the impeachment power in his constitutional law treatise. He was particularly concerned to rebut the claim that impeachable offenses were limited to ordinary criminal offenses:[41]

> We must adopt the . . . more enlarged theory, because it is in strict harmony with the general design of the organic law, and

because it alone will effectively protect the rights and liberties of the people against the unlawful encroachments of power. Narrow the scope of impeachment, and the restraint over the acts of rulers is lessened. If any fact respecting the Constitution is incontrovertible, it is that the convention which framed, and the people who adopted it, while providing a government sufficiently stable and strong, intended to deprive all officers, from the highest to the lowest, of any opportunity to violate their public duties, to enlarge their authority, and thus to encroach gradually or suddenly upon the liberties of the citizens.[42]

Pomeroy contended that the history and design of the Constitution led to the conclusion that an officer is impeachable "for very many breaches of public duty," such as exercising pardon power "in a manner which would destroy the efficacy of the criminal law, and evince a design on his part to subvert the very foundations of justice," a "rash, headstrong, willful course" of action "against the best and plainest interests of the country, although without any traitorous design, he might plunge the nation into a most unnecessary and disastrous war," if he were to "bring defeat, disgrace, and ruin upon his country" through stubbornness and willfulness, though not from "a mere mistake in the exercise of his discretion."[43]

Clear violations of the Constitution by presidents have been relatively rare, but abuses of power have been more common. Most of those abuses might not necessitate or justify impeachment, but presidents exercising discretion within their quite expansive lawful authority create plenty of opportunities for abuses. Presidents are entrusted by both the Constitution and statute with a great deal of unilateral power, which can be exercised for either good or ill, wisely or unwisely, to advance the national interest or not.

Judicial review has become our primary method for addressing constitutional violations, but it offers little help in addressing abuse of power. The concern regarding those who abuse power is not that they are exceeding the powers of their office; it is that they are exercising their lawful discretion in a manner that is inconsistent with the larger purposes of their commission. Abuse of power implies the exercise of powers that are lawfully possessed. Courts are very useful for patrolling the boundaries of lawful powers and declaring when officers have crossed those boundaries. They are much less useful for hearing complaints of how power is exercised within those boundaries. The abuse of power cannot be identified and corrected by courts.

Elections are a much more promising vehicle for addressing abuses of power. The electoral mechanism was put in place precisely to try to align the interests of government officials with those of the citizenry. Whereas lords and kings were in a position to abuse power with impunity, a republican form of government sought to make government leaders responsible to those who bore the brunt of governmental actions, rendering such abuses less likely and more redressable.

There are limits to how effectively elections can remedy abuses of lawful discretion by high government officials, however. The most immediate problem is one of timing. Federal judges, of course, are not subject to election at all, and the impeachment power has most frequently been turned on them. Presidents are subject to an electoral check, but presidential elections are not frequent. It was a maxim of politics at the time of the American founding that "where annual elections end, tyranny begins."[44] The office of the president proposed by the Federalists was a sharp departure from that conventional wisdom. An abusive president might not face the voters for years to come, which created seemingly intolerable risks. The president's long term of office meant that elections were "not a sufficient security" against presidential misconduct.[45] When an election is near, the need to turn to the impeachment power is lessened, but when Election Day is still far away, the need to contemplate the use of the impeachment power to rein in abuses is much more pressing.

There are other potential limitations on the utility of elections for remedying the abuse of power. Some abuses of power might

be of little interest to voters. As the constitutional framers themselves recognized, the electorate could not be relied upon to remedy
all forms of constitutional mischief. Notably, the different branches
of government would have to be armed with "the necessary constitutional means and personal motives to resist encroachments of the
others."[46] If a president were to obstruct the constitutional function
of Congress by, for example, refusing to cooperate with congressional investigations, ignoring subpoenas, and making expansive
claims of executive privilege to shield the activities of the executive branch from outside scrutiny, Congress itself is the aggrieved
party. Such actions by the president might undermine legislative
prerogatives and corrupt the constitutional order without arous-
ing the anger of the electorate. The electoral check on such abuses
might well be unavailing.

Worse yet, the bulk of the electorate might approve of abuses
by a sitting president. James Madison was particularly incisive in
pointing out that the "relief" from political mischief can be "supplied by the republican principle" only when the source of the
mischief is a small faction of the society. When the faction is sufficiently large, however, the republican principle of free and fair
elections cannot be counted on "to secure the public good and
private rights against the danger."[47] A president might, with the
apparent approval of a populace stirred by fear and passion, direct
that American citizens whose family origin could be traced to an
enemy nation be interned in camps for the duration of a war, for
example. We might well think that such a wartime action is within
the discretion of a president acting as commander in chief.[48] Unfortunately, Congress might not be any more inclined than the
electorate to take action to stop the abuse. Such are the challenges
of trying to find "a republican remedy for the diseases most incident to republican government."[49] But because impeachment
might also prove to be an unavailing remedy does not alter the fact
that there are circumstances in which elections might be an adequate means for correcting abuses of power—and circumstances
when they are not.

Elections and impeachments are both blunt instruments. In order to address an abuse of power, they provide the means for removing the abusive official. As in the case of constitutional violations, removal of the offender might sometimes be necessary to address the enormity of the constitutional breach and prevent its repetition. But in other cases, the loss of the officer's services might not be warranted. As in the case of constitutional violations, it might sometimes be possible—even desirable—to counter the particular abuses while leaving the officer in place.

In many cases, Congress can take statutory steps to ameliorate abuses of discretion. The opportunity for abuse of power arises from discretionary authority that comes with delegated power. When the source of that discretion is to be found in legislation, then the options for restricting its scope are fairly straightforward. When the source of that discretion is to be found in the terms of the Constitution itself, then the options for a legislative response might be more limited. Even in those circumstances, however, Congress might not be without an array of carrots and sticks to encourage a president to more faithfully conduct the duties of office.

The power of the purse is one of the most fundamental powers of Congress, and it has traditionally been understood to be a key check on executive power. The constitutional framers imposed an important qualification on the power of the purse in order to secure the independence of the executive from an overweening legislature: Congress can neither increase nor decrease the salary of the president during the presidential term of service.[50] Beyond that constitutional limitation, Congress has substantial authority to make spending decisions that might influence presidential behavior or restrict the president's ability to act on any malignant motives.

The modern Congress has often been reluctant to take full advantage of those tools, but they can be a more targeted approach to addressing perceived abuses of power than the use of the impeachment power. In practice, Congress has chosen to give the president substantial discretionary authority over how appropriated funds are spent. If that discretion is abused, it can be removed. A president might, for example, take advantage of existing statutory authority to declare a national emergency as a pretext to shift the spending of funds appropriated for national defense toward the construction of a border wall to impede the flow of illegal immigrants. Such a decision might well be within the lawful discretion provided by the broadly worded grants of legislative authority, but might nonetheless be viewed as an egregious abuse of delegated discretion. It is within the power of Congress to restrict such an expenditure of funds through statute so as to end the immediate abuse and the opportunity to repeat it.

The power of the purse can also be used as an offensive weapon by Congress to induce better presidential compliance with the legislature's goals. Presidents ultimately can do little on their own. They need resources and staff to implement policies and advance the presidential agenda. While the president's personal salary is beyond the scope of the power of the purse, the rest of the executive branch is not. Even decisions by the president about how to use the unilateral constitutional powers afforded the office can be influenced by tugging at the purse strings.

Of course, Congress has other legislative tools to influence presidential behavior in addition to the power of the purse. Such tools have long formed the normal give-and-take of interbranch relations. The Senate can hold presidential nominations hostage. Congress can refuse to advance the president's legislative priorities. Congress can remove administrative discretion by which the president pursues policy goals. Congress can impose political costs on an administration through hearings and other efforts at public messaging and publicity. Disputes over assertions of executive privilege, for example, have historically been resolved through the use of such tools and negotiation and accommodation between the White House and Congress.[51] While the threat of impeachment hovers in the background as a potential weapon for Congress to use if such interbranch battles escalate, it is one particularly powerful weapon among others.[52] Whether it needs to be used is a judgment that Congress can reasonably make, based not simply on the gravity or impeachability of the abusive behavior at issue but also on the relative efficacy of the available remedies.

Congress might also make use of purely political tools to attempt to rein in a misbehaving government official. Members of Congress not only have the formal powers that the Constitution has entrusted to them; they also exercise a range of informal powers that reflect their capacity and skills as political leaders. As the congressional scholar David Mayhew has detailed, members of Congress perform "conspicuous actions" in the public sphere.[53] They do so, of course, for such mundane reasons as elevating their own political profiles and advancing their careers. More interestingly, they also do so in order to influence public opinion, shape the political agenda, mobilize supporters, and put pressure on other political actors. Politicians use their own forms of "soft power," which in the context of international relations has been understood as "the ability to get what you want through attraction rather than coercion or payments."[54] Or, as presidential scholar Richard Neustadt famously observed, "presidential power is the power to persuade."[55] Political leaders lead by influencing rather than commanding.

Congress might deploy such tools to attempt to directly influence the wayward officer, to persuade others not to cooperate in the misbehavior, or to counter the questionable actions of the officer. Congress might act collectively to adopt resolutions and other forms of "soft law" to signal its own views about preferred behavior and to encourage others to adopt them.[56] Congress might attempt to shore up broken political norms by engaging in political reprisals against those who violate them, by performatively reaffirming those norms and their importance through their own actions, and by encouraging others to continue to adhere to those norms even if some officials, such as the president, are violating them. Political norms and conventions are established and preserved through the cooperative behavior of political elites. If particular individuals violate them, the priority should generally be on pursuing actions aimed at keeping the norms resilient.[57] Impeachments might be a vehicle for doing that, but it is not the only means by which norms can be bolstered when they come under pressure.

President Donald Trump's second impeachment revolved around his responsibility for the storming of the Capitol by his supporters on January 6, 2021. The violent attack on Congress as it attempted to perform its constitutional duty of counting the ballots of the Electoral College and declaring the winner of the 2020 presidential election necessitated a forceful constitutional response by Congress. If there had been no riot, there never would have been a second impeachment. Trump's own postelection behavior, however, would have been the same, and presumably would have been just as condemnable even if it had not actually led to violence. Trump shattered norms of appropriate presidential behavior by doing all he could to delegitimize American elections, his political opponents, and his successor. Indeed, he had spent four years engaging in similar departures from expectations about presidential rhetoric and vilifying the press, the judiciary, and others. Such behavior is grossly incompatible with the office of the presidency and abusive of the platform that the president commands (though perhaps not the lawful powers that he exercises). Presidential rhetoric is best countered by rhetorical countermeasures. Other political leaders had a responsibility to actively and "conspicuously" speak in opposition to the president, to isolate and marginalize him, to work to persuade the public that the president was wrong. Perhaps the president could have and should have been impeached for his demagoguery and rhetorical abuses, but those high crimes might have been better and more effectively addressed by concerted and early action to meet the president in the public sphere.

Presidents, along with other government officials, have ample opportunity to abuse their discretionary authority, and sometimes they do. Impeachment is one tool for addressing such abuses, but it is not the only tool. Although minor abuses might not need to be remedied by the impeachment power, the gravity of the offense is not the only or even the critical question in determining when abuses of power merit the use of the impeachment power. Even if conduct could be addressed by the impeachment power, there is a further question of whether the misconduct in question could be effectively, and perhaps even more effectively, remedied by the use of other political tools.

6

Can the Supreme Court
Intervene in an Impeachment?

IN 2019, the Trump administration was barraged by speculation that the president would soon be impeached. In the 2018 midterm elections, the Democrats had wrested control of the House of Representatives from the Republicans and were threatening to turn up the political pressure on and intensify the congressional oversight of the president. In the spring of that year, special counsel Robert Mueller filed his report with the Department of Justice, detailing the Trump campaign's shocking indifference to whether a hostile foreign power was meddling in domestic American politics, but not finding the evidence of a conspiracy to steal an election that many Democrats expected. Potentially more damaging was the second volume of the Mueller report, which focused on the president's repeated efforts to bring the investigation of the 2016 election to a rapid conclusion. Whether or not the president's actions met the criminal standard for obstruction of justice, they certainly seemed inappropriate to many congressional Democrats and potentially impeachable. Many thought the Mueller report itself, like the report of independent counsel Kenneth Starr during the Clinton administration, was written as a road map for a House impeachment. The dust had barely cleared from the release of the Mueller report when Trump was caught up in a new controversy over his efforts to persuade Ukrainian president Volodymyr Zelensky to announce a criminal investigation of the son of Trump's likely 2020 presidential challenger, Joe Biden. Trump insisted that his conversation with the Ukrainian president about whether the American president would release the aid that Congress had appropriated for the embattled Russian neighbor had been a "perfect phone call." Observers outside Trump's immediate orbit were not reassured by that characterization.

In response to the impeachment speculation, President Trump floated an unusual idea. Once the Mueller report was released to the public, the president took to Twitter to declare, "If the partisan Dems ever tried to Impeach, I would first head to the U.S. Supreme Court."[1] Later he dismissed the idea of an impeachment, asserting that since he had not committed any crimes, there was no basis for an impeachment. "I can't imagine the courts allowing it."[2] Trump was famously litigious, and he was prone to bragging that the judges he appointed to the federal judiciary would be his reliable friends, so it is perhaps not surprising that he would look to the courts to save him from an impeachment. But the president had not come up with the idea on his own. Harvard Law School professor Alan Dershowitz had become a close adviser to Trump and would later serve on his defense team at his impeachment trial. Dershowitz had proposed that the president could and should refuse "to leave office on the ground that his impeachment and removal were unconstitutional." No impeachment process could be final until "the Supreme Court affirmed his removal." Given Dershowitz's own narrow understanding of impeachable offenses, he announced that he expected the court to swiftly overrule an "unconstitutional" impeachment.[3]

Dershowitz was not the first to imagine that the judiciary might have something to say about how the impeachment process was conducted, though his particular argument is unusually stark. Since the longtime criminal defense attorney had the ear of a sitting president, the possibility of judicial review of congressional actions during an impeachment has a new prominence and is unlikely to simply fade away. It is worth evaluating the strength of the claim.

Political Questions

Separate from the question of what counts as an impeachable offense is who gets to decide what counts as an impeachable offense. The traditional answer to that question has been that Congress gets to decide. The House gets to choose who it wants to impeach, and in an impeachment trial the Senate gets to make the final judgment on whether the House's action was justified.

But perhaps impeached officers do not have to leave their fate in the hands of the House and Senate. If the president thought that the House had overstepped its constitutional bounds by undertaking a presidential impeachment for something that is not an impeachable offense, the president might file an immediate motion in the courts to try to enjoin a Senate trial and have the House's articles of impeachment declared constitutionally invalid. If that fails, the president might make a motion to the chief justice, who presides over the Senate trial in a presidential impeachment, seeking to have the case dismissed in the Senate on the grounds that the charges do not meet the legal definition of an impeachable offense. The chief justice as presiding officer in a presidential impeachment trial would be asked to declare that, given the House's articles of impeachment, the senators could not properly vote to convict given their oath "to do impartial justice according to the Constitution and the law." (However the presiding officer rules on such a motion, a majority of the senators could overturn that ruling. If a majority of the senators thought at that stage of the proceedings that no impeachable offenses were being charged on the face of the House's articles, then acquittal is a foregone conclusion in any case. The interesting question is what happens if a majority of the senators think the articles of impeachment are constitutionally valid.) If the chief justice failed to grant the motion to dismiss, or if the majority of the senators overruled the presiding officer on that question, then the defense attorneys might again attempt to have the courts intervene to put an end to the trial. If that effort failed and the Senate continued to final judgment on the merits of the case and convicted the president of high crimes and misdemeanors, the president might then seek relief from the federal judiciary, contending that his conviction in the Senate was not constitutionally valid and should be declared null and void.

Most remarkably, Dershowitz added an extraordinarily dangerous wrinkle. If the Senate were to hold a trial and convict, Dershowitz suggested, the president should simply refuse to leave office and insist that the Supreme Court adjudicate his claim that his conviction violated the Constitution. Dershowitz staked out the strongest possible claim for judicial supremacy. The Supreme Court and the Supreme Court alone should resolve all disagreements about constitutional meaning, and the president should simply defy Congress until the court interceded.

To be clear, Dershowitz was encouraging the president to instigate a constitutional crisis in the hope that it would force the Supreme Court's hand to the benefit of the president.[4] Why he thought as either a legal or political matter the justices would want to back a president who had defied a conviction by two-thirds of the sitting senators and was refusing to voluntarily leave the White House is not at all clear. Why he thought that a president who had been encouraged to refuse to accept his conviction and removal by the Senate would suddenly acquiesce to the judgment of a court that affirmed his conviction and removal is perhaps even less clear. (Dershowitz hinted that the president's public approval would collapse if the Supreme Court ruled against him but not if the Senate convicted him. Presumably, the president would be forced to concede defeat at that point, though Dershowitz did not explain why either was likely.) Why he thought that advising a president—who liked to reflect on having the support of "the tough people" who could make things "very bad, very bad" if pushed beyond "a certain point"—that he could reasonably refuse to leave office after conviction in a Senate trial is bewildering.[5]

One of the problems with the rhetoric of a constitutional crisis is that it encourages political actors to imagine that the gloves have come off, that the rules no longer apply. Likewise, they may also imagine that any action they might take in response would be justified in the exceptional circumstances of the crisis, even if it would be unconscionable in the ordinary circumstances of normal politics taking place within the constitutional rules. It is wise to be extraordinarily cautious before suggesting to a sitting president that they alone are acting within their rights and that everyone else is behaving illegitimately and illegally.

Dershowitz may have been imprudent in advising President Trump to play this card, but it turned out to be unnecessary to attempt this gambit since the president was never in danger of being convicted by the Senate. The president did not even attempt to "head to the U.S. Supreme Court" after his first impeachment by the House, likely because he had good reason for confidence in how the impeachment trial would go in the Senate. Perhaps a future president, or other impeached officer, will not be so fortunate in the Senate and will be tempted to follow the path that Dershowitz laid out for Trump. What are the courts likely to do with such a case?

Dershowitz is right to suggest that there are trends in the Supreme Court's jurisprudence that make judicial intervention in an impeachment dispute more plausible than once might have been the case. The court generally has become more insistent on its own authority to resolve contested constitutional questions. More specifically, the court has steadily weakened the jurisprudential doctrine that might keep impeachment disputes off the judicial docket. Even so, there are reasons for thinking that the court will continue to avoid taking on impeachment controversies.

The court has for several decades made bold claims on behalf of its own authority. Early in the nation's history, Chief Justice John Marshall tapped into a broad political consensus that supported the judiciary's role in interpreting the Constitution. As Marshall explained, courts must not "close their eyes on the constitution, and see only the" statutes passed by Congress. If the Constitution is the supreme law of the land, then "what part of it are [judges] forbidden to read or to obey?" The judges could not be the only government officials blind to the requirements of the Constitution, and if judges were to do their duty as interpreters of the law, then they would have to take the Constitution into account while doing their work. "It is emphatically the province and duty of the judicial department to say what the law is," so judges must be able to identify occasions when "two laws conflict with each other" and resolve the conflict so as to apply the law to the case at hand. When the Constitution conflicts with mere legislation, the court should follow the Constitution.[6]

Marshall's explanation of the power of judicial review within a constitutional republic is anodyne but eloquent. It illustrates the important principle that courts could refuse to follow legislative directions when they conflict with the superior mandates of the Constitution. In recent decades, the courts have made far more of it than that. They have built up a mythic narrative around John Marshall's decision and his rhetoric. In this retelling of the case of *Marbury v. Madison*, Marshall's declaration that it was the emphatic duty of the courts "to say what the law is" was meant to convey that the judges were the special guardians of the Constitution.[7] The courts did not simply have an obligation not to follow unconstitutional legislation. They had the responsibility and authority to look into every part of the Constitution and declare its meaning and to supervise every action of government officials and declare them valid or invalid.

The modern Supreme Court makes far less modest claims for itself than it once did. The court triumphantly moved out of the battles over desegregation, proclaiming "that the federal judiciary is supreme in the exposition of the law of the Constitution."[8] The justices had concluded that the constitutional rules could only be meaningful and effective if the court assumed the role of "the ultimate interpreter of the Constitution."[9] Dershowitz pointed to the court's intervention in the 2000 presidential election dispute in *Bush v. Gore* as evidence that the court would not sit on the sidelines as a constitutional crisis unfolds. The case is certainly emblematic of the court's stature in the modern constitutional scheme. Neither the public nor the politicians wanted Congress to have the final say over how the 2000 presidential election dispute would be resolved. The court was expected to bear the load and bring finality to a volatile situation.[10]

There is a more specific jurisprudential obstacle to the Supreme Court involving itself in impeachment controversies. The political question doctrine has long been used by the court to describe a type of constitutional controversy that the judiciary should refrain from trying to resolve. When constitutional questions are entrusted to a different institution or when there are no constitutional standards that could adequately guide a judicial inquiry, the court has said that judges should forgo trying to impose a resolution to a dispute. Such questions are political, not justiciable.

The Lessons of *Nixon*

The Supreme Court has specifically pointed to the political question doctrine to explain why courts should not intervene in controversies involving the impeachment power. U.S. district judge Walter Nixon was impeached by the House in 1989 after he had been convicted in criminal court for making false statements to a grand jury. The Senate made use of its new rule allowing for an impeachment committee to collect evidence before the full Senate heard closing arguments. Nixon was convicted of high crimes and misdemeanors and removed from office. He filed suit in federal court seeking to regain his judicial office on the grounds that the Senate had not met the constitutional requirements of an impeachment trial.

When Nixon's case reached the Supreme Court, the Court declined to second-guess how the Senate conducted its impeachment trials. Writing for the court in 1993, Chief Justice William Rehnquist found that the constitutional questions surrounding impeachment trials were exclusively committed to the Senate by the Constitution itself.

The parties do not offer evidence of a single word in the history of the Constitutional Convention or in contemporary commentary that even alludes to the possibility of judicial review in the context of the impeachment powers. . . . Nixon's argument would place final reviewing authority with respect to impeachments in the hands of the same body that the impeachment process is meant to regulate.[11]

If the Senate were to convict a Supreme Court justice in an impeachment trial, could the justice appeal to the other justices on the court to have the verdict overturned? Rehnquist thought such a possibility was absurd. Nixon could not appeal from the constitutional court of impeachment to the ordinary courts. The meaning of the impeachment power was a political question that the courts should not attempt to answer.

The Supreme Court seems to have closed the door on the kind of maneuver that Dershowitz was contemplating. But perhaps we should not be too hasty in believing that *Nixon* settled the matter. Justice Byron White wrote separately for himself and Justice Harry Blackmun to say that they were willing to have courts review the constitutional validity of the Senate's actions, though in this case they thought the Senate had successfully met the constitutional requirements for an impeachment trial. Likewise, Justice David Souter wrote separately to say that he could "envision different and unusual circumstances that might justify more searching review of impeachment proceedings" and situations where "judicial interference might well be appropriate."[12] Thus, three of the nine justices seemed to leave the door slightly ajar in 1993.

Perhaps the court would decide *Nixon* differently today, or so Dershowitz would assert. Of the justices who heard the *Nixon* case, only Justice Clarence Thomas remains on the court, and he had joined Rehnquist's opinion declaring impeachment controversies to be political questions. Perhaps the current justices would see things more like White and Souter than like Rehnquist. Scholars have chronicled the general "fall of the political question doctrine" on the court. The recent tendency of the Supreme Court to think "that it alone among the three branches of government has the power and competency to provide the full substantive meaning of all constitutional provisions" might suggest that a majority of the court would not be as deferential as Chief Justice Rehnquist if the question were raised anew.[13] Myriad issues that the courts once avoided, from election disputes to legislative apportionment to executive privilege battles, are now routinely resolved in a courtroom rather than a legislature. Would courts be willing to wade into an impeachment fight as well? The Supreme Court's general embrace of judicial supremacy and the specific withering of the political question doctrine gives impeached officers some hope that they can continue the fight even after the Senate has pronounced judgment.

There are probably special reasons to think that the court would not attempt to throw a lifeline to an impeached president, even though it has shown itself willing to be more intrusive in political debates than once might have been the case. The political question doctrine has always had a jurisdictional and a prudential logic, and in his opinion for the court in *Nixon*, Rehnquist appealed to both. With regard to jurisdictional logic, is this the kind of question that the Constitution has assigned to another branch of government to resolve? As the Supreme Court emphasized in one landmark nineteenth-century case, while the court "should always be ready to meet any question confided to it by the Constitution, it is equally its duty not to pass beyond its appropriate sphere of action, and to take care not to involve itself in discussions which properly belong to other forums."[14] On this point, Chief Justice Rehnquist asked, What part of "sole power to try all impeachments" did former judge Nixon not understand?

> "Sole" is defined as "having no companion," "solitary," "being the only one," and "functioning . . . independently and without assistance or interference." . . . If the courts may review the actions of the Senate in order to determine whether that body

"tried" an impeached official, it is difficult to see how the Senate would be "functioning . . . independently and without assistance or interference."[15]

Constitutional, legal, and factual questions were all within the sole jurisdiction of the constitutional court of impeachment—the Senate. On matters relating to impeachment, the Senate and not the Supreme Court is the court of last resort.

With regard to the prudential logic of the political question doctrine, the courts should refrain from becoming involved in some kinds of controversies because judicial involvement would be counterproductive at best. When the Supreme Court was asked in the early twentieth century to declare that the adoption of initiative and referendum mechanisms for making law was inconsistent with the federal Constitution's guarantee that the states would have "a Republican Form of Government," Chief Justice Edward Douglass White emphasized the "ruinous destruction of legislative authority in matters purely political" if the justices were to give in to the temptation to embark on an "inconceivable expansion of the judicial power." If the judiciary could hear cases questioning whether state governments were sufficiently republican, "anarchy" would ensue. He said the court should avoid creating "these strange, far-reaching and injurious results" and leave such questions to the other branches of government to decide.[16]

In the *Nixon* case, Chief Justice Rehnquist invoked this prudential logic as well, warning courts to stay out of impeachment controversies:

We agree with the Court of Appeals that opening the door of judicial review to the procedures used by the Senate in trying impeachments would "expose the political life of the country to months, or perhaps years, of chaos." . . . This lack of finality would manifest itself most dramatically if the President were impeached. The legitimacy of any successor, and hence his effectiveness, would be impaired severely, not merely while the judicial process was running its course, but during any retrial that a differently constituted Senate might conduct if its first judgment of conviction were invalidated.[17]

If the courts were willing to hear the kinds of cases that Dershowitz wanted to bring, Rehnquist warned, chaos would ensue. The stability of the American political system required that questions about the impeachment process be settled once and for all in the same constitutional court of impeachment that would judge whether an officer was guilty of high crimes and misdemeanors and should be removed from office. The nation could not wake up the day after an impeachment judgment in the Senate and not know who should be exercising the powers of the office of the president. The courts should not encourage a president who has been convicted in the Senate to refuse to vacate the White House in the hope that the judiciary might salvage their presidency. At the moment the Senate declares judgment on a president, there should be no controversy over whether the vice president takes the reins of the executive branch of the federal government.

The Limits of Judicial Supremacy

Even if the Supreme Court has become less committed to the jurisdictional logic of the political question doctrine, it should not waver on the prudential logic, at least not in the case of impeachments.

Let us imagine the extreme case where the House impeaches the president for something that no one reasonably believes is an impeachable offense under the Constitution and the Senate convicts on that charge. Make it simple: the president is impeached and convicted for a fashion crime—wearing a tan suit or a navy blue suit jacket with black slacks in the White House, or wearing white after Labor Day. Or imagine that the Senate convicted the president with no semblance of a trial. The House managers simply walked into the chamber and presented the articles of impeachment, and the Senate immediately took a voice vote declaring the president guilty and removed from office. Observers, including judges, would reasonably conclude that Congress was badly abusing its constitutional power and not even making a pretense of adhering to a good-faith interpretation of the Constitution. Confronted with such a runaway Congress, judges might even be tempted to try to ride to the president's rescue and inform Congress that it was violating the constitutional rules.

This is where politics comes into play and stresses one strand of the prudential logic of the political question doctrine. A Congress willing to impeach and remove a sitting president on such an obvious pretext could hardly be trusted to sit idly by while the justices attempted to reinstall that president in the White House. If a court were to intervene in such a scenario, the justices might well find themselves next on the chopping block. The justices might at this point recall the words of Chief Justice Salmon Chase when the court was asked to order President Andrew Johnson not to enforce the Reconstruction Acts in Mississippi after the Civil War:

> The impropriety of such interference will be clearly seen upon consideration of its possible consequences. . . . Suppose the bill filed and the injunction prayed for allowed. If the President refuse obedience, it is needless to observe that the court is without power to enforce its process. If, on the other hand, the President complies with the order of the court and refuses to execute the acts of Congress, is it not clear that a collision may occur between the executive and legislative departments of the government? May not the House of Representatives impeach the President for such refusal? And in that case could this court interfere, in behalf of the President, thus endangered by compliance with its mandate, and restrain by injunction the Senate of the United States from sitting as a court of impeachment? Would the strange spectacle be offered to the public world of an attempt by this court to arrest proceedings in that court?

"These questions answer themselves," Chase concluded.[18] Indeed. The power of the judiciary has its practical limits.

We might well believe that such an impeachment and conviction would itself amount to a constitutional crisis. I would call it a crisis of fidelity, as Congress would simply be ignoring the relevant constitutional rule regarding impeachable offenses or impeachment trials.[19] It is the nature of a constitutional crisis that the country would no longer be playing by the constitutional rules. Whether judicial intervention would be helpful in such a moment is ultimately a pragmatic matter rather than something directed by the Constitution itself. It seems unlikely that a Congress able to overcome the supermajority hurdle for conviction would be cowed by an opinion issued by the Supreme Court. Perhaps the justices would convince themselves that they could help calm the situation by intervening on behalf of the embattled president against the overreaching Congress. The chief justice might look in the mirror and think that the nation turns its lonely eyes to you. Dershowitz imagined that "if you had a standstill, Congress saying he's removed and the president remaining in the White House, only one institution could resolve the issue of whether or not you need a crime for there to be an impeachable and removeable offense."[20] This is a rather heroic vision of the Supreme Court, and Justices White and Souter seemed to have had a similar view of the Supreme Court as a potential savior of a crumbling republic in a constitutionally misguided impeachment. This strikes me as a hopelessly naive view of the power of the judiciary.[21] If the country reaches a point at which an impeached and convicted president refuses to step down and barricades the Oval Office doors, there will be a lot of other players to take into account before the justices would even have their say.

But let us leave the seminar room behind and consider the real world. In the real world, there is no possibility that the president would be impeached, let alone convicted, for fashion crimes. Instead, presidents are at risk of being impeached for offenses that only those holding fairly extreme views about the impeachment power—people like Alan Dershowitz—think are outside its constitutional scope. At best, the president would be at risk of being impeached for offenses about which there can be reasonable disagreement on whether they rise to the level of high crimes and misdemeanors. There would be no answer in black-and-white as to whether the House was acting beyond its constitutional powers; it would all be in shades of gray.

The constitutional case for impeachment in those more realistic circumstances might not be easy, but it would certainly not be crazy. No justice has ever suggested that the Supreme Court should intervene in such ordinary disputes. No justice has ever suggested that it would be a constitutional crisis if the House impeached and the Senate convicted on the basis of charges about which there could be reasonable disagreement. It is not a crisis just because one side did not get its way. The only person initiating a constitutional crisis in the real world would be a president who refused to leave office after conviction by the Senate. It is simply not credible to attempt to shift the blame for such a crisis to the Congress.

Not every constitutionally controversial action the House and Senate might take when exercising the impeachment power goes to the very core of that power, however. The Supreme Court would be intruding very deeply into the jurisdiction of the Senate if it were to try to give the Senate instructions on what constituted high crimes and misdemeanors or what constituted a constitutionally valid Senate trial. Other questions that might come up are more marginal. They might not challenge the House and Senate so directly, and they might well involve less politically contentious cases and controversies. The judiciary's practical political power is at its nadir when it directly confronts Congress or the president on matters that are politically important to those politicians and their constituents. Telling the Senate that it cannot remove a president that the Senate believes has committed high crimes and misdemeanors is as politically risky as telling Congress it cannot create legal tender during the Civil War or cannot authorize the president to suspend the gold standard during the Great Depression.[22] The justices prefer not to take such political risks. Leaving Congress alone when it takes such make-or-break actions lets the court survive to fight constitutional battles another day.

Not everything involving the impeachment power has such high stakes. Some questions relating to impeachment are more marginal or less politically consequential. The Senate might be less defensive about its prerogative to determine the rules of evidence in an impeachment trial than it would be about determining the scope of impeachable offenses. The House might be less invested in its own conclusions about whether it has to hold a preliminary vote to authorize an impeachment inquiry than it would be on who counted as an officer subject to the impeachment power. It is certainly likely that impeachment cases involving district court judges would be less politically sensitive than impeachment cases involving presidents or Supreme Court justices. Some collateral issues that might arise in an impeachment might seem conducive to judicial exposition. If, for example, a president were impeached for inciting a riot but the speech in question would be constitutionally protected if the case involved a private citizen facing a criminal prosecution, could the Supreme Court instruct the Senate on the proper application of the First Amendment to an impeachment case?[23] If a president claimed that executive privilege or legislative overreach justified a refusal to cooperate with congressional oversight committees, could the Supreme Court instruct the Senate on the scope of executive privilege as it might be used in an impeachment defense?[24] If witnesses refused to testify in a Senate impeachment trial on the grounds that the testimony might put them in legal jeopardy, could the Supreme Court instruct the Senate on the significance of the Fifth Amendment in an impeachment trial? If a president offered as a defense in an impeachment trial that refusal to comply with a statute was based on the president's belief that it impinged on presidential authority under Article II of the Constitution, could the Supreme Court inform the Senate on whether or not the statute was constitutionally valid?[25]

None of that would change the jurisdictional logic of the political question doctrine. It might well be the case that the Constitution has established the Senate acting as the constitutional court of impeachment to be the final arbiter on any such disputes, at least as far as they implicated the exercise of the impeachment power. It might, however, affect the prudential logic of the political question doctrine. The House or the Senate might accept, in a particular instance, an interlocutory appeal during impeachment proceedings that allowed the Court to weigh in on some disputed procedural or substantive question about which the members of Congress had no strong views. Chief Justice Rehnquist, however, took a longer view of the political risks. It might be tempting for the court to intercede in a low-profile impeachment controversy where the immediate repercussions were likely to be limited, but if they did so, they would be opening the door to politicians seeking to draw the court into far more politically exposed controversies. Justice White worried that the court might be inviting bad behavior by Congress if the justices made plain that they would not serve as a backstop to any errors that might be committed during the impeachment process. If Congress knew that judges would not be checking their work, legislators might get careless. But by demonstrating a willingness to review the actions of the constitutional court of impeachment at all, the justices might be inviting the far more worrisome prospect of an impeached officer, such as a president, choosing to defy the authority of the House and Senate. Rehnquist warned that any judicial meddling in the impeachment process would create a "lack of finality" that could be debilitating to the operation of the government. Finality is an important attribute of some legal and political decisions, and impeachment is the type of decision that puts a premium on a clear finality of judgment.

Both White and Souter thought it would be useful for the Supreme Court to hold open the possibility of judicial review of matters relating to impeachment because they did not want to "issue an invitation to the Senate to find an excuse . . . to be dismissive of its critical role in the impeachment process." They imagined that Congress would be more faithful to its own constitutional duties if legislators had some fear that the Supreme Court might someday review their work. There might be circumstances in which that is true, but impeachment is probably not one of them.[26] In any case, White and Souter only posited the possibility of the court's involvement in the most extreme of circumstances. As White himself admitted, "as a practical matter, it will likely make little difference whether the Court's or my view controls the case" because it would be "extremely unlikely" that the Congress would go so far beyond the bounds of the "very wide discretion" it had regarding the impeachment power. Justice John Paul Stevens, who also wrote a separate opinion in the *Nixon* case, thought it unhelpful and inappropriate to pontificate on such "improbable hypotheticals." In the real world of likely impeachments, even White and Souter were urging a standard of extreme judicial deference to congressional judgments about how to use the impeachment power. That is, even if you took White's and Souter's view of the judiciary's role in the impeachment process as controlling, you should not think the courts should intervene given any of the impeachment charges that are realistically going to be on the table. The fact that Dershowitz was advising a sitting president that he could defy a conviction in a Senate impeachment trial underlined Justice Stevens's point. White and Souter might have thought that they were just cautioning the House and Senate to act responsibly, but in doing so they might have been encouraging presidents to act irresponsibly. Sometimes the justices should leave certain things unsaid.

Justice White seemed particularly offended by the idea of the Senate making a clear constitutional error without the possibility of the Supreme Court correcting it.[27] But the justices rarely pause to contemplate that others might feel the same way about the Supreme Court itself. It is judicial hubris to imagine the court would never make mistakes or that only judicial mistakes should be tolerated. Someone will have the last word, and whoever that is, they might make a mistake. The point of the political question doctrine is to identify the occasions when the institution that, whether for good or for ill, finally settles some constitutional questions would be an elected one rather than a judicial one.

Significantly, Chief Justice Rehnquist did not bother to address what should happen if Congress went completely off the constitutional rails, but his point about the fundamental constitutional design was in sharp contrast to White's and Dershowitz's vision of a constitutional edifice that rests on the backs of the justices. The founders, Rehnquist thought, had not entrusted the Constitution to the courts. Indeed, they had done the opposite. They gave Congress the ultimate check on the courts—the power of impeachment. It was to the popularly elected legislative branch that the constitutional drafters gave the ultimate weapon. It was to the popularly accountable Congress that they gave the final responsibility for resolving constitutional controversies and exercising constitutional discretion in the case of impeachments.

To empower the justices to sit in judgment of whether Congress was using the impeachment power correctly would be to turn the Constitution on its head. It would transform a constitutional system that ultimately rested on the people into a constitutional system in which everyone ultimately answered to the judges. If we are to worry about checks and balances, then we should pay attention to the checks and balances that the framers built into the impeachment power itself. The impeachment power was distributed across a bicameral elected legislature and pivoted on a hard-to-reach supermajority in the Senate. The protection against the abuse of the impeachment power does not depend on the whims of five Supreme Court justices but on the need for a two-thirds vote in the Senate. If the president were to lose the support of more than a third of their own party caucus in a Senate trial (as would usually be the case for conviction), then it would be implausible to contend that the president had simply been railroaded by a Senate intent on subverting the Constitution. A president in such a position should not expect the Supreme Court to ride to the rescue.

Conclusion

FROM A CHECKS and balances perspective, the impeachment power is the greatest power that Congress possesses. Unlike other great constitutional powers that can be exercised by Congress, the impeachment power does not require the cooperation of any other political body. Constitutional amendments must be ratified by the states. Laws must be presented to the president and survive review by the courts. The impeachment power rests in the hands of the Congress alone. There is no appeal from the constitutional court of impeachment.

The impeachment power symbolizes the ultimate preeminence of the first branch of government, the republican branch that is closest to the people. It uniquely gives Congress the power to re-move members of the other two branches of government. It em-powers Congress to peer into the workings of the other branches and to remedy misconduct. It gives Congress the ultimate trump card in conflicts with the other branches of government. Alexan-der Hamilton predicted that "there can never be danger that the judges" would encroach on the powers of Congress, because the legislature had "a complete security" from such threats—Congress alone possessed the "important constitutional check," the "power of instituting impeachments."[1] The Constitution entrusts Con-gress with the authority to act swiftly to right the ship of state when others are derelict in their duty or abusive of their office. It gives Congress the power to reinforce or reconfigure constitutional norms and transform constitutional understandings.

The three great branches of government are separate, independent, and coordinate, but that does not mean that they are coequal. When James Madison was explaining the proposed Constitution to the skeptical anti-Federalists, he admitted that "in republican government, the legislative authority necessarily predominates." The executive and the judiciary could be "fortified" so that they could help check the legislature, but "it is not possible to give each department an equal power of self-defense."[2] Congress occupied a special place in a constitutional republic. Months before he would be turned out of office in the election of 1860, President James Buchanan protested that the House of Representatives had appointed a committee to investigate "the President of the United States or any other officer of the Government" for exercising improper influence over proposed legislation. Buchanan contended that "as a coordinate branch of the Government he is their equal," and thus should not be subjected to such congressional harassment. But in the same breath, Buchanan admitted as "the high impeaching power of the country," the House could call even the president to account. The House pushed back—hard. "The conduct of the President is always subject to the constitutional supervision and judgment of Congress; whilst he, on the contrary, has no such power over either branch of that body. He is left, under the law, without shield or protection of any kind, except such as borne by all." The House Judiciary Committee went further:

> The President affirms, with seeming seriousness, in comparing himself with the House of Representatives, that, "as a coordinate branch of the government, he is their equal." This is denied in emphatic terms. He is "co-ordinate" but not coequal. He is "co-ordinate," for he "holds the same rank," but he is not coequal, for his immunities and powers are less. The members of the House may claim a privilege, whether right or wrong,

which he cannot, and the executive or law-making power must always be inferior to the legislative or law-making power. The latter is omnipotent within the limits of the Constitution; the former is subject not only to the Constitution, but to the determination of the latter also. To repeat the point: the President is not, in any respect, superior to the citizen, merely because he is bound to discharge more numerous duties; and he is not co-equal with that branch of government which helps to impose and define those duties.[3]

The Constitution begins by describing the organization and power of the legislative branch. The other branches follow downstream from that starting point.

If the constitutional system is to function properly, and if republican government more broadly is to function properly, Congress must understand its own authority within that system and be prepared to fulfill its responsibilities. Understanding is the first step. The impeachment power is not a familiar power. It was not familiar to the founders either. It is not a power that a legislature should be expected to use routinely. Impeachments should be extraordinary events, necessary because something has gone wrong— perhaps terribly wrong. An impeachment exercises legislative muscles that are not used to the exertion. The hope is that those muscles have not atrophied during the downtime.

Of course, like any other political power, the impeachment power can be misused or abused. If we do not understand the power properly, if we do not appreciate what it should be used for and what it should not, it is more likely to be misused. There are sins of both omission and commission. Congress might not be ready to deploy the impeachment power when it should be deployed. But Congress might also use it too readily, or use it badly. Congress might fail to appreciate what the impeachment power can do and might also fail to respect the limits of what it can reasonably accomplish.

Understanding is at best only half the battle. The impeachment power is ultimately a political tool to be wielded by political actors. They must not only understand what they are doing; they must also have the will and the desire to use their powers responsibly and appropriately. In the end, the elected members of the legislature are accountable not just to their consciences but to the people. If elected legislators fail to act appropriately or fail to act at all when action is needed, they must explain themselves to the electorate and face the consequences of their choices. If the people themselves do not demand appropriate behavior from their elected leaders, they are unlikely to get it.

This raises a more fundamental possibility. Perhaps the impeachment power is outdated and no longer matters. Certainly, our recent experience with the impeachment power does not breed confidence that it is a meaningful feature of our modern constitutional system. Whatever the founders might have hoped for when bestowing this power on Congress, the modern legislature might not be up to the task of employing it and perhaps the country is no longer ready to see it employed.

One can imagine both attractive and much less attractive reasons for why that might be the case. Perhaps the best news would be that we have simply outgrown the impeachment power. The English Parliament has moved beyond the impeachment power. Ministers are now held accountable to parliamentary majorities in more effective ways. Working at the dawn of constitutional democracy, the American framers looked for what tools they had to restrain government officials and remedy abuses. From their standpoint, the impeachment power might have seemed indispensable, but from our standpoint more than two centuries later, we might have learned other, more efficient and more effective, ways to solve those kinds of political problems.

That would indeed be great news, and it is at least partly true. As discussed earlier, the framers were probably too pessimistic about the modes of correcting constitutional abuses and violations. It turns out that constitutional and political errors can often be corrected without taking the dramatic step of impeaching an incumbent official. The emergence of judicial review as a routine feature of American constitutional governance has provided a regular, fine-grained check on the executive that has reduced some of the pressure that might otherwise have fallen on Congress to engage in diligent oversight of executive officers. The impeachment power is potent but crude. The workings of a system of constitutional checks and balances can sometimes result in pitched battles between the branches, but for the most part American politicians have discovered how to operate the constitutional system with somewhat less *Sturm und Drang*. If political problems can be remedied without Congress having to deploy the heavy artillery of impeachment, then so much the better.

This happy rationale for consigning the impeachment power to the ash heap of history is only partly persuasive. The impeachment power still has its uses even after the development of more subtle political tools. Sometimes judges who cannot be trusted to continue to exercise the authority of their office simply refuse to resign. So long as we have a system of lifetime tenure for judges, some mechanism for forcing them off the bench against their will is necessary. Even if the federal system eventually followed the model of the states and moved away from lifetime appointments and toward a system of lengthy terms of office, it would still be necessary to have some means for removing an obstinate judge before their term expired. Likewise, the fundamental concern that motivated the constitutional drafters in Philadelphia has not gone away. Perhaps we are further removed from the kind of monarchical intrigues that filled their nightmares and do not have to worry quite so much about a president selling the office to foreign powers. Perhaps. But the presidency is an even mightier office now than it was imagined to be in 1787, and four years can be a very long time to tolerate a brute occupying the White House. The Constitution would be deficient if it did not have a fail-safe to address an intolerable situation. The Constitution is not a suicide pact, and if the impeachment power did not exist, a would-be dictator would have to be dealt with by some extraconstitutional means. Best to keep your powder dry.

It might also be happy news if the impeachment power has become outdated because our democratic sensibilities have outpaced it, but in that case the news probably would not be entirely good. But how can the flowering of our democratic norms be less than happy news? Of course, generally that has been a clear virtue. America is a more robustly democratic nation than it was at the end of the eighteenth century, and that is a good thing. But it might not be an unalloyed good thing.

Those democratic sensibilities can be leveraged in ways that subvert the *constitutional* aspects of our constitutional democracy. When talk of impeachment got serious during the Trump presidency, Fox News personality (and Trump confidant) Sean Hannity took to the airwaves to inform the viewers that he would no longer refer to the impeachment inquiry as a "political witch hunt" but rather as an "attempted coup of a duly elected president." Hannity was not exactly breaking new ground. Some two decades earlier, Democratic representative Jerry Nadler labeled President Bill Clinton's impeachment "a thinly veiled coup d'etat." Nadler, a future House manager in the Trump impeachment, was hardly alone in feeding Clinton supporters that particular narrative.[4]

Coup talk is inflammatory—and is meant to be—but it also taps into real political, and democratic, sensibilities. The impeachment power is a vestige of an eighteenth-century constitutionalism that preferred mechanisms of indirect democracy. We cut the indirect election of U.S. senators out of the Constitution through amendment, and we cut the indirect election of the president out of our constitutional practice by emasculating presidential electors.[5] The country quailed at the thought of resolving the 2000 presidential dispute by a vote in Congress.[6] In the modern era of a "plebiscitary presidency," the people may have come to conceptualize their own relationship with the president as so direct and immediate that no intermediary should appropriately intercede.

Who are the members of Congress to "overturn the results of the election" by impeaching a sitting president? The Argentinean political scientist Guillermo O'Donnell has described the darker side of this impulse. In what he calls "delegative democracies," presidents exalt in their popular mandate, and horizontal checks on their power are shrugged off as an unnecessary hindrance.[7] Such democracies are often not very stable. Once elevated, such presidential strongmen are tempted to discard the vertical check of elections as well. The democratic sensibility in such situations is real but not entirely healthy or sustainable. If our democratic sentiments have truly outpaced the impeachment power, it would be a short step from there to presidents insisting that neither should they be bound by the decrees of nine unelected justices or be hindered by obstructionist legislators. The American constitutional democracy is not the only form of democracy that exists in the world.

Does the impeachment power survive as a kind of constitutional vestigial organ, like presidential electors? Could it not be expected to function without provoking a legitimacy crisis? Although presidential impeachments remain difficult, it seems unlikely that they should be regarded as broadly illegitimate and incompatible with our contemporary constitutional practices and values. As the example of Jerry Nadler demonstrates, the modern partisan distrust of the impeachment power tends to be situational. The impeachment power is great when it is aimed at our foes but troubling when aimed at our allies. Certainly, the impeachment power is not likely to be regarded as off-limits if Congress turns its attention to removing a judge or executive officer. Removing a president is a much tougher political task, but it probably should be. The House and Senate should recognize that a significant portion of the American public will greet an impeachment inquiry aimed at the president with great skepticism. The House will bear a significant burden of proof when it comes to persuading the average voter, even if it does not have much difficulty persuading the median legislator. Circumstances matter. If the House seems hell-bent on removing a president by any means necessary, if it seems unconstrained by any evidence or constitutional principles, if it seems too eager to take the decision of whether to keep an incumbent president out of the hands of the electorate, then presidential declarations that the House is pursuing a bloodless coup will find a sympathetic audience. If Congress proceeds with great deliberation and makes the effort to win public opinion to its side, then such rhetoric might instead ring hollow. That presidential impeachments are difficult or controversial or rare does not mean that they are illegitimate. Supporters of a sitting president might prefer that the chief executive be answerable solely to the voters at the ballot box, but the American system is one of constitutional checks and balances and not just one of democratic elections. It is not yet evident that the people have abandoned that ideal.

It would not be good news at all if the impeachment power has become outdated because our *partisan* sensibilities have overwhelmed it. The impeachment power fits more neatly into a world without political parties. At least in their more high-minded moments, the framers might have imagined the members of Congress simply deliberating together on how best to advance the public good and forging a consensus through good argument and persuasion. We do not live in a nonpartisan world. Partisan feelings and commitments are all too real. The incentives driving legislative action are often deeply partisan ones.

There is no question that partisanship is a problem for the smooth functioning of the impeachment power. As Thomas Jefferson feared, the impeachment power can become a formidable weapon of faction. Partisans might be quick to think that government officials hailing from the other political party are richly deserving of impeachment. They might be so quick to think so that we begin to question their judgment, if not their sincerity. On the other hand, partisanship can also be a powerful shield against impeachment. As Bill Clinton and Donald Trump discovered, partisans can be made to rally around the flag of an embattled president.

The sitting president can count on a significant portion of the American public to be implacably opposed to any impeachment effort. Partisan legislators can be motivated to fall into line as well, at least so long as their partisan base remains in the president's corner. This is hardly a new discovery. Republican representative Amos Granger railed against Democratic president James Buchanan in 1858, but his party did not yet control the House and could not turn his words into actions. Baited by a member of the president's party, Granger retorted that there was "more truth than poetry" in the suggestion that the proper remedy to Buchanan's alleged misbehavior was impeachment:

> True, sir, impeachment would be resorted to as the most important and effectual remedy but for the presence of the demon, *party*, who stands here with his cloven foot and pitchforks to defend and protect the *guilty*. Sir, there never was a fairer candidate for impeachment, and for more than one specification that we can produce. In the purer days of the Republic, no Congress would have submitted to what we have.[8]

We have always been tempted to pine for the purer days of the republic, but nostalgia is no substitute for political stratagem. For better or for worse, the game of impeachment takes place on a partisan playing field.

If partisanship is a problem for the impeachment power, it does no good to try to wish it away. The question is not whether voters and legislators will rise above partisanship. The question is whether the impeachment power can still be meaningful when party spirit rides high. Even in our partisan world, the impeachment power is not obsolete.

And the impeachment power might still be able to channel partisan forces in a productive way. It is easy to forget that most impeachments are robustly bipartisan affairs. That is true in no small part because most impeachments have not been politically divisive or especially politically salient. Time and time again, Congress has proven itself capable of evaluating allegations of misconduct leveled against lower-court judges. It could probably do the same if it were necessary to turn to the impeachment power to rid the executive branch of some abusive but relatively insignificant officer. Such impeachments fly under the political radar, and they can still be moments in which the members of Congress are capable of rising above their normal partisan animosities.

Matters are considerably more complicated when impeachments are highly consequential politically. Presidents, justices, and cabinet officers inevitably stir partisan passions. In a sufficiently partisan environment, even low-level officers might inspire a partisan defense. Federalists in Congress rallied to the defense of the admittedly impaired district judge John Pickering in 1803. They might have done so with some real embarrassment and misgivings, but they also could not stomach creating a vacancy on even a trial court bench for their hated foe President Thomas Jefferson to fill. It is not easy to peel away partisan support from an incumbent president or a Supreme Court justice. Not easy, but not impossible. President Richard Nixon's support in the Senate crumbled when the revelations about his behavior threatened to sink the Republican Party as a whole. It became necessary to cauterize the political wound. Bill Clinton and Donald Trump were able to shore up their partisan support by appealing directly to the people, but one can imagine such efforts falling short. They made it work, but that gambit is hardly a sure thing. At the same time, partisan incentives can be leveraged to move an impeachment effort along. Without the added nudge of partisanship, members of Congress might be willing to overlook the misconduct of government officials in the other branches. The possibility of some partisan benefit from exposing the wrongdoing of the other side might make some members of Congress more vigilant than they otherwise would be.

If the sole purpose of an impeachment is to remove a president, then partisanship is often an insuperable obstacle. If an impeachment inquiry serves other goals, however, partisanship might be a spur to undertaking the project. When the House Judiciary

Committee threw President James Buchanan's protest back in his face, it no doubt helped that the newly emergent Republican Party had won the House in the midterm election and Buchanan was a Democrat. Nineteenth-century constitutional sensibilities did not do all the work when a House committee declared, "There is no judge presiding over the representatives of the sovereign people, of the sovereign States, to teach and inculcate legal proprieties."[9] Partisan as well as institutional loyalties can sometimes stiffen the spine of the members of Congress, even if partisan loyalties sometimes render members of Congress spineless.

The impeachment power has been a meaningful tool in the American constitutional system, and it can be in the future. We should not let disappointment with any particular impeachment episode or frustration with any particular impeachment effort lead us to distort our constitutional inheritance. Senators were asked in the first Trump impeachment, for example, to adopt a standard of impeachable offenses that would neuter to a significant degree the legislature's ability to address the problem of abusive officers. Going along with such suggestions might be the easy way out for senators looking for a credible excuse to cast a vote in the way that their partisan base is demanding. But the easy way out of a short-term dilemma can undermine the strength of our constitutional protections in the long term. It is necessary to adhere to an appropriate understanding of the impeachment power even when it is inconvenient in the moment or even when a particular impeachment effort seems misguided. How members of Congress turn aside entreaties for impeachment or conviction matters for how the impeachment power is understood going forward. Even when Congress is not willing to impeach or remove an official today, it should preserve the power unimpaired for a possible occasion in the future.

It is tempting to think of the impeachment power as primarily a matter of law. Crimes shall be prosecuted, and the guilty shall be punished. There is hope that impeachable offenses could be reduced to an identifiable list, borrowing from the criminal code. Such hopes are unlikely to be fulfilled.

The impeachment power is inescapably political. It is exercised by politicians and aimed at government officials. It exists in order to remedy political problems. When politicians consider launching an impeachment inquiry, they should be thinking primarily in political terms—not the low politics of public approval and electoral fortunes but the high politics of advancing the public good and preserving the constitutional order. Legislators who find themselves called upon to consider making use of the impeachment power have an obligation to think through some basic questions: What is an impeachable offense? Is this kind of behavior impeachable? Does this instance of misconduct justify impeachment? What is Congress trying to achieve? Might other tools be more effective at realizing those goals? Lawyers can help answer some of those questions, but they mostly require political judgment.

FURTHER READING

AN EXCELLENT primer on the modern impeachment process is Michael J. Gerhardt, *Impeachment: What Everyone Needs to Know* (New York: Oxford University Press, 2018). See also Gerhardt's *The Federal Impeachment Process: A Constitutional and Historical Analysis*, 3rd ed. (Chicago: University of Chicago Press, 2019).

On how the impeachment power should be understood and should be used, see Charles L. Black, Jr., *Impeachment: A Handbook* (New Haven, CT: Yale University Press, 1974); Cass R. Sunstein, *Impeachment: A Citizen's Guide* (Cambridge, MA: Harvard University Press, 2017); Joshua Matz and Laurence Tribe, *To End a Presidency: The Power of Impeachment* (New York: Basic Books, 2018); Gene Healy, *Indispensable Remedy: The Broad Scope of the Constitution's Impeachment Power* (Washington, D.C.: Cato Institute, 2018).

There are a number of useful studies of the history of the impeachment power. In British history, those include A. H. Dodd, *The Growth of Responsible Government: From James the First to Victoria* (London: Routledge & Paul, 1956); P. J. Marshall, *The Impeachment of Warren Hastings* (London: Oxford University Press, 1965); Clayton Roberts, *The Growth of Responsible Government in Stuart England* (Cambridge, UK: Cambridge University Press, 1966); Colin G. C. Tite, *Impeachment and Parliamentary Judicature in Early Stuart England* (London: Athlone Press, 1974). In American history, those include David E. Kyvig, *The Age of Impeachment: American Constitutional Culture since 1960* (Lawrence: University

Press of Kansas, 2008); Raoul Berger, *Impeachment: The Constitutional Problems* (Cambridge, MA: Harvard University Press, 1974); Peter Charles Hoffer and N.E.H. Hull, *Impeachment in America, 1635–1805* (New Haven, CT: Yale University Press, 1984); Eleanore Bushnell, *Crimes, Follies, and Misfortunes: The Federal Impeachment Trials* (Urbana: University of Illinois Press, 1992); Keith E. Whittington, *Constitutional Construction: Divided Powers and Constitutional Meaning* (Cambridge, MA: Harvard University Press, 1999); Frank O. Bowman III, *High Crimes and Misdemeanors: A History of Impeachment for the Age of Trump* (New York: Cambridge University Press, 2019).

Deep dives into particular impeachment episodes and near impeachments include Buckner F. Melton, Jr., *The First Impeachment: The Constitution's Framers and the Case of Senator William Blount* (Macon, GA: Mercer University Press, 1998); Richard E. Ellis, *The Jeffersonian Crisis: Courts and Politics in the Young Republic* (New York: Oxford University Press, 1971); William H. Rehnquist, *Grand Inquests: The Historic Impeachments of Justice Samuel Chase and President Andrew Johnson* (New York: Morrow, 1992); Michael Les Benedict, *The Impeachment and Trial of Andrew Johnson* (New York: Norton, 1973); Hans Louis Trefousse, *Impeachment of a President: Andrew Johnson, the Blacks, and Reconstruction* (Knoxville: University of Tennessee Press, 1975); Brenda Wineapple, *The Impeachers: The Trial of Andrew Johnson and the Dream of a Just Nation* (New York: Random House, 2019); Robert S. Levine, *The Failed Promise: Reconstruction, Frederick Douglass, and the Impeachment of Andrew Johnson* (New York: Norton, 2021); Joshua E. Kastenberg, *The Campaign to Impeach Justice William O. Douglas: Nixon, Vietnam, and the Conservative Attack on Judicial Independence* (Lawrence: University Press of Kansas, 2019); John R. Labovitz, *Presidential Impeachment* (New Haven, CT: Yale University Press, 1978); Stanley I. Kutler, *The Wars of Watergate: The Last Crisis of Richard Nixon* (New York: Knopf, 1990); Richard A. Posner, *An Affair of State: The Investigation, Impeachment, and Trial of President Clinton* (Cambridge, MA: Harvard University Press, 2000); Peter

Baker, *The Breach: Inside the Impeachment and Trial of William Jefferson Clinton* (New York: Scribner, 2000); Michael D'Antonio and Peter Eisner, *High Crimes: The Corruption, Impunity, and Impeachment of Donald Trump* (New York: Thomas Dunne Books, 2020); Rachael Bade and Karoun Demirjian, *Unchecked: The Untold Story behind Congress's Botched Impeachments of Donald Trump* (New York: William Morrow, 2022).

For a more political analysis, see Daniel P. Franklin, Stanley M. Caress, Robert M. Sanders, and Cole D. Taratoot, *The Politics of Presidential Impeachment* (Albany: SUNY Press, 2020). For a comparative context, see Aníbal S. Pérez-Liñán, *Presidential Impeachment and the New Political Instability in Latin America* (New York: Cambridge University Press, 2007); Omololu Fagbadebo, *Impeachment in the Nigerian Presidential System: Challenges, Successes, and the Way Forward* (Singapore: Palgrave Macmillan, 2020).

On the related question of removing incapacitated presidents, see Brian C. Kalt, *Constitutional Cliffhangers: A Legal Guide for Presidents and Their Enemies* (New Haven, CT: Yale University Press, 2012); David Priess, *How to Get Rid of a President: History's Guide to Removing Unpopular, Unable, or Unfit Chief Executives* (New York: PublicAffairs, 2018); and Kalt's *Unable: The Law, Politics, and Limits of Section 4 of the Twenty-Fifth Amendment* (New York: Oxford University Press, 2019).

Ever since the impeachment of President Bill Clinton, there has been a cottage industry of books calling for the impeachment of the sitting president. A sampling includes Ann H. Coulter, *High Crimes and Misdemeanors: The Case against Bill Clinton* (Washington, D.C.: Regnery, 1998); John Nichols, *The Genius of Impeachment: The Founders' Cure for Royalism* (New York: New Press, 2006); Andrew C. McCarthy, *Faithless Execution: Building the Political Case for Obama's Impeachment* (New York: Encounter Books, 2014); Allan J. Lichtman, *The Case for Impeachment* (London: William Collins, 2017). Somewhat unusual is the preemptive defense of Donald Trump in Alan Dershowitz, *The Case against Impeaching Trump* (New York: Hot Books, 2018).

ACKNOWLEDGMENTS

PASSAGES OF THIS BOOK have been drawn from some of my previous publications, and I appreciate the permission to use them here. They include items in *Lawfare, The Atlantic,* and *The Volokh Conspiracy,* as well as "Bill Clinton Was No Andrew Johnson: Comparing Two Impeachments," *University of Pennsylvania Journal of Constitutional Law* 2 (2000): 422; "Impeachment in a System of Checks and Balances," *Missouri Law Review* 87 (2022): 1171; "Is Presidential Impeachment Like a Coup?," *Georgetown Journal of Law and Public Policy* 18 (2020): 669; and "A Formidable Weapon of Faction? The Law and Politics of Impeachment," *Wake Forest Law Review* 55 (2020): 381.

NOTES

Introduction

1. For those interested, with particular attention to the 1804 impeachment of Justice Samuel Chase, the 1868 impeachment of President Andrew Johnson, and the near impeachment of President Richard Nixon in 1974, see Keith E. Whittington, *Constitutional Construction* (Cambridge, MA: Harvard University Press, 1999).

2. *Trial of Andrew Johnson*, vol. 3 (Washington, D.C.: Government Printing Office, 1868), 175.

3. George Ticknor Curtis, *Constitutional History of the United States*, vol. 2 (New York: Harper & Brothers, 1896), 701.

4. John W. Burgess, *Reconstruction and the Constitution* (New York: Charles Scribner's Sons, 1903), 145. The court reporter recorded the attorney general's argument a bit differently: Mississippi v. Johnson, 71 U.S. 475, 501 (1866).

5. *The History of the Trial of Warren Hastings, Esq.*, part 4 (London: J. Debrett, and Vernor and Hood, 1796), 25.

Chapter One: What Is the Impeachment Process?

1. Edward Hyde, Earl of Clarendon, *The History of the Rebellion and Civil Wars in England*, new ed., vol. 1 (Oxford, UK: Clarendon Press, 1826), 41.

2. King James I, *The Political Works of James I*, ed. Charles Howard McIlwain, vol. 1 (Cambridge, MA: Harvard University Press, 1918), 20.

3. Quoted in Clayton Roberts, *The Growth of Responsible Government in Stuart England* (London: Cambridge University Press, 1966), 13.

4. *Proceedings in Parliament, 1614 (House of Commons)*, ed. Maija Jansson (Philadelphia: American Philosophical Society, 1988), 420.

5. *Foedera*, ed. Thomas Rymer, vol. 17 (London: J. Tonson, 1727), 275.

6. *Proceedings and Debates of the House of Commons, in 1620 and 1621*, vol. 2 (Oxford, UK: Clarendon Press, 1766), 360.

7. *Commons Debates, 1621*, ed. Wallace Notestein, Frances Helen Relf, and Hartley Simpson, vol. 2 (New Haven, CT: Yale University Press, 1935), 148–149.

8. *Proceedings and Debates, in 1620 and 1621*, 1:117.

9. *Commons Debates, 1621*, 2:303. Later in the session, Pym included in his summation of the House's accomplishments that it had revived a power "which hath slept this 300 years and is the greatest benefit that may be" (3:353) and "to the terror" (5:185) of offenders against the Parliament.

10. "May 29, 1624, Journal of Sir Simonds D'Ewes," in *Proceedings in Parliament: 1624: The House of Commons*, ed. Philip Baker, 129–130; *British History Online* (http://www.british-history.ac.uk/no-series/proceedings-1624-parl/may-29).

11. *Commons Debates, 1621*, 3:30.

12. William Cobbett, *Cobbett's Parliamentary History of England*, vol. 2 (London: R. Bagshaw, 1803), 36–37.

13. Quoted in Christopher Hill, *The Century of Revolution*, 2nd ed. (New York: Routledge, 2002), 72.

14. *Basilika: The Works of King Charles the Martyr*, ed. William Fulman and Richard Perrinchief, 2nd ed. (London: Richard Chiswell, 1687), 253.

15. *Mr. Burnet's Defence: Or, More Reasons for an Impeachment* (London: J. Roberts, 1715), 33.

16. Thomas Erskine May, *A Treatise upon the Law, Privileges, Proceedings and Usage of Parliament* (London: Charles Knight & Co, 1844), 374.

17. Earl Grey, *Parliamentary Government Considered with Reference to a Reform of Parliament* (London: Richard Bentley, 1858), 4.

18. James Madison, *Notes of Debates in the Federal Convention of 1787*, ed. Adrienne Koch (New York: W. W. Norton, 1987), 42, 82, 88. Madison had proposed a congressional veto over state legislation, echoing the power that the king's Privy Council had exercised over the colonial assemblies prior to American independence. The convention settled on a constitutional clause specifying that the federal constitution and laws made pursuant to it were to be supreme to state laws. Federal and state judges alike were "bound" to act accordingly in the cases that came before them.

19. Madison, 61–63.

20. Madison, 338.

21. Dallas Woodhouse, "State House Republicans Hold Ultimate Ace to Stop N. C. Supreme Court Madness," *Carolina Journal* (October 21, 2021).

22. The issue of the timing of Trump's impeachment was first raised by Noah Feldman: "Trump Isn't Impeached until the House Tells the Senate," *Bloomberg* (December 19, 2019). That position was disputed by others: Jonathan Turley, "Trump Stands Impeached: A Response to Noah Feldman," *JonathanTurley.org* (December 20, 2019); Adam Liptak, "A Law Professor's Provocative Argument: Trump Has Not Yet Been Impeached," *New York Times* (December 20, 2019). I argued that Feldman was mostly right: Keith E. Whittington, "When Is an Officer Impeached?," *Volokh Conspiracy*, parts I (December 20, 2019), II (December 20, 2019), III (December 21, 2019), and IV (December 22, 2019).

23. 48 *Cong. Record* (July 11, 1912), 8934; Charles W. Johnson, John V. Sullivan, and Thomas J. Wickham, Jr., *House Practice* (Washington, D.C.: U.S. Government Publishing Office, 2017), 604. In Judge Archbald's case, the House approved articles of impeachment along with a resolution of impeachment. In other cases, the House sometimes adopted a resolution of impeachment before drafting any articles of impeachment, and sometimes sent a representative to the Senate to impeach an officer before any articles of impeachment had been drafted. The articles were something the House needed for the Senate to proceed to trial, but not necessarily something the House needed in order to accomplish an impeachment.

24. William Blackstone, *Commentaries on the Laws of England*, 8th ed., vol. 4 (Oxford, UK: Clarendon Press, 1778), 256; William Rawle, *A View of the Constitution of the United States of America* (Philadelphia: H. C. Carey and I. Lea, 1825), 199.

25. 7 *Annals of Cong.* (July 7, 1797), 39.

26. It is worth noting that if we think the Senate's impeachment power depends on the House having completed a constitutionally valid impeachment, and we think that the House can only impeach current officers, and we think that an impeachment occurs when the House addresses itself to the Senate, then the House would create a jurisdictional problem for itself if it waits until an individual has left office before going to the Senate. Of course, this is exactly what the House did in Trump's second impeachment. See Keith E. Whittington, "When Is an Officer Impeached? V" *Volokh Conspiracy* (January 16, 2021).

27. *Cannon's Precedents of the House of Representatives of the United States*, vol. 6 (Washington, D.C.: Government Printing Office, 1936), 512; H. Rep. 946, 62nd Cong., 2nd Sess. (July 8, 1912), 27.

28. For details on the English and state practice of so-called late impeachments, see Brian C. Kalt, "The Constitutional Case for the Impeachability of Former Federal Officials: An Analysis of the Law, History, and Practice of Late Impeachment," *Texas Review of Law and Politics* 6 (2001): 13.

29. For discussion, see Michael J. Gerhardt, *The Federal Impeachment Process*, 2nd ed. (Chicago: University of Chicago Press, 2000), 77–79.

Chapter Two: What Is a Fair Impeachment Process?

1. For the classic account of the early antipathy toward political parties, see Richard Hofstadter, *The Idea of a Party System* (Berkeley: University of California Press, 1970). For a somewhat idiosyncratic critique of the conventional wisdom, see Robert E. Ross, *The Framers' Intentions* (Notre Dame, IN: University of Notre Dame, 2019).

2. Alexander Hamilton, "No. 1," in *The Federalist Papers*, ed. Clinton Rossiter (New York: New American Library, 1961), 34; James Madison, *Notes of Debates in the Federal Convention of 1787*, ed. Adrienne Koch (New York: W. W. Norton, 1987), 137.

3. *Notes of Debates*, 52.

4. George Washington, *The Writings of George Washington*, ed. Worthington Chauncey Ford, vol. 12 (New York: G. P. Putnam's Sons, 1891), 465, 466; vol. 13, 301–304.

5. Washington, 13:305.

6. Thomas Jefferson, *Memoir, Correspondence, and Miscellanies*, ed. Thomas Jefferson Randolph, vol. 4 (Charlottesville, VA.: F. Carr, 1829), 202, 204; Thomas Jefferson, *The Writings of Thomas Jefferson*, ed. Paul Leicester Ford, vol. 12 (New York: G. P. Putnam's Sons, 1905), 375.

7. Jefferson, *Writings*, 7:114.

8. Jefferson, *Writings*, 7:120, 76; Thomas Jefferson, *A Manual of Parliamentary Practice* (Philadelphia: Parrish, Dunning, and Mears, 1858), v, 13, 14.

9. Jefferson, *Writings*, 7:190.

10. Jefferson, *Writings*, 7:202–203.

11. Jefferson, *Writings*, 7:207–208.

12. Jefferson, *Writings*, 7:195.

13. *Proceedings on the Impeachment of William Blount* (Philadelphia: Joseph Gales, 1799), 61–62, 102.

14. Any relief Jefferson might have felt was only temporary. Months after the House presented articles of impeachment against Blount to the Senate, Congress passed the Sedition Act of 1798, which Jefferson and his allies thought was an even more despotic tool of faction and "so palpably in the teeth of the Constitution as to shew they mean to pay no respect to it" (Jefferson, *Writings*, 7:267).

15. St. George Tucker, *Blackstone's Commentaries*, vol. 1 (Philadelphia: William Young Birch and Abraham Small, 1802), 295.

16. Joseph Story, *Commentaries on the Constitution of the United States*, 3rd ed., vol. 2 (Boston: Little, Brown, 1858), 239.

17. James Madison, "No. 44," *Federalist Papers*, 282.

18. "A Resolution Expressing the Sense of the Senate that the House of Representatives Should, Consistent with Long-Standing Practice and Precedent, Prior to Proceeding Any Further with Its Impeachment Investigation into President Donald J. Trump, Vote to Open a Formal Impeachment Inquiry and Provide President Trump with Fundamental Constitutional Protections," S. Res. 378, 116th Cong. (2019).

19. White House counsel Pat Cipollone, letter to Speaker of the House Nancy Pelosi (October 8, 2019).

20. House minority leader Kevin McCarthy, letter to Speaker of the House Nancy Pelosi (October 3, 2019).

21. 26 *Cong. Globe* (February 9, 1857), 628, 629.

22. "Constitutional hardball" is a phrase invented by Mark Tushnet to describe actions that are within the constitutional rules but violate earlier widespread assumptions about how government officials are supposed to conduct themselves within those rules: "Constitutional Hardball," *John Marshall Law Review* 37 (2004): 523.

23. Thomas Hart Benton, *Thirty Years' View*, vol. 2 (New York: D. Appleton, 1856), 629.

24. Mathews v. Eldridge, 424 U.S. 319, 335 (1976).

25. Morrissey v. Brewer, 408 U.S. 471, 481 (1972).

26. Dent v. West Virginia, 129 U.S. 114, 124 (1889).

27. Joint Anti-Fascist Refugee Committee v. McGrath, 341 U.S. 123, 161, 172 (1951) (Frankfurter, J., concurring).

28. Palko v. Connecticut, 302 U.S. 319, 327 (1937).

29. Joint Anti-Fascist Refugee Committee, 172.

30. "'Politics,' he says, 'ain't bean bag. 'Tis a man's game; an' women, childher, an' pro-hybitionists'd do well to keep out iv it'": Finley Peter Dunne, *Mr. Dooley in Peace and in War* (Boston: Small, Maynard, 1899), xiii. "Mr. Dooley" was a popular fictional Irish bartender in Chicago created by the Gilded Age humorist Dunne.

31. Veronica Stracqualursi, "'I'm Not Trying to Pretend to Be a Fair Juror Here': Graham Predicts Trump Impeachment Will 'Die Quickly' in Senate," CNN (December 14, 2019).

32. Naomi Lim and Joseph Simonson, "Elizabeth Warren Says She's Seen Enough Evidence to Convict Trump in Senate Impeachment Trial," *Washington Examiner* (October 4, 2019).

33. Keith E. Whittington, *Constitutional Construction* (Cambridge, MA: Harvard University Press, 1999), 149; *Trial of Andrew Johnson*, vol. 1 (Washington, D.C.: Government Printing Office, 1868), 91, 93.

34. *Deschler's Precedents of the U.S. House of Representatives*, vol. 3 (Washington, D.C.: Government Printing Office, 1994), 2125–2126.

35. Mark Nevin, "Nixon Loyalists, Barry Goldwater, and Republican Support for President Nixon during Watergate," *Journal of Policy History* 29 (2017): 403.

36. The concerns with trial committees are carefully examined in Michael J. Gerhardt, *The Federal Impeachment Process*, 2nd ed. (Chicago: University of Chicago Press, 2000).

Chapter Three: What Is the Impeachment Power For?

1. On the Clinton impeachment, see also Keith Whittington, "Bill Clinton Was No Andrew Johnson: Comparing Two Impeachments," *University of Pennsylvania Journal of Constitutional Law* 2 (2000): 422; Keith E. Whittington, "'High Crimes' after Clinton: Deciding What's Impeachable," *Policy Review* 99 (2000): 27.

2. On the centrality of the demands for explanation to legislative behavior, see John W. Kingdon, *Congressmen's Voting Decisions*, 3rd ed. (Ann Arbor: University of Michigan Press, 1989); Richard F. Fenno, Jr., *Home Style* (Boston: Little, Brown, 1978); R. Douglas Arnold, *The Logic of Congressional Action* (New Haven, CT.: Yale University Press, 1990); William T. Bianco, *Trust* (Ann Arbor: University of Michigan Press, 1994).

3. Gene Healy, *Indispensable Remedy* (Washington, D.C.: Cato Institute, 2018).

4. James Madison, *Notes of Debates in the Federal Convention of 1787*, ed. Adrienne Koch (New York: W. W. Norton, 1987), 332, 52.

5. 10 *Cong. Globe* (September 10, 1841), 449.

6. 39 *Cong. Record* (January 16, 1905), 945.

7. 156 *Cong. Record* (December 8, 2010), 594.

8. Madison, *Notes of Debates*, 334.

9. Committee on the Judiciary, "Trial of Good Behavior of Certain Federal Judges," H. Rep. 921, 77th Cong., 1st Sess. (July 10, 1941). See also Tara Leigh Grove, "The Origins (and Fragility) of Judicial Independence," *Vanderbilt Law Review* 71 (2018): 485–486.

10. 1 *Annals of Cong.* (May 19, 1789), 387.

11. 1 *Annals of Cong.*, 387.

12. H. Res. 24, 117th Cong., 1st Sess. (January 25, 2021).

13. On the scope of the impeachment disqualification clause, see Brian C. Kalt, "The Constitutional Case for the Impeachability of Former Federal Officials: An Analysis of the Law, History, and Practice of Late Impeachment," *Texas Review of Law and Politics* 6 (2001): 13; Benjamin Cassady, "'You've Got Your Crook, I've Got Mine': Why the Disqualification Clause Doesn't (Always) Disqualify," 32 *Quinnipiac Law Review* 32 (2014): 209; Michael Stern, "An Exchange on the Disqualification Clause," *Quinnipiac Law Review* 33 (2014): 1; Seth Barrett Tillman and Josh Blackman, "Offices and Officers of the Constitution, Part III: The Appointments, Impeachment, Commissions, and Oath or Affirmation Clauses," *South Texas Law Review* 62 (2023): 349.

14. 3 U.S.C. 102 note.

15. 13 *Annals of Cong.* (January 4, 1804), 319.

16. Charles Howard McIlwain, *The High Court of Parliament and Its Supremacy* (New Haven, CT: Yale University Press, 1910), 189.

17. 21 *Annals of Cong.* (April 3, 1810), 1736, 1741.

18. 5 *Annals of Cong.* (March 7, 1796), 444.

19. 4 *Annals of Cong.* (November 26, 1794), 930.

20. 29 *Cong. Globe* (March 12, 1860), 110.

21. 1 *Annals of Cong.* (May 19, 1789), 394–395.

22. Massachusetts Constitution of 1780, Chap. I, Sec. 3, Art. VI.

23. Healy, *Indispensable Remedy*, 85.

24. On impeachment as an emergency measure, see Laurence H. Tribe and Joshua Matz, *To End a Presidency* (New York: Basic Books, 2018), xii. For my doubts about the wisdom of too-frequent impeachments, see Keith E. Whittington, "Presidential Impeachments Should Not Be Normalized," in *Debating Reform*, eds. Richard J. Ellis and Michael Nelson, 4th ed. (Washington, D.C.: CQ Press, 2020).

25. Thomas M. Cooley, *A Treatise on Constitutional Limitations*, 4th ed. (Boston: Little, Brown, 1878), 3.

26. A. V. Dicey, *Lectures Introductory to the Study of the Law of the Constitution* (London: Macmillan, 1885), 25.

27. On the Chase and Johnson impeachments, see Keith E. Whittington, *Constitutional Construction* (Cambridge, MA: Harvard University Press, 1999).

28. James Madison, "No. 48," in *The Federalist Papers*, ed. Clinton Rossiter (New York: New American Library, 1961), 309.

29. "Articles of Impeachment against Donald John Trump," H. Res. 755, 116th Cong., 1st Sess. (December 18, 2019).

30. 5 *Annals of Cong.* (1796), 759, 760, 773, 760, 774.

31. White House to Congress, October 8, 2019, in "White House Letter to Congress on Impeachment Inquiry," *Lawfare* (October 8, 2019) (https://www.lawfareblog.com/white-house-letter-congress-impeachment-inquiry).

32. Josh Chafetz, *Congress's Constitution* (New Haven, CT: Yale University Press, 2017).

33. James Madison, *The Writings of James Madison*, ed. Gaillard Hunt, vol. 5 (New York: G. P. Putnam's Sons, 1904), 404.

Chapter Four: What Are High Crimes and Misdemeanors?

1. Italics in original; Thomas Jefferson, *The Writings of Thomas Jefferson*, ed. Paul Leicester Ford, vol. 3 (New York: G. P. Putnam's Sons, 1894), 224.

2. Alexander Hamilton, "No. 9," in *The Federalist Papers*, ed. Clinton Rossiter (New York: New American Library, 1961), 72, 71.

3. James Madison, "No. 48," *Federalist Papers*, 308; "No. 51," 320, 322.

4. Hamilton, "No. 9," *Federalist Papers*, 71; James Madison, *Notes of Debates in the Federal Convention of 1787*, ed. Adrienne Koch (New York: W. W. Norton, 1987), 135, 312, 42.

5. Madison, *Notes of Debates*, 332–334.

6. See, e.g., Keith E. Whittington, "'High Crimes' after Clinton: Deciding What's Impeachable," *Policy Review* 99 (2000): 27; Michael J. Gerhardt, *Impeachment: What Everyone Needs to Know* (New York: Oxford University Press, 2018), 59–65; Frank O. Bowman III, *High Crimes and Misdemeanors* (New York: Cambridge University Press, 2019), 244–252.

7. Jonathan H. Adler, "'High Crimes and Misdemeanors' as an Inkblot," *Volokh Conspiracy* (December 13, 2019) (https://reason.com/2019/12/13/high-crimes-and-misdemeanors-as-an-inkblot/).

8. *Nomination of Robert H. Bork to Be Associate Justice of the Supreme Court of the United States, Hearings before the Committee of the Judiciary*, 100th Cong., 1st Sess. (1987), 249.

9. *Nomination of Robert H. Bork*, 250.

10. Nietzsche, *On the Genealogy of Morals and Ecce Homo*, trans. Walter Kaufmann and R. J. Hollingdale (New York: Vintage Books, 1969), 150.

11. 116 *Cong. Record* (April 15, 1970), H3113.

12. "Impeachment of the President," H. Rep. 7, 40th Cong., 1st Sess. (November 25, 1867), 60.

13. 39 *Cong. Globe* App. (December 6, 1867), 63.

14. *Trial of Samuel Chase, an Associate Justice of the Supreme Court of the United States*, vol. 1 (Washington, D.C.: Samuel H. Smith, 1805), 47. On the Chase impeachment and its legacy, see Keith E. Whittington, *Constitutional Construction* (Cambridge, MA: Harvard University Press, 1999).

15. Alan Dershowitz, *The Case against Impeaching Trump* (New York: Hot Books, 2018).

16. *Proceedings of the United States Senate in the Impeachment Trial of President Donald John Trump*, vol. 1, S. Doc. 116–18, 116th Cong., 2nd Sess. (January 31, 2020), 216.

17. "Impeachment of the President," 60.

18. Joseph Story, *Commentaries on the Constitution of the United States*, 3rd ed., vol. 1 (Boston: Little, Brown, 1858), 553.

19. Story, 554.

20. Story, 556, 557.

21. 39 *Cong. Globe* App. (December 6, 1867), 64.

22. 39 *Cong. Record* (February 23, 1905), 3179.

23. John Hatsell, *Precedents of Proceedings in the House of Commons*, vol. 4 (London: T. Payne, T. Cadell, and W. Davies, 1796), 63.

24. Cass R. Sunstein, *Impeachment: A Citizen's Guide* (Cambridge, MA: Harvard University Press, 2017), 18–19.

25. On high crimes and misdemeanors as a term of art from British parliamentary practice, see James C. Phillips and John C. Yoo, "You're Fired: The Original Meaning of Presidential Impeachment," *Southern California Law Review* 94 (2021): 1191.

26. William Blackstone, *Commentaries on the Laws of England*, 8th ed., vol. 4 (Oxford, UK: Clarendon Press, 1778), 141.

27. Samuel March Phillipps, ed., *State Trials*, vol. 1 (London: W. Walker, 1826), 100.

28. *Journals of the House of Commons*, vol. 42 (April 25, 1787), 670.

29. Delaware Const., Art. 23 (1776).

30. New York Const., Art. 33 (1777).

31. Massachusetts Const., Chap. 1, Sec. 2, Art. VIII (1780).

32. Virginia Const. (1776).

33. Madison, *Notes of Debates*, 139.

34. Madison, 331–335.

35. Madison, 605.

36. Hamilton, "No. 65," *Federalist Papers*, 396.

37. Jonathan Elliot, ed., *The Debates in the Several State Conventions of the Adoption of the Federal Constitution*, 2nd ed., vol. 4 (Washington, D.C.: Jonathan Elliot, 1836), 281.

38. Elliot, 4:276, 34, 113–114.

39. Elliot, 3:512.

40. Elliot, 3:17, 368, 486.

41. James Wilson, *The Works of the Honourable James Wilson, L.L.D.*, vol. 2 (Philadelphia: Lorenzo Press, 1804), 166.

42. St. George Tucker, *Blackstone's Commentaries*, vol. 1 (Philadelphia: William Young Birch and Abraham Small, 1802), 178.

43. Joseph Story, *Commentaries on the Constitution of the United States*, 2nd ed., vol. 2 (Boston: Charles C. Little and James Brown, 1851), 532.

44. William Rawle, *A View of the Constitution of the United States of America* (Philadelphia: H. C. Carey and I. Lea, 1825), 207, 204, 208.

45. Thomas M. Cooley, *The General Principles of Constitutional Law in the United States of America* (Boston: Little, Brown, 1880), 159.

46. Charles W. Johnson, John V. Sullivan, and Thomas J. Wickham, Jr., *House Practice* (Washington, D.C.: U.S. Government Publishing Office, 2017), 592, 593, 596.

47. See, e.g., Marc W. Kruman, *Between Authority and Liberty* (Chapel Hill: University of North Carolina Press, 1997), 123–130.

48. John Norton Pomeroy, *An Introduction to the Constitutional Law of the United States*, 3rd ed. (New York: Hurd and Houghton, 1875), 484.

49. John Randolph Tucker, *The Constitution of the United States*, vol. 1 (Chicago: Callaghan, 1899), 419–420.

50. Thomas Jefferson, *The Writings of Thomas Jefferson*, ed. Paul Leicester Ford, vol. 7 (New York: G. P. Putnam's Sons, 1905), 202.

51. See, e.g., Virginia Constitution of 1776 ("The Governor, when he is out of office, and others, offending against the State, either by mal-administration, corruption, or other means, by which the safety of the State may be endangered, shall be impeachable by the House of Delegates"); New York Constitution of 1777 ("That the power of impeaching all officers of the State, for mal and corrupt conduct in their respective offices, be vested in the representatives of the people in assembly"); North Carolina Constitution of 1776 ("The Governor, and other officers, offending against the State, by violating any part of this Constitution, mal-administration, or corruption, may be prosecuted, on the impeachment of the General Assembly").

52. Laurence Tribe and Joshua Matz, *To End a Presidency* (New York: Basic Books, 2018), 8.

53. Gene Healy, *Indispensable Remedy* (Washington, D.C.: Cato Institute, 2018), 36.

54. Sunstein, *Impeachment*, 12; Gerhardt, *Impeachment*, 2.

55. Charles L. Black, Jr., *Impeachment: A Handbook* (New Haven, CT: Yale University Press, 1974), 33.

56. Black, *Impeachment*, 34.

57. Tribe and Matz, *To End a Presidency*, 39, 42.

58. Sunstein, *Impeachment*, 125.

59. On disagreement as central to politics, see Jeremy Waldron, *Law and Disagreement* (New York: Oxford University Press, 1999), 102.

60. Patriot Front Manifesto (https://patriotfront.us/manifesto/).

61. Political disagreement raises its head again even in imagining the hypotheticals, however. If the Supreme Court had not ducked in the Gold Clause Cases and President Franklin Roosevelt had delivered the message he had prepared, declaring that the national interest as he understood it took priority over obeying edicts of the U.S. Supreme Court, it is not obvious that a majority of the House of Representatives in the summer of 1935 would have been more inclined to impeach Roosevelt than Justice James McReynolds. On the Gold Clause Cases, see David Glick, "Conditional Strategic Retreat: The Court's Concession in the 1935 Gold Clause Cases," *Journal of Politics* 71 (2009): 806; Keith E. Whittington, *Political Foundations of Judicial Supremacy* (Princeton, NJ: Princeton University Press, 2007), 36–38.

62. Black, *Impeachment*, 36.

63. Sunstein, *Impeachment*, 134.

64. Black, *Impeachment*, 36.

65. Sunstein, *Impeachment*, 133.

66. Williams v. State, 142 Tex. Crim. 155, 160 (1941).

Chapter Five: When Does Abuse of Power Justify Impeachment?

1. Edmund Burke, "Reflections on the Revolution in France," in *Revolutionary Writings*, ed. Iain Hampsher-Monk (New York: Cambridge University Press, 2014), 32.

2. Thomas Gordon, *The Works of Tacitus*, vol. 2 (London: Thomas Woodward, 1721), 39.

3. Montesquieu, *The Spirit of the Laws*, trans. Thomas Nugent, vol. 1 (London: J. Nourse and P. Vaillant, 1750), 220.

4. *Journals of the House of Commons*, vol. 10 (January 13, 1691), 626.

5. Joseph Story, *Commentaries on the Constitution of the United States*, 3rd ed., vol. 1 (Boston: Little, Brown, 1858), 559, 544, 546.

6. On impeachment as a fail-safe, see Cass R. Sunstein, *Impeachment: A Citizen's Guide* (Cambridge, MA: Harvard University Press, 2017), 174. On impeachment as a mechanism for securing the state, see Story, *Commentaries on the Constitution*, 1:280. On impeachment as an alternative to waiting until the next election, see Laurence Tribe and Joshua Matz, *To End a Presidency* (New York: Basic Books, 2018), 8.

7. Story, *Commentaries on the Constitution*, 1:545.

8. Charles W. Johnson, John V. Sullivan, and Thomas J. Wickham, Jr., *House Practice* (Washington, D.C.: U.S. Government Publishing Office, 2017), 603, 608.

9. James Madison, *Letters and Other Writings of James Madison*, vol. 3 (Philadelphia: J. B. Lippincott, 1865), 659; vol. 4, 355, 9, 299.

10. Madison, 4:239.

11. James Madison, *The Writings of James Madison*, ed. Gaillard Hunt, vol. 6 (New York: G. P. Putnam's Sons, 1906), 389.

12. Richard A. Posner, *An Affair of State* (Cambridge, MA: Harvard University Press, 1999), 152.

13. *Trial of Andrew Johnson*, ed. Benjamin Perley Poore, vol. 1 (Washington, D.C.: Government Printing Office, 1868), 50–52, 115–116; vol. 2, 378; Keith E. Whittington, *Constitutional Construction* (Cambridge, MA: Harvard University Press, 1999), 132–139.

14. Henry Clay, *The Papers of Henry Clay*, ed. Robert Seager II, vol. 8 (Lexington: University Press of Kentucky, 1984), 643.

15. Madison, *Letters and Other Writings*, 4:299–300.

16. *Constitutionality of the President's "Pocket Veto" Power: Hearing before the Subcommittee on Separation of Powers*, U.S. Senate, 92nd Cong., 1st Sess. (January 26, 1971), 207, 209.

17. James Madison, "No. 48," in *The Federalist Papers*, ed. Clinton Rossiter (New York: New American Library, 1961), 308.

18. On the Madisonian and Marshallian strategies, see Keith E. Whittington, *Constitutional Crises, Real and Imagined* (forthcoming); George Thomas, *The Madisonian Constitution* (Baltimore: Johns Hopkins University Press, 2008), 16–38.

19. Madison, *Letters and Other Writings*, 4:299.

20. Madison, 4:105.

21. Madison, *Writings of James Madison*, 6:328.

22. Youngstown Sheet & Tube Co. v. Sawyer, 343 U.S. 579, 637 (1952).

23. Charles L. Black, Jr., *Impeachment: A Handbook* (New Haven, CT: Yale University Press, 1974), 33–34.

24. Charles W. Johnson, John V. Sullivan, and Thomas J. Wickham, Jr., *House Practice* (Washington, D.C.: U.S. Government Publishing Office, 2017), 608.

25. Madison, *Writings of James Madison*, 9:597.

26. Story, *Commentaries on the Constitution*, 1:553.

27. Alexander Hamilton, "No. 78," *Federalist Papers*, 465.

28. John Winthrop, *The History of New England from 1630 to 1649*, ed. James Savage, vol. 2 (Boston: Little, Brown, 1853), 280.

29. Algernon Sidney, *Discourses Concerning Government*, 2nd ed. (Edinburgh: G. Hamilton and J. Balfour, 1750), 40.

30. John Locke, *Two Treatises of Government*, ed. Peter Laslett (New York: Cambridge University Press, 1988), 397.

31. David Hume, *Hume: Political Essays*, ed. Knud Haakonssen (New York: Cambridge University Press, 1994), 184.

32. St. George Tucker, *Blackstone's Commentaries*, vol. 1 (Philadelphia: William Young Birch and Abraham Small, 1803), xvi.

33. See Georg Vanberg, *The Politics of Constitutional Review in Germany* (New York: Cambridge University Press, 2004); Jeffrey K. Staton, *Judicial Power and Strategic Communication in Mexico* (New York: Cambridge University Press, 2010); David S. Law, "A Theory of Judicial Power and Judicial Review," *Georgetown Law Journal* 97 (2009): 723.

34. James R. Rogers, "Information and Judicial Review: A Signaling Game of Legislative-Executive Interaction," *American Journal of Political Science* 45 (2001): 84; Keith E. Whittington, "'Interpose Your Friendly Hand': Political Supports for the Exercise of Judicial Review by the United States Supreme Court," *American Political Science Review* 99 (2005): 583.

35. Jeremy Waldron, *Law and Disagreement* (New York: Oxford University Press, 1999); Mark Tushnet, *Taking the Constitution Away from the Courts* (Princeton, NJ: Princeton University Press, 2000).

36. See also Keith E. Whittington, "Is Presidential Impeachment Like a Coup?," *Georgetown Journal of Law & Public Policy* 18 (2020): 1.

37. Madison, *Writings of James Madison*, 5:504.

38. E. A. Bond, ed., *Speeches of the Managers and Counsel in the Trial of Warren Hastings*, vol. 1 (London: Longman, Brown, Green, Longmans & Roberts, 1859), 4.

39. Madison, *Writings of James Madison*, 5:364; Alexander Hamilton, "No. 65," *Federalist Papers*, 396; Tucker, *Blackstone's Commentaries*, 1:178; Story, *Commentaries on the Constitution*, 2:532; John Randolph Tucker, *The Constitution of the United States*, vol. 1 (Chicago: Callaghan, 1899), 418–420; Thomas M. Cooley, *The General Principles of Constitutional Law in the United States of America* (Boston: Little, Brown, 1880), 158–159; William Howard Taft, "The Selection and Tenure of Judges," *American Bar Association Reports*, 36 (1913): 430; Edward S. Corwin, *John Marshall and the Constitution* (New Haven, CT: Yale University Press, 1919), 78.

40. Cooley, *General Principles of Constitutional Law*, 159.

41. The opposite case had been advanced by Columbia Law School dean Theodore W. Dwight and had played a role in Johnson's impeachment defense: Dwight, *Trial by Impeachment* (Philadelphia: E. C. Markley & Sons, 1867), 268–269.

42. John Norton Pomeroy, *An Introduction to the Constitutional Law of the United States*, 3rd ed. (New York: Hurd and Houghton, 1875), 490.

43. Pomeroy, 484.

44. Madison, "No. 53," *Federalist Papers*, 330.

45. James Madison, *Notes of Debates in the Federal Convention of 1787*, ed. Adrienne Koch (New York: W. W. Norton, 1987), 332.

46. Madison, "No. 51," *Federalist Papers*, 321–322.

47. James Madison, "No. 10," *Federalist Papers*, 80.

48. Korematsu v. United States, 323 U.S. 214 (1944).

49. James Madison, "No. 10," *Federalist Papers*, 84.

50. U.S. Const., Art. II, Sec. 1.

51. See Peter M. Shane, "Legal Disagreement and Negotiation in a Government of Laws: The Case of Executive Privilege Claims against Congress," *Minnesota Law Review* 71 (1987): 461; Randall K. Miller, "Congressional Inquests: Suffocating the Constitutional Prerogative of Executive Privilege," *Minnesota Law Review* 81 (1997): 632.

52. David E. Pozen, "Self-Help and the Separation of Powers," *Yale Law Journal* 124 (2014): 2.

53. David R. Mayhew, *America's Congress* (New Haven, CT: Yale University Press, 2000), 30.

54. Joseph S. Nye, Jr., *Soft Power* (New York: PublicAffairs, 2004), x.

55. Richard E. Neustadt, *Presidential Power* (New York: John Wiley & Sons, 1960), 10.

56. Jacob E. Gersen and Eric A. Posner, "Soft Law: Lessons from Congressional Practice," *Stanford Law Review* 61 (2008): 573; Jonathan S. Gould, "Codifying Constitutional Norms," *Georgetown Law Journal* 109 (2021): 703.

57. On constitutional norms, see Daphna Renan, "Presidential Norms and Article II," *Harvard Law Review* 131 (2018): 2187; Neil S. Siegel, "Political Norms, Constitutional Conventions, and President Donald Trump," *Indiana Law Journal* 93 (2018): 177; Keith E. Whittington, "The Status of Unwritten Constitutional Conventions in the United States," *University of Illinois Law Review* (2013): 1847.

Chapter Six: Can the Supreme Court Intervene in an Impeachment?

1. https://twitter.com/realDonaldTrump/status/1121023509029892096 (April 24, 2019).

2. Elizabeth Thomas and Katherine Faulders, "Trump Attacks Mueller, Calls Him 'a True Never Trumper,'" *ABC News* (May 30, 2019).

3. Alan Dershowitz, *The Case against Impeaching Trump* (New York: Hot Books, 2018), 22.

4. On the concept of a constitutional crisis, see Keith E. Whittington, *Constitutional Crises, Real and Imagined* (forthcoming); Sanford Levinson and Jack M. Balkin, "Constitutional Crises," *University of Pennsylvania Law Review* 157 (2009): 707.

5. "Exclusive—Trump on Campus Free Speech Executive Order: 'We're Going to Do a Very Big Number' Probably 'Next Week,'" *Breitbart.com* (March 12, 2019).

6. Marbury v. Madison, 5 U.S. 137, 177 (1803).

7. See Keith E. Whittington and Amanda Rinderle, "Making a Mountain Out of a Molehill? *Marbury* and the Construction of the Constitutional Canon," *Hastings Constitutional Law Quarterly* 39 (2012): 823.

8. Cooper v. Aaron, 358 U.S. 1, 17–18 (1958).

9. Baker v. Carr, 369 U.S. 186, 211 (1962).

10. See also Keith E. Whittington, *Political Foundations of Judicial Supremacy* (Princeton, NJ: Princeton University Press, 2007), 230–232.

11. Nixon v. United States, 506 U.S. 224, 233, 235 (1993).

12. Nixon v. United States, 253.

13. On the health of the political question doctrine, see Rachel E. Barkow, "More Supreme Than Court? The Fall of the Political Question Doctrine and the Rise of Judicial Supremacy," *Columbia Law Review* 102 (2002): 237; Louis Henkin, "Is There a 'Political Question' Doctrine?," *Yale Law Journal* 85 (1976): 597; Gwynne Skinner, "Misunderstood, Misconstrued, and Now Clearly Dead: The 'Political Question Doctrine' as a Justiciability Doctrine," *Journal of Law & Politics* 29 (2014): 427; Tara Leigh Grove, "The Lost History of the Political Question Doctrine," *New York University Law Review* 90 (2015): 1908.

14. Luther v. Borden, 48 U.S. 1, 46 (1849).

15. Nixon v. United States, 231. Rehnquist also devoted part of his opinion to rebutting Nixon's arguments about what "try" means in the constitutional grant to the Senate to "try all impeachments." By addressing the substance of Nixon's dispute, and finding that the Senate was operating within a reasonable interpretation of the constitutional language, Rehnquist might have implied that a future court could look at a similar dispute and reach a different substantive conclusion about whether the House or the Senate was adhering to the constitutional rules. One signal of the weakening, or the mirage, of the political question doctrine is that the court does not content itself with saying that a case poses a question that the judiciary cannot answer but often goes on to say, or says instead, that the court thinks another branch has landed on the correct constitutional answer. Rehnquist might have been more emphatic about the jurisdictional claim if he had just left it there and refused to say anything at all about the reasonableness of the Senate making use of an impeachment committee.

16. Pacific States Telephone & Telegraph Co. v. Oregon, 223 U.S. 118, 141, 142 (1912).

17. Nixon v. United States, 236.

18. Mississippi v. Johnson, 71 U.S. 475, 501–502 (1867).

19. Keith E. Whittington, "Yet Another Constitutional Crisis?," *William & Mary Law Review* 43 (2002): 2019–2118.

20. Alan Dershowitz, "What Constitutes an Impeachable Offense?," *We the People* podcast (August 30, 2018) (https://constitutioncenter.org/news-debate/podcasts/what-constitutes-an-impeachable-offense).

21. I have written about the limits of judicial power elsewhere. See Keith E. Whittington, "Legislative Sanctions and the Strategic Environment of Judicial Review," *International Journal of Constitutional Law* 1 (2003): 446; *Political Foundations of Judicial Supremacy* (Princeton, NJ: Princeton University Press, 2007).

22. See Whittington, *Repugnant Laws* (Lawrence: University Press of Kansas, 2019).

23. Whittington, "Is There a Free Speech Defense to an Impeachment?," *Lawfare* (January 19, 2021).

24. Whittington, "Trump's Defiance Is Destroying Congress's Power," *The Atlantic* (October 14, 2019).

25. Whittington, *Constitutional Construction* (Cambridge, MA: Harvard University Press, 1999), 141–151.

26. See also Whittington, "James Madison Has Left the Building," *University of Chicago Law Review* 72 (2005): 1137; Whittington, *Constitutional Construction*.

27. Nixon v. United States, 239, 238.

Conclusion

1. Alexander Hamilton, "No. 81," in *The Federalist Papers*, ed. Clinton Rossiter (New York: New American Library, 1961), 485.

2. James Madison, "No. 51," *Federalist Papers*, 322.

3. James Buchanan, "Protests, March 28, 1860," in *A Compilation of the Messages and Papers of the Presidents*, ed. James D. Richardson, vol. 5 (New York: Bureau of National Literature, 1897), 617; Committee on the Judiciary, "Protest of the President against Certain Proceedings of the House of Representatives," Rep. 394, 36th Cong., 1st Sess. (April 9, 1860), 2–3.

4. See Keith E. Whittington, "Is Presidential Impeachment Like a Coup?," *Georgetown Journal of Law and Public Policy* 18 (2020): 670.

5. On presidential electors, see Whittington, "Originalism, Constitutional Construction, and the Problem of Faithless Electors," *Arizona Law Review* 59 (2017): 903.

6. On the 2000 election, see Whittington, "Yet Another Constitutional Crisis?," *William & Mary Law Review* 43 (2002): 2093.

7. Guillermo O'Donnell, "Delegative Democracy," *Journal of Democracy* 5 (1994): 55.

8. Italics in original; 27 *Cong. Globe* 1526 (April 7, 1858).

9. Committee on the Judiciary, "Protest of the President against Certain Proceedings," 4.

INDEX

abuse, impeachment power, 16–17, 176

abuse of power: abuses of discretion and, 181–82; boundaries of political power and, 117, 161; Congressional tools for addressing, 181–84; constitutional culture and, 160; elections for addressing, 179–81; exercising unlawful power as, 165–75; James Madison on, 159–60; judicial review and, 172–74, 178–79; lessons from Europe on, 150–52; question of most effective remedies for, 152–59; remedies for, 175–85

abuses of discretion, 181–82

acceptable political behavior, impeachment establishing norms of, 105–8

accountability, 15–16

Adams, John, 41–43

Alien and Sedition Act of 1798, 166

American government: accountability in, 15–16; checks and balances in, 14–16, 108–15, 180, 204–5, 207–8; Congressional tools in, 181–84; impeachment power in, 3–4, 12–14; political parties and, 40–42. *See also* Constitution, U.S.; House of Representatives, U.S.; Senate, U.S.

anti-Federalists, 132, 205

Archbald, Robert W., 24, 32–33, 34, 93, 225n23

Articles of Confederation, 132

articles of impeachment, 18, 20, 22, 24–25

authorization votes, 52–55

autogolpe, 77

Belknap, William, 34

Biden, Joe, 2, 23, 75, 95, 187

bills of attainder, 47, 98

Black, Charles, 139, 142, 146, 168

Blackmun, Harry, 193

Blackstone, William, 25, 129

Blount, Thomas, 70

Blount, William, 25, 43–45, 61, 70, 166

Bork, Robert, 120–21

boundaries of political power, 117, 161

Boyce, William, 57

break glass in case of emergency, impeachment power, 138–49

bribery, 30–31

British Parliament, impeachment in the: abuse of, 128–29; definition of, 21; as model for the U.S. Constitution, 7–13, 150–52, 176–77; punishments following, 37, 38; scope of, 34–35

Buchanan, James, 205, 212, 214

Burke, Edmund, 150, 176–77

Bush, George W., 143

Bush v. Gore, 191–92

Butler, Benjamin, 70

Charles I, King, 7–12
Chase, Salmon, 197
Chase, Samuel, 90, 107, 123, 143
checks and balances in American
    government, 14–16, 108–15, 180,
    204–5, 207–8
Cipollone, Pat, 51, 53, 112, 113, 114
Claiborne, Harry, 92
Clay, Henry, 163–64
Clinton, Bill, 145, 161, 209; impeachment
    of, 19, 51, 61, 79–82; independent
    counsel report on, 186; partisanship
    and, 211, 213
Coke, Edward, 9–10, 21
consequences of impeachment,
    36–39
Constitution, U.S., 3–4, 12–17; abuse of
    power addressed by, 151–52, 160–65;
    checks and balances in, 14–16, 108–15,
    204–5, 207–8; on consequences of
    impeachment, 36–37; giving power
    to impeach to the House, 3–4, 17–26,
    205–6; on impeaching former offi-
    cers, 31–36; judicial review and,
    172–74, 178–79, 191; language used in,
    21; on limits of presidential power,
    168–69; Senate impeachment trials
    under, 3–4, 19–22; text on impeach-
    ment power in, 26–29; timing of
    violations to, 174–75; on who can
    be impeached, 29–31. See also
    House of Representatives, U.S.;
    Senate, U.S.
constitutional culture, 160
constitutions, state, 21–24, 129–30
Cooley, Thomas, 105–6, 134, 177
Corwin, Edward, 177
Cranfield, Lionel, 7

Debs, Eugene, 141
dereliction of duty, 138–49
Dershowitz, Alan, 123, 125–26, 187,
    189–93, 196, 198, 202–3
Dicey, A. V., 106
discretion, abuses of, 181–82

disqualification from public office,
    92–97
Douglas, William O., 121–22

ejusdem generis, 124
elections, for addressing abuse of
    power, 179–81
elective despotism, 116
English, George, 61
Evans, Lemuel, 57

fast impeachments, 72–77
Fawkes, Guy, 8
Federalists, 14, 45, 90, 109, 116, 132,
    213
Fifth Amendment, 47, 68
First Amendment, 166
Ford, Gerald, 121–22, 123
former officers, impeachment of,
    31–36
Fourteenth Amendment, 94
Franklin, Benjamin, 14, 40–41, 119
future officeholders, impeachment
    sending messages to, 103–5

George III, King, 151
Gerry, Elbridge, 14, 119
Glorious Revolution of 1688, 150
Goldwater, Barry, 71
Gordon, Thomas, 151
Graham, Lindsey, 51, 69
grand inquests, 97–103
Granger, Amos, 212
Grant, Ulysses S., 68
Great Remonstrance of 1641, 11–12
Green, Al, 73–74

Hamilton, Alexander, 40, 117, 130, 131,
    170, 177
Hannity, Sean, 209
Hastings, Warren, 129, 176
Healy, Gene, 103
Henry, Patrick, 132–33
high crimes and misdemeanors, 119,
    142; inkblot theory of, 120–22;

ordinary crimes answer to, 123–27; political offenses answer to, 127–38
House of Commons, British, 7–13, 21, 34–35, 102, 176–77. *See also* Britain, impeachment in
House of Lords, British, 37. *See also* Britain, impeachment in
House of Representatives, U.S.: authorization votes in, 52–55; cooperation with the Senate in impeachments, 19–26; grand jury analogy of process in, 55–56; impeachment investigations in, 55, 97–103; impeachment process in, 51–59; Judiciary Committee, 205–6; as partisan institution, 57–59, 210–2112; power to impeach in, 17–26, 162–63; prosecutor role of, 27; U.S. Supreme Court and, 188. *See also* Senate, U.S.
House Practice Manual, 24, 158–59, 166
Hume, David, 171
Humphreys, West, 35, 90, 92, 93, 144

impeachable offenses, 16, 30–31, 70–71, 73–74, 79–81, 109–10, 155–59, 177–78, 214–15; abuse of power (*See* abuse of power); break glass in case of emergency, 138–49; inkblot theory of, 120–22; maladministration, 129–30, 131, 135, 137, 138; ordinary crimes answer to, 123–27; political offenses answer to, 127–38; U.S. Supreme Court and questions of, 188–92
impeachable persons, 29–31
impeachment, 1–6; allowed under the Constitution, 3–4, 12–17; articles of, 20; in Britain (*See* British Parliament, impeachment in the); burden of proof for, 18–19; consequences of, 36–39, 104; cooperation between the House and Senate in, 19–26;

danger of frequent, 176; decisions to pursue, 81–82, 157–58; as effective remedy for abuse of power, 152–59, 167; end goals of, 78–79; establishing norms of acceptable political behavior, 105–8; first trial in U.S., 43–45; of former officers, 31–36; judicial review and, 172–74, 178–79; misuse and abuse of, 16–17; as political tool, 15, 20, 57–59, 84–86, 154–55, 207; power in the House, 17–26; power in the Senate, 3–4, 26–29; procedural constraints on, 18; public skepticism about, 210–11; for removal of misbehaving individuals, 86–92, 155–56; for removing individuals from public life, 92–97; sending a message to future office-holders, 103–5; state constitutions and, 21–24; when accomplished, 23–26; who can be subject to, 29–31
impeachment process: amount of procedure due in, 66–69; conflicts of interest and, 69–70; duty of impartiality in, 70–71; fast trials in, 72–77; grand inquests in, 97–103; in the House, 51–59; limits of judicial supremacy and, 196–203; partisanship in, 40–42, 57–59, 136–37, 210–14; for political misdeeds, 46–50; political parties and, 40–42; removal by address and, 46; in the Senate, 59–72; trial of William Blount and, 43–45
inkblot theory of impeachable offenses, 120–22
investigations, impeachment, 55
Iredell, James, 132

Jackson, Andrew, 163–64
Jackson, Robert, 168
James I, King, 7–12, 15
James II, King, 150
January 6, 2021, attacks, 23, 75–76, 94, 95, 100, 162, 184

Jay Treaty of 1795, 110–11

Jefferson, Thomas, 213; on democracy, 116; impeachment trial of William Blount and, 43–45; political parties and, 41–43; as vice president, 42–43; worries about impeachment as a weapon, 136, 211

Johnson, Andrew, 3–4, 122, 143, 166, 177; conflicts of interest of Senators during trial of, 69–70; eleven articles of impeachment against, 60–61; impeachable offenses of, 80, 90, 125, 127, 135–36; Reconstruction Acts and, 197; Republican National Convention during impeachment trial of, 68; on right to free speech, 161; term finished out by, 75, 107

Jones, Isaac, 85

judicial review, 172–74, 178–79, 191

Kennedy, Edward, 164–65

Kent, Samuel, 92

late impeachments, 31–36

legislative tools, Congressional, 182–83

Lincoln, Abraham, 69–70

Maclaine, Archibald, 132

Madden, John, 78

Madison, James, 88, 113, 115, 142, 151, 177, 205; on abuse of power, 159–60, 163–65; on boundaries of government, 117; on constitutional rights and responsibilities of various branches of government, 111–12; criticism of George Washington, 41; on defending the community against the chief executive, 130–31; desire to provide Congress with check against mischief of the states, 14, 108–9; on impeachable offenses, 169–70; on impeachment power, 84; on presidential responsibility, 100; on the republican principle, 180; worries

about Legislature tendencies to absorb power, 15

maladministration, 129–30, 131, 135, 137, 138

Mann Act, 146

Marbury v. Madison, 191

Marshall, John, 165–66, 190–91

Mason, George, 118, 130–31, 138

Massachusetts Bay Colony, 171

Mayhew, David, 183

McCarthy, Kevin, 51–52

Mississippi v. Johnson, 4, 197

Mompesson, Giles, 9–10

Montesquieu, 151

Mueller, Robert, 101, 186

Mueller Report, 186–87

Nadler, Jerry, 209, 210

Neustadt, Richard, 183

Nicholas, George, 133

Nietzsche, Friedrich, 121

Ninth Amendment, 120–21

Nixon, Richard, 35–36, 51, 71, 164–65, 213

Nixon, Walter, 192–96, 202

Nixon v. United States, 192–196, 201–202

Obama, Barack, 143

O'Donnell, Guillermo, 210

ordinary crimes answer, 123–27

Palmer, Henry W., 127–28

pardon power, presidential, 38

partisanship, 40–42, 57–59, 136–37, 210–14

Pelosi, Nancy, 23–24, 29, 51, 113–14

Pence, Mike, 91

persuasion, 82–83

Philadelphia Convention, 13, 30, 87, 116, 130–31

Phillip II, King, 9

Pickering, John, 90, 98, 143, 213

Pinckney, Charles, 131–32

political misdeeds, impeachment process for, 46–50
political offenses answer, 127–38
political parties, 40–42
political question doctrine, 102, 149, 188–202, 236n15
political speeches, 139–41
political tool, impeachment as, 15, 20, 57–59, 84–86, 207
Pomeroy, John Norton, 135–36, 177–78
Porteous, G. Thomas, Jr., 86, 93
Posner, Richard, 161
power of the purse, 182–83
presidential powers, 182–83; for pardons, 38
Pym, John, 10–11

Randolph, Edmund, 13, 119, 130, 133
Rawle, William, 25, 134
Reconstruction Act, 197
Rehnquist, William, 192–96, 201, 203, 236n15
removal by address, 46
removal of misbehaving individuals by impeachment, 86–92
republican principle, 180
Roberts, John, 28
Rutledge, Edward, 132

Scott, Hugh, 71
Senate, U.S.: amount of procedure due in, 66–69; conducting normal legislative business alongside trials, 68–69; conflicts of interest in, 69–70; cooperation with the House in impeachments, 19–26; court role of, 27–28; duty to impartial justice in, 70–71; as empowered, not mandated to have trials, 60; impeachment process in, 59–72; power to reject impeachment charges, 62–65; power to try all impeachments in, 3–4, 26–29; procedural bar for conviction in, 56; quick convictions in, 65–66; special committees for hearing evidence in, 71–72; U.S. Supreme Court and, 188–92. *See also* House of Representatives, U.S.

Shakespeare, William, 8
Sitgreaves, Samuel, 25
Sixth Amendment, 21
social media, 76, 187
Souter, David, 193, 198, 201–2
Starr, Kenneth, 82, 186
Stephens, Alexander, 141
Stevens, John Paul, 202
Story, Joseph, 47, 125–28, 134, 153, 177
Sunstein, Cass, 146
Supreme Court, U.S.: Donald Trump and, 187, 190; limits of judicial supremacy and, 196–203; political questions on impeachable offenses and, 188–92; U.S. district judge Walter Nixon and, 192–96
suspension powers, 22–23
Swayne, Charles, 85, 127–28
Sydney, Algernon, 171

Tacitus, 151
Taft, William Howard, 177
Texas Revolution, 56–57
Third Amendment, 168
Thomas, Clarence, 193
treason, 30–31
Trump, Donald, 2, 28, 31, 53, 68, 69, 80, 82, 113; abbreviated trial of, in the Senate, 61; Charlottesville riots and, 140–41; fast second impeachment and trial of, 75–76; grand inquest into, 101–2; impeachable offenses of, 73–74, 90–91, 125; January 6, 2021, attacks and, 23, 75–76, 94, 95, 100, 184; Mueller Report on, 186–87; norms broken by, 162; ordinary crimes answer to impeachable offenses of, 123–24; partisanship and, 59, 211, 213; response to congressional

Trump, Donald (*continued*)
  inquiry, 109–10, 113–15; Sean
  Hannity on, 209; single article of
  impeachment against, 94–95; social
  media use by, 76, 187; timing of
  impeachment of, 23–24; U.S.
  Supreme Court and, 187, 190
Tucker, John Randolph, 136, 177
Tucker, St. George, 47, 133, 171, 177
Twenty-Fifth Amendment, 76,
  138–39
Twitter, 76, 187
Tyler, John, 61–62, 85

Ukraine, 186–87

Villiers, George, 7
Virginia Plan, 13

voter ID law, 22
votes, authorization, 52–55

Wade, Benjamin, 69
Warren, Elizabeth, 69
Washington, George, 41, 103, 111–12
Washington Post, 168
Watrous, John, 56–57
White, Byron, 193, 198, 201–3
White, Edward Douglass, 195
Williamson, Hugh, 13–14
Wilson, James (Supreme Court
  justice), 14, 133
Wilson, James F. (member of
  Congress), 122, 124, 127
Winthrop, John, 171

Zelensky, Volodymyr, 186–87

A NOTE ON THE TYPE

This book has been composed in Arno, an Old-style serif typeface in the
classic Venetian tradition, designed by Robert Slimbach at Adobe.